The Destruction of the Bison

The Destruction of the Bison explains the decline of the North American bison population from an estimated 30 million in 1800 to fewer than 1000 a century later. In this wide-ranging, interdisciplinary study, Andrew C. Isenberg argues that the cultural and ecological encounter between Native Americans and Euroamericans in the Great Plains was the central cause of the near-extinction of the bison. Cultural and ecological interactions created new types of bison hunters on both sides of the encounter: mounted Indian nomads and Euroamerican industrial hidemen. Together with environmental pressures, these hunters nearly extinguished the bison. In the early twentieth century, nostalgia about the very cultural strife that first threatened the bison became, ironically, an important impetus to its preservation.

Andrew C. Isenberg is Assistant Professor of History at Princeton University.

STUDIES IN ENVIRONMENT AND HISTORY

Editors

Donald Worster, University of Kansas
Alfred W. Crosby, University of Texas at Austin

The Destruction of the Bison

An Environmental History, 1750–1920

ANDREW C. ISENBERG

Princeton University

CAMBRIDGE
UNIVERSITY PRESS

CAMBRIDGE UNIVERSITY PRESS
Cambridge, New York, Melbourne, Madrid, Cape Town, Singapore,
São Paulo, Delhi, Dubai, Tokyo, Mexico City

Cambridge University Press
32 Avenue of the Americas, New York, NY 10013-2473, USA

www.cambridge.org
Information on this title: www.cambridge.org/9780521003483

First published 2000
First paperback edition 2001
11th printing 2010

A catalog record for this publication is available from the British Library.

Library of Congress Cataloging in Publication Data

Isenberg, Andrew C. (Andrew Christian)
The destruction of the bison : an environmental history, 1750–1920
/ Andrew C. Isenberg.
p. cm – (Studies in environment and history)
Includes index.
ISBN 0-521-77172-2
1. American bison.   2. American bison hunting – History.
3. Nature – Effect of human beings on – North America.   I. Title.
QL737.U531834   2000
333.95'9643'0978 – dc21   99–37543
CIP

ISBN 978-0-521-77172-6 Hardback
ISBN 978-0-521-00348-3 Paperback

For Petra

Contents

Acknowledgments

In this book I have tried to account for the often unacknowledged interconnections among living things, and I therefore take special pleasure in acknowledging the many people who have contributed to its making.

I began work on this book as a doctoral candidate at Northwestern University, where, to my immense good fortune, my adviser was Arthur McEvoy. I determined then, and remain convinced now, that no graduate student ever had a better mentor. I cannot begin to recount the insights I have learned from Art, or the number of times I have returned to them. I am also thankful to James Oakes, who held me to his own high standards and believed that I could achieve them. Frederick Hoxie was a patient and generous teacher who gave this manuscript a close, insightful reading that strengthened it considerably.

Cambridge University Press has been unfailingly supportive. The advice of Frank Smith, Donald Worster, and Alfred Crosby has improved this book tremendously.

I revised many of my ideas during a year as a fellow at the Shelby Cullom Davis Center for Historical Studies at Princeton University. I am indebted to the Director of the Davis Center, William Chester Jordan, and to the fellows Katherine Grier, William Hallo, Richard Hoffman, Karen Rader, Nigel Rothfels, and Edward Steinhart for their readiness to read, discuss, and comment on this project. I finished the book as a member of the Princeton Department of History, a uniquely stimulating and supportive environment in which to work. My colleagues Peter Brown, Angela Creager, Hendrik Hartog, William Howarth, Emmanuel Kreike, James McPherson, Kenneth Mills, John Murrin, and Daniel Rodgers have provided me with indispensable critical insights.

A small army of scholars read all or part of this book in its formative stages. I am grateful to Volker Berghahn, James Campbell, William Cronon, Kurk Dorsey, Dan Flores, Ari Kelman, Naomi Lamoreaux, Nancy MacLean, Jenny Price, Hal Rothman, Louis Warren, and Richard White.

I was fortunate to spend two years during the early stages of the project as a member of the faculty at the University of Puget Sound. I am indebted to all my colleagues there, but particularly to Suzanne Barnett, William Barry, William

Breitenbach, Nancy Bristow, Terry Cooney, Mott Greene, John Lear, David Smith, and Peter Wimberger.

This project reflects much of what I learned about the study of history from several gifted teachers, particularly Josef Barton, Henry Binford, T. H. Breen, Tim Harris, Frank Safford, Michael Sherry, and John Tutino.

I leaned, heavily at times, on friends during the course of writing this book, among them Katey Anderson and William Trischuk, Mike Angell, Bruce Buttny, Jim and Terry Denegre, Sarah Feltes, John and Lynn Hillman, Kari Hoover, Greg Lind, Joel Schorn, Georg Schmundt-Thomas and Katrin Thomas, Susan Smulyan, and Bettina Westerhoff.

My most important thanks are to my family. I cannot adequately thank my parents for their boundless support. Rather than distractions, my son, Kai, and daughter, Elena, have been inspirations. Finally, my wife, Petra Gödde, took time away from work on her own book to help me complete mine. Our life together has largely overlapped with this project, and it is for her.

Earlier versions of portions of this book have appeared in different form as journal articles. They are reprinted with permission. Early formulations of the arguments in the first half of this book appeared in "Toward a Policy of Destruction: Buffaloes, Law, and the Market, 1803–1883," *Great Plains Quarterly*, 12 (Fall 1992), 227–241; and "Conservation and Equality: The Bison as a Natural Resource," in Kelly G. Wadsworth and Richard E. McCabe, eds., *Transactions of the Sixtieth North American Wildlife and Natural Resources Conference* (Washington, D.C.: Wildlife Management Institute, 1995), 550–556. A different version of Chapter Six, titled, "The Returns of the Bison: Profit, Nostalgia, and Preservation," was published in *Environmental History*, 2 (April 1997), 179–196.

Introduction

Before Europeans brought the horse to the New World, Native Americans in the Great Plains hunted bison from foot. Their technique was ingenious: by making a fire or creating a ruckus near a herd of bison, they stampeded the skittish animals toward a bluff. The Indians lined the route to the bison "jump" with fallen trees or thicket and waved robes to shoo the beasts toward their destination. If the hunters dared to risk a general conflagration, they set more fires to direct the herd. Once they had stampeded the bison over the precipice, they peppered the crippled animals with arrows. For the bison, the stampede to the bluff was probably a disorienting experience. As they hurried toward their deaths, the more perceptive among them might have wondered, "Where is all this commotion leading me?" As readers of this book consider – among other things – grassland ecology, horses, smallpox, the fur trade, and gender roles in Indian and Euroamerican societies, they may find themselves pondering the same question. Nonetheless, just as pedestrian hunters herded their prey to their deaths, this book eventually leads to the destruction of the bison.

Why consider so many seemingly disparate subjects? Because, a host of economic, cultural, and ecological factors herded the bison toward their near-extinction. That diverse assembly of factors first emerged in the middle of the eighteenth century from ongoing encounters among Indians, Euroamericans, and the Great Plains environment. Those encounters were both a *process* of intercultural and ecological exchange and an interaction between people and a *place*, the nonhuman natural environment.[1]

---

[1] For the American West as a place, see Donald Worster, "New West, True West," *Western Historical Quarterly*, 18 (April 1987), 141–156; for process, see William Cronon, "Revisiting the Vanishing Frontier: The Legacy of Frederick Jackson Turner," Ibid., 157–176. For the interaction of ecology, economy, and culture, see Arthur F. McEvoy, *The Fisherman's Problem: Ecology and Law in the California Fisheries, 1850–1980* (New York: Cambridge University Press, 1986), 3–16; McEvoy, "Toward an Interactive Theory of Nature and Culture: Ecology, Production, and Cognition in the California Fishing Industry," in *The Ends of the Earth: Perspectives in Modern Environmental History*, ed. Worster (New York: Cambridge University Press, 1988), 211–229. Also see Carolyn Merchant, *Ecological Revolutions: Nature, Gender, and Science in New England* (Chapel Hill: University of North Carolina Press, 1989), 1–26. My understanding of environmental history has been profoundly influenced by the work of Richard White, particularly *The Roots of Dependency: Subsistence, Environment, and Social Change among the Choctaws, Pawnees, and Navajos* (Lincoln: University of Nebraska Press, 1983).

On its surface, the encounter between the Old and New Worlds that led to the destruction of the bison appears to be a simple matter: Indian and Euroamerican hunters pushed the species to the brink of extinction for commercial profit. In the nineteenth century, they slaughtered millions of bison and brought to market the animals' hides, meat, tongues, and bones. Like other environmental catastrophes in the American West – the depletion of the California fisheries, the deforestation of the Great Lakes region and Pacific Northwest, and the "dust bowl" of the southern plains in the 1930s – the destruction of the bison was, in part, the result of the unsustainable exploitation of natural resources.[2] Yet, as in the California fisheries, the wheat fields of the dust bowl, and elsewhere, more than a capitalist economy's demand for natural resources caused the near-extinction of the bison. The volatile grassland environment itself was a factor; drought, cold, predators, and the competition of other grazing animals accounted for much of the decline.

The Great Plains environment influenced the fate of not only the bison but the human inhabitants of the region, particularly mounted, bison-hunting Indian societies. In the eighteenth and nineteenth centuries, the hunters adjusted their social structures and resource strategies to the ecology of the grasslands. Just as important, the Indians adapted to the ecological and economic changes that resulted from the arrival of Euroamericans in the West. Largely in reaction to the Europeans' introduction of the horse (which facilitated bison hunting), Old World diseases (which discouraged a sedentary life), and the fur trade (which encouraged specialization as hunters), some Indian groups reinvented themselves as equestrian nomads in the high plains.[3] These adaptations

[2] For the California fisheries, see McEvoy, *Fisherman's Problem*; for deforestation, see Richard White, "The Altered Landscape: Social Change and the Land in the Pacific Northwest," in William G. Robbins, Robert J. Frank, and Richard E. Ross, eds., *Regionalism and the Pacific Northwest* (Corvallis: Oregon State University Press, 1983), 109–127; for a masterful treatment of the transformation of the Western environment in the nineteenth century, see William Cronon, *Nature's Metropolis: Chicago and the Great West* (New York: Norton, 1991); for an equally insightful history of environmental change in the twentieth-century West, see Donald Worster, *Dust Bowl: The Southern Plains in the 1930s* (New York: Oxford University Press, 1979). The degradation of the environment is an important theme of recent works in Western history. See Wilbur Jacobs, "The Great Despoliation: Environmental Themes in American Frontier History," *Pacific Historical Review*, 47 (February 1978), 1–26; Worster, "Beyond the Agrarian Myth," and White, "Trashing the Trails," in Patricia Nelson Limerick, Clyde A. Milner II, and Charles E. Rankin, eds., *Trails: Toward a New Western History* (Lawrence: University Press of Kansas, 1991), 18–21, 26–39.

[3] The first important study of the impact of imported biota on a previously isolated community was Charles S. Elton, *The Ecology of Invasions by Plants and Animals* (London: Chapman and Hall, 1958). The historian Alfred W. Crosby has integrated the science of ecological invasions with the history of European exploration and colonialism in several major books and essays. See Crosby, *Ecological Imperialism: The Biological Expansion of Europe, 900–1900* (New York: Cambridge University Press, 1986); Crosby, *Germs, Seeds, & Animals: Studies in Ecological History* (Armonk, N.Y.: M. E. Sharpe, 1994); Crosby, *The Columbian Exchange: Biological and Cultural Consequences of 1492* (Westport: Greenwood Press, 1972). Indian history has been revitalized in recent years by studies that have analyzed Indian societies that reinvented themselves in response to European colonialism. According to this perspective, the changes attendant on the arrival of Europeans were so extensive that not just the colonists, but Indians as well, found themselves in a "new

left the newly nomadic societies dependent on the bison, a species vulnerable to depletion by overhunting and drought. In the mid-nineteenth century, the combination of Indian predation and environmental change decimated the bison.

Cultural and ecological encounters also shaped the Euroamerican destruction and, later, preservation of the bison. Beginning in the 1840s, the presence of increasing numbers of Euroamericans in the plains displaced the bison from their customary habitats. Livestock belonging to Euroamerican emigrants on the Oregon-California and Santa Fe trails degraded the valleys of the Platte and Arkansas rivers.[4] More important, between 1870 and 1883, Euroamerican hunters slaughtered millions of bison. Federal authorities supported the hunt because they saw the extermination of the bison as a means to force Indians to submit to the reservation system.[5] The hunters, aided by drought, blizzards, and other environmental factors, nearly destroyed the Indians' primary resource. Although Eastern preservationists at the turn of the century decried the wastefulness of the hide hunters, they nonetheless yearned for the bygone era that the hide hunters had epitomized. Their desire to preserve the bison as a living memorial to a romanticized frontier of Euroamerican conquest animated their mission to save the species from extinction.

So many subjects are considered in the following pages that it is necessary briefly to define the confines of this study. Although this book analyzes the changing apprehensions of the bison in American culture, it is not an exhaustive history of the bison as an artifact of American folklore. Readers interested in the cultural mythology of the bison can consult other studies.[6] This book relies heavily on environmental science, but it is neither a natural history nor a biological study of the bison. Such studies of the species already exist.[7] This book is not

---

world." See James H. Merrell, *The Indians' New World: Catawbas and Their Neighbors from European Contact through the Era of Removal* (New York: Norton, 1989).

[4] See Elliott West, *The Way to the West: Essays on the Central Plains* (Albuquerque: University of New Mexico Press, 1995), 51–83.

[5] See Andrew C. Isenberg, "Toward a Policy of Destruction: Buffaloes, Law, and the Market, 1803–1883," *Great Plains Quarterly*, 12 (Fall 1992), 227–241. For a recent summary of writings on the bison, see Isenberg's introduction to the new edition of E. Douglas Branch, *The Hunting of the Buffalo* (Lincoln: University of Nebraska Press, 1997), ix–xvi.

[6] See Valerius Geist, *Buffalo Nation: History and Legend of the North American Bison* (Stillwater, Minn.: Voyageur Press, 1996); David A. Dary, *The Buffalo Book: The Saga of an American Symbol* (New York: Avon, 1974). See also Larry Barsness, *The Bison in Art: A Graphic Chronicle of the American Bison* (Flagstaff, Ariz.: Northland, 1977); Barsness, *Heads, Hides & Horns: The Compleat Buffalo Book* (Fort Worth, Tex.: Texas Christian University Press, 1985); Mari Sandoz, *The Buffalo Hunters: The Story of the Hide Men* (New York: Hastings, 1954).

[7] Joel A. Allen, *The American Bisons, Living and Extinct* (Cambridge: Harvard University Press, 1876); Frank Gilbert Roe, *The North American Buffalo: A Critical Study of the Species in Its Wild State* (Toronto: University of Toronto Press, 1951); Jerry N. McDonald, *North American Bison: Their Classification and Evolution* (Berkeley: University of California Press, 1981); Joel Berger and Carol Cunningham, *Bison: Mating and Conservation in Small Populations* (New York: Columbia University Press, 1994); Tom McHugh, *The Time of the Buffalo* (Lincoln: University of Nebraska Press, 1972); Margaret Mary Meagher, *The Bison of Yellowstone National Park.*

an environmental history of the grasslands. Like the bison, it occasionally strays from the American Great Plains to Canada, Mexico, and the eastern United States. Moreover, a comprehensive environmental history of the plains would necessarily include species other than the bison – among them the antelope and the prairie dog – and resource uses other than bison hunting – including ranching, farming, and oil exploitation.[8] This book is a history of the interactions among ecology, economy, and culture that led to the near-extermination of the bison, the dominant species of the historic Great Plains. As such, it approaches the destruction of the bison as a social and ecological problem.

Most historical studies of the bison, since they first appeared in the late nineteenth century, have been of two types. One emerged from the late nineteenth- and early twentieth-century movement to preserve the species from extinction. Written by officers of the American Bison Society, a private philanthropic organization devoted to the preservation of the bison, these studies deplored the wastefulness of late nineteenth-century Euroamerican bison hunters and concluded with a hopeful and self-congratulatory assessment of their own efforts at preservation. They presented the salvation of the species as a salutary example of elitist philanthropy and Progressive-era good government.[9]

Concurrently, another type of study integrated the near-extinction of the bison into the prevailing understanding of the history of the American West. That interpretation, epitomized by the late nineteenth-century historians Frederick Jackson Turner and Theodore Roosevelt, viewed the West as, in Turner's words, "the meeting point between savagery and civilization." The conquest of the Indians and the wilderness shaped not only the American character – hardy, individualistic, and pragmatic – but American institutions and ideologies as well – democracy, ruralism, and nationalism.[10] Although Turner's frontier thesis

---

National Park Service Scientific Monographs Series, 1 (Washington, D.C.: Government Printing Office, 1973).

[8] See Cronon, *Nature's Metropolis*, 97–147, 207–259; Worster, *Dust Bowl*; Walter Prescott Webb, *The Great Plains* (Boston: Ginn and Company, 1931); James Malin, *The Grassland of North America: Prolegomena to its History* (Lawrence, Kansas, 1948); Rodman Paul, *The Far West and Great Plains in Transition, 1859–1900* (New York: Harper and Row, 1988); Terry G. Jordan, *North American Cattle-Ranching Frontiers: Origins, Diffusion, Differentiation* (Albuquerque: University of New Mexico Press, 1993), 208–240, 267–307.

[9] For an early example, see William T. Hornaday, "The Extermination of the American Bison, with a Sketch of its Discovery and Life History," *Annual Report of the Smithsonian Institution, 1887*, vol. II (Washington, Government Printing Office, 1889), 367–548. See also Martin S. Garretson, *The American Bison: The Story of its Extermination as a Wild Species and its Restoration under Federal Protection* (New York: New York Zoological Society, 1938). See also American Bison Society, *Annual Report*. 13 vols. (New York, 1907–31). A historian who followed in this tradition was Branch, *Hunting of the Buffalo*.

[10] See Frederick Jackson Turner, "The Significance of the Frontier in American History," American Historical Association *Annual Report* (1893), 199–227; Theodore Roosevelt, *The Winning of the West*, 7 vol. (New York: G. P. Putnam's Sons, 1907); Richard Slotkin, *Gunfighter Nation: The Myth of the Frontier in Twentieth-Century America* (New York: HarperCollins, 1992), 29–62; James R. Grossman, ed., *The Frontier in American Culture: Essays by Richard White and Patricia Nelson Limerick* (Berkeley: University of California Press, 1994), 7–65.

went out of fashion in the first half of the twentieth century, it returned, infused by Cold War nationalism, in the 1950s. During this renaissance of the frontier thesis a number of histories of the destruction of the bison appeared. They were followed in succeeding decades by a handful of studies that, without abandoning the perspectives of frontier history, were somewhat more sympathetic to the Indians of the western plains. These studies presented Indians not as savage impediments to progress but as colorful primitives doomed to defeat by their clash with civilization. All the frontier histories viewed the near-extermination of the herds as a sanguine example of the Euroamerican conquest.[11]

Both the preservationist and the frontier historians of the bison analyzed the near-extinction and preservation of the species from the perspective of dynamic Euroamericans who shaped a passive nature and overwhelmed culturally static Indians. Both interpretations also saw in the near-extinction of the bison the inevitable triumph of Euroamerican society. Many frontier historians applauded the destruction of the bison as the removal of an obstacle to Euroamerican expansion. The preservationists denounced the slaughter of the bison but celebrated their rescue as an example of Progressive-era benevolence. Both interpretations steered their narratives toward happy endings: the triumph of either Euroamerican settlement or preservationism.

Most studies of the decline and return of the bison preceded the development in recent decades of the fields of social, cultural, labor, and gender history. Insights from those fields suggest far greater complexities in the relationships of Indians and Euroamericans to the bison than historians formerly supposed. They suggest, for instance, the significance of cultural constructions of gender in Indian and Euroamerican societies. The Indians of the western plains who produced bison robes for the market relied on a gendered division of labor; men hunted while women dressed skins. The acceleration of the robe trade in the mid-nineteenth century resulted in the impressment of greater numbers of women into the dressing of robes. Cultural constructions of gender were no less significant in Euroamericans' relationship to the bison. In the 1870s and early 1880s, the effort by the newly founded Society for the Prevention of Cruelty to Animals to halt Euroamerican hide hunters' destruction of the bison reflected the emergence of a feminized rhetoric of moral reform. The installation of bison in managed preserves in the early twentieth century by the American Bison Society emerged from a concern by the officers of that organization that masculine virtues were on the wane in urban America. To reverse that decline, the Society resolved to preserve the bison as a reminder of frontier manliness. Altogether, the collapse and revival of the bison population were entangled in social

---

[11] For such histories, see Carl Coke Rister, "The Significance of the Destruction of the Buffalo in the Southwest," *Southwestern Historical Quarterly*, 33 (July 1929), 34–49; Wayne Gard, *The Great Buffalo Hunt* (Lincoln: University of Nebraska Press, 1959). Studies more sympathetic to the Indians were Francis Haines, *The Buffalo* (New York: Crowell, 1975); Sandoz, *Buffalo Hunters*; and Dary, *Buffalo Book*.

and cultural changes – particularly changes in cultural constructions of gender –
in complex and important ways.

Many histories of the bison also appeared before the emergence of the field of
environmental history. The destruction of the bison was part of a global decline
of mammalian diversity in the nineteenth century. The combination of European ecological expansion and European and American economic expansion in
this period extinguished or marginalized dozens of species of feral megafauna.
European colonists afterward replaced these wild animals with domesticated
species. Certainly nineteenth-century hunters and ranchers epitomized this
trend. But this meta-narrative of the decline of feral species and the rise of
domesticates both preceded and followed the late nineteenth century. Indians in
the plains initiated the decline of the bison when they adopted that most useful
of Old World domesticated species, the horse. In the plains, horses not only facilitated hunting, but they competed with the bison for scarce water and forage. In
the late nineteenth and early twentieth centuries, bison preservationists saw their
work as a repudiation of the commercial slaughter of the herds. Yet in important
ways they were complicit in the transformation of plains fauna from feral to
domesticated. The enclosed, managed preserves they established made semi-
domesticates of the remnant bison who had survived the nineteenth century.

In recent years, a number of excellent essays have argued that the decline of
the bison was a consequence of environmental factors in the plains.[12] This is
an important and previously overlooked factor. However, the influence of the
environment was not by any means the sole or even primary cause of the near-
extinction of the herds. Environmental factors such as overgrazing and diseases
brought by domestic livestock certainly contributed to the destruction of the
bison, but they were inextricably connected to the human economies that introduced domesticated species to the plains. Human societies were so bound to the
plains environment in the nineteenth century that there were few purely environmental or anthropogenic causes of the bison's destruction.

As the foregoing indicates, Indians are an important part of this history, and it
is therefore necessary to define how they are delimited and understood. Much of
this study concerns the equestrian, bison-hunting, Indian societies of the western shortgrass and mixed-grass plains: the Arapahos, Assiniboines, Atsinas,
Blackfeet, Cheyennes, Comanches, Crows, Kiowas, and Sioux. This study does
not analyze all Indian bison hunters, however, only those who both inhabited the
western plains year-round and subsisted primarily on the bison. Although the

---

[12] For the environmental factors that contributed to the diminution of the bison, see Rudolph W.
Koucky, "The Buffalo Disaster of 1882," *North Dakota History*, 50 (Winter 1982), 23–30. The
best such studies are Dan Flores, "Bison Ecology and Bison Diplomacy: The Southern Plains
from 1800 to 1850," *Journal of American History*, 78 (September 1991), 482; White, "Animals and
Enterprise," in *The Oxford History of the American West* ed. Clyde A. Milner, et al. (New York:
Oxford University Press, 1994), 249; and West, *Way to the West*, 72–83.

Shoshones and Flatheads of the northern Rockies periodically hunted bison in the grassland, they did not primarily inhabit the plains. Neither did the occasional bison hunters of the Southwest, except for the small group of Jicarilla Apaches who confederated with the Kiowas in the early eighteenth century and thereafter remained in the plains. Although the Indians of the Missouri River watershed such as the Arikaras, Caddos, Hidatsas, Mandans, Omahas, Osages, Pawnees, Poncas, and Wichitas regularly left their cornfields in the river valleys to hunt bison in the high plains, they were primarily agriculturalists who combined seasonal bison hunting with farming. The historian Richard White has written an excellent analysis of the Pawnees; rather than duplicate White's study of the villagers this book complements it by focusing on those Plains Indians who were year-round bison hunters.[13]

Ethnically and culturally, the western plains bison hunters were diverse. The Assiniboines, Crows, and Sioux spoke Siouan languages; the Arapahos, Atsinas, Blackfeet, and Cheyennes were Algonquians; the Comanches spoke a Shoshonean language; the Kiowa language is related to Tanoan of the Southwestern Pueblos. Yet the bison hunters shared the western plains environment, from the Blackfeet in the north to the Comanches in the south. Although the western plains vary in climate and vegetation over this extent, they nonetheless offered similar opportunities and imposed similar constraints on all the societies that inhabited the region. The Indians of the western plains also shared the timing of their arrival in the region. Unlike the villagers whose habitation of the Missouri River valley was centuries old, most of the equestrian bison hunters of the western plains were relative newcomers to grassland; they converged upon the western plains after the diffusion of horses northward from the Spanish colonies in New Mexico. Only the Crows, who separated from the Hidatsas in the seventeenth century, were early inhabitants of the high plains. Other societies of the western plains migrated there in the eighteenth century from either the Rocky Mountains or the Eastern woodlands. Such movements of indigenous populations were common in North America, particularly after the coming of European colonists. Two recent works by Richard White and Stephen Aron have described similar migrations of Indian groups to the Great Lakes region and Kentucky in the seventeenth and eighteenth centuries.[14] Like the migrants in the Trans-Appalachian West, the newcomers to the western plains, although culturally diverse, were united by time and space.

Although they maintained their separate cultural identities, shared experiences common to their environment and their era shaped the western plains

---

[13] White, *Roots of Dependency*.

[14] White, *The Middle Ground: Indians, Empires, and Republics in the Great Lakes Region, 1650–1815* (New York: Cambridge University Press, 1991); Stephen Aron, *How the West Was Lost: The Transformation of Kentucky from Daniel Boone to Henry Clay* (Baltimore: Johns Hopkins University Press, 1996).

bison-hunting societies. The emergence of such societies was not unlike the rapid development of pastoral nomadism in the Central Eurasian grasslands among former Chinese farmers, Siberian forest hunters, and others in the second half of the first millennium B.C.E. The bison hunters might also be compared to the mounted hunters of South America such as the Tehuelches, Puelches, and Querandí of the Argentine pampas. In the eighteenth century, responding to the same European ecological invasion that brought the horse to North America, they adopted the use of the horse to hunt the guanaco (*Lama guanicoe*) and feral cattle. Like the horse nomads of the North American plains, the nomads of Eurasia and South America eventually developed segmentary, patrilineal social organizations.[15] Whether in the grasslands of Central Eurasia or the Americas, the exigencies of resource use transcended ethnicity.

Above all, the Indians of the western plains, like the nomadic herders of the Eurasian steppes and the guanaco hunters of the pampas, shared a similar land use strategy: hunting bison from horseback. Despite the cultural differences among nomadic groups in the western plains, the demands of the two grazing animals essential to the Indians' subsistence – the bison and the horse – imposed similar conditions on all. Mobility was the most important of those conditions. Bison migrated frequently in search of forage and water. Indians moved their camps not only to maintain access to the bison, but also when the pressure of their own hunting reduced the density of the herds. Moreover, they were forced to move often enough to provide forage and water for their horses. The hunters stored little game, except after their fall hunts to see them through the winter, because the demands of mobility kept their provisions limited. Anthropologists distinguish between this strategy of "immediate return" common to mobile foragers and the "delayed return" of agriculturalists and pure pastoralists.[16] In sum, the interaction of the bison's migrations and the Indians' hunting strategies combined to keep the largest animals in the Great Plains – bison, horses, and humans – on the move.

Despite these similarities, generalizing about the land use of the Indians of the western plains is not easy. They are most often referred to as "Plains Indians," a term that includes the farmers of the Missouri River valley whose resource strategy was notably unlike that of the mobile hunters of the high plains. Missouri River farmers, like many Indian groups of the Eastern woodlands, seasonally left their villages to hunt. The mounted hunters of the high plains, however, had no

---

[15] For an overview of the horse in history, see Harold Barclay, *The Role of the Horse in Man's Culture* (London: J. A. Allen, 1980), 82–101, 164–188. For Eurasian nomads, see Owen Lattimore, *Inner Asian Frontiers of China* (New York: American Geographical Society, 1940), 58–66. For South American nomads, see Ronald E. Gregson, "The Importance of the Horse in Indian Cultures of Lowland South America," *Ethnohistory*, 16 (Winter 1969), 33–50; Julian H. Steward and Louis C. Faron, *Native Peoples of South America* (New York: McGraw-Hill, 1959), 408–413; John M. Cooper, "The Patagonian and Pampean Hunters," in Steward, ed., *Handbook of South American Indians, Vol. I: The Marginal Tribes* (Washington, D.C.: Government Printing Office, 1946), 127–164.

[16] For a discussion of these strategies, see Robert Brightman, *Grateful Prey: Rock Cree Human-Animal Relationships* (Berkeley: University of California Press, 1993), 320, 354.

permanent village sites to which to return.[17] One might call the western plains Indians "bison hunters," but the Indians of the river valleys, the Rocky Mountains, and the Southwest, to say nothing of Euroamericans, also periodically hunted bison. For the same reason, the Indian groups of the western plains were not distinguished as mere "equestrian societies." Scholars of Eurasian and African pastoralism and pastoral nomadism generally reserve the term "pastoralist" for societies that raised stock for food, not as a hunting tool.[18] Though they maintained herds of horses, the bison provided the Indians' subsistence; the horse was merely a means to that end. Indians invested considerable time and effort in maintaining their horses, but this activity was nonetheless secondary to the production of bison meat and hides.

The bison, above all, was mobile, indeed, quite unpredictably so. This mobility was the greatest challenge to the bison hunters' subsistence. The inevitable consequence of the western plains Indians' year-round reliance on the bison was nearly year-round mobility. The eighteenth- and nineteenth-century equestrian bison hunters of the western plains are therefore best described as *nomads*: groups with no fixed abodes who moved from place to place in search of food and grazing land. In the context of the Great Plains, the term "nomad" is illuminating, because it captures the centrality of the relationship among people, animals, and the land in the eighteenth and nineteenth centuries. It is also problematic, because social theorists once disparaged nomadism as a primitive stage in human development. The residue of that low esteem remains in popular culture. However, the century-old canard that described stages of civilization proceeding from primitive nomads to civilized agriculturalists is most dubious in the semi-arid Great Plains. The drought-prone western plains suffered one of the worst agricultural disasters in world history under putatively civilized management: the "dust bowl" of the 1930s.[19] Many of the nomadic societies of the western plains – the Crows, Cheyennes, Arapahos, Atsinas, and Sioux – had once been agriculturalists. By the nineteenth century, however, they had come to understand that, although equestrian bison hunting was not problem-free, it was more reliable than farming in the semi-arid environment of the high plains. These nomads knew how to farm but knew better than to attempt it in the grasslands. (The few surviving nomadic hunting societies in the late twentieth century likewise inhabit marginal, arid, semi-arid, or Arctic environments ill-suited to agriculture.) Moreover, nomadic groups in the western plains can hardly be described as primitive. They had neither an indeterminate sense of their territory nor a haphazard strategy of exploiting resources. They did not

---

[17] For the Eastern woodland Indians, see Cronon, *Changes in the Land: Indians, Colonists, and the Ecology of New England* (New York: Hill and Wang, 1983); Timothy Silver, *A New Face on the Countryside: Indians, Colonists, and Slaves in South Atlantic Forests, 1500–1800* (New York: Cambridge University Press, 1990); White, *Roots of Dependency*, 1–146.

[18] See A.M. Khazanov, *Nomads and the Outside World* (New York: Cambridge University Press, 1984), 15–16; Philip Carl Salzman, "Is 'Nomadism' a Useful Concept?" *Nomadic Peoples*, 6 (June 1980), 2.

[19] Worster, *Dust Bowl*.

wander. They knew their land well, defended it from outsiders, and made ingenious use of resources to maximize productivity: for example, firing grasses to attract game and anticipating the bison's seasonal movements between river valleys and high plains. Like nomads of Eurasia and Africa, they did not exist in isolation from sedentary societies; indeed, they relied on trade contacts with agriculturalists. They had no permanent homes, but they were not homeless; they made habitual use of their favorite sites for winter and summer camps. The Indians' mobility was not primitive but a creative use of the land.[20]

If nomadic equestrian bison hunting in the Great Plains was not primitive, neither was it idyllic. Since the 1960s, certain writers, some strongly influenced by romantic elements of the environmental movement, have sought to depict Indian land use strategies as models of sustainability and harmony between people and nature.[21] The nineteenth-century plains nomads, popularly regarded as the archetypal Native Americans, have been seen as particularly sensitive to their environment. Certainly, many Indian resource strategies were sensible and their beliefs about nature inspirational to modern environmentalists. Yet the apotheosis of the "aboriginal ecologist" has proceeded without regard to historical accuracy. Insofar as the nomads of the western plains are concerned, the notion of aboriginal environmentalism holds that the Indians hunted bison only when necessary and wasted no parts of their kills. Mounted bison hunting was not a time-honored practice, however, but rather an eighteenth-century improvisation that the western plains Indians continued to revise during the nineteenth century. Moreover, like other Native American groups that relied on the hunting of large mammals – whales, seals, and caribou, for instance – the nomadic bison hunters sometimes wasted large amounts of their kills.[22]

Indeed, Indian hunters had a hand in the bison's decline, particularly during the height of the bison robe trade in the middle of the nineteenth century. The decline of the bison was not, however, the end of western plains Indian cultures.[23] Indians of the western plains accommodated themselves to the economic and ecological realities of the late nineteenth and early twentieth centuries – significant numbers of nomads became cowboys, for instance – just as they had adapted to the arrival of the horse in the eighteenth century.[24] After the destruction of

---

[20] For a brief, comparative overview of nomadism, see Thomas J. Barfield, *The Nomadic Alternative* (Englewood Cliffs, N.J.: Prentice-Hall, 1993).

[21] See J. Donald Hughes, *American Indian Ecology* (El Paso: Texas Western Press, 1983), 42; Christopher Vecsey and Robert W. Venables, eds., *American Indian Environments: Ecological Issues in Native American History* (Syracuse: Syracuse University Press, 1980).

[22] For wasteful hunting, see Tim Ingold, *Hunters, Pastoralists, and Ranchers: Reindeer Economies and their Transformations* (Cambridge: Cambridge University Press, 1980), 69–75.

[23] Peter Farb, *Man's Rise to Civilization As Shown by the Indians of North America from Primeval Times to the Coming of the Industrial State* (New York: E. P. Dutton, 1968), 112–132, notwithstanding.

[24] Peter Iverson, *When Indians Became Cowboys: Native Peoples and Cattle Ranching in the American West* (Norman: University of Oklahoma Press, 1994), 52–85. See also Frederick Hoxie, *Parading Through History: The Making of the Crow Nation in America, 1805–1935* (New York: Cambridge University Press, 1995), 266–296.

the bison, nomadism was untenable, but the Sioux, Cheyennes, and others persisted by adapting to new uses of animals and the land.

Just as change characterized Indian societies in the western plains, it characterized the western plains environment. Most environmental historians imagine nonhuman nature as a dynamic agent in human history, inherently prone to unpredictable changes in climate, vegetation, and animal populations, among other things. This conception of nature has significant implications; it means, in short, that the nonhuman natural world has its own history. It rejects the romantic dualism between cyclical nature and linear human history. If one believes that nature is essentially stable and orderly, then environmental change such as the near-extinction of the bison in the nineteenth century must emerge from human action, and environmental history becomes a story of a dynamic human society altering (usually for the worse) an otherwise stable and harmonious nonhuman natural world. Such a history would, in its broad outlines, argue that although periodically depleted by drought or other environmental factors, the bison was a resilient species that always returned to dominance in the western plains until Indians and Euroamericans nearly exterminated the species in the nineteenth century.

On its surface, the bison-shortgrass partnership in the western plains suggests permanence and stability. Adapted to each other and the semi-arid climate, the shortgrasses and the bison dominated the plains from the end of the last Ice Age until the nineteenth century, preventing the intrusion of other animal and vegetable species. The hardy shortgrasses endured despite low precipitation; the bison survived on the meager carbohydrates and the sparse water that the region offered. When Euroamericans first came to the Great Plains, the bison–shortgrass environment was well over 10,000 years old. Yet the semi-arid climate also periodically wreaked havoc on its dominant plant and animal species. In wet years tall grasses invaded the western plains. During droughts, both shortgrasses and considerable numbers of bison died. The western plains, from this perspective, were prone to frequent and pronounced ecological instability. Although one's impression of the western plains depends largely on the breadth of one's view – the last 10,000 years or the last 200 – such changes contradict the notion of self-regulating equilibrium inherent in early twentieth-century ecologists' concepts of "climax community" and "ecosystem." In recent years, particularly as "chaos theory" has become an important part of scientific study, ecologists have shifted away from the idea of self-regulating equilibrium in nature and toward a conception of nature as prone to unpredictable change.[25]

[25] Worster, "The Ecology of Order and Chaos," in *The Wealth of Nature: Environmental History and the Ecological Imagination* (New York: Oxford University Press, 1993), 156–170; Daniel Botkin, *Our Natural History: The Lessons of Lewis and Clark* (New York: G. P. Putnam's Sons, 1995), 14; and Botkin, *Discordant Harmonies: A New Ecology for the Twenty-first Century* (New York: Oxford University Press, 1990), 9. For chaos theory, see James Gleick, *Chaos: Making a New Science* (New York: Viking, 1987).

The historic Great Plains environment was characterized by both stability and dramatic, frequent, and destructive change. The evidence of overexploitation of the bison by nineteenth-century hunters is irrefutable. Without human predators, the bison would not have become nearly extinct. Yet the notion of an orderly shortgrass–bison biome destroyed by humanity's destabilizing influence posits an unconvincing disjuncture between nature and people. In the last 10,000 years, the Great Plains have never been without human influences; the very dominance of the bison in the eighteenth and nineteenth centuries owed itself, in part, to the hunters who, at the end of the last Ice Age, helped to kill off giant herbivores and thereby opened a niche for the bison. For as long as they have existed, people have inhabited, altered, and been affected by the nonhuman natural world. Even such precapitalist societies as the equestrian bison hunters of the Great Plains were sometimes given to waste and degradation of the resources upon which they depended. To assume an unchanging, harmonious relationship between Indians and the Great Plains environment classes both Indian culture and nature as static.

The concept of a stable plains environment also ignores persuasive evidence of dynamism and instability. Drought and other environmental factors doubtless contributed to the decline of the bison in the nineteenth century. Some students of environmental history may be loathe to abandon the notion of natural stability because a dynamic nature can be seen as exculpating human society for its degradation of the environment. If drought or bovine disease were even partly responsible for the destruction of the bison, so this argument goes, then Euroamerican hide hunters cannot alone be held accountable for the near-extinction of the species.[26] But there is no reason why environmental change and human agency should not both be taken into account. Environmental history properly understood is the story of the interaction of dynamic forces, with both nature and human society contributing to change.[27]

The destruction of the bison is about such change. The central transformation that concerns the pages that follow is the decline of the bison population from as many as 30 million in the mid-eighteenth century to a few hundred by the early twentieth century. That transformation was a consequence of the encounter between Indians and Euroamericans in the Great Plains – an encounter in which the interactions of indigenous and Euroamerican ecologies were as significant as, and inextricably bound to, economic and cultural exchanges.

[26] Koucky, "Buffalo Disaster," 28.
[27] McEvoy, *Fisherman's Problem*, 14–15; Cronon, "The Uses of Environmental History," *Environmental History Review*, 17 (Fall 1993), 14.

1

The Grassland Environment

The Great Plains, extending from the Missouri River valley in the east to the base of the Rocky Mountains in the west, and from Canada south to Mexico, is the largest biome in North America.[1] Although flatness is popularly believed to be the distinguishing characteristic of the plains, its topography is quite varied. Between 50 and 70 million years ago, surging molten rock from beneath the earth's surface created the Black Hills of western South Dakota and several ranges in Montana, among them the Highwood, Bearpaw, Judith, and Crazy Mountains. During the last five to ten million years, geological forces have carved a multitude of hills and bluffs in the region, from the Badlands of South Dakota to the Flint Hills of Kansas. Generally, the area between the Rocky Mountains and the Missouri River slopes from 5,000 feet above sea level at the base of the mountains to 2,000 feet above sea level at the Missouri.[2] An ubiquitous flatness exists only to the east of the Missouri and in the Llano Estacado, or Staked Plains of west Texas. In general, the region consists of many landscapes: primarily shortgrass and mixed-grass rolling plains but also wooded river valleys and high, forested hills.(See Map 1.1.)

The Mandan Indians, whose villages on the banks of the Missouri date from at least the thirteenth century, attributed the variety of the western Great Plains landscape to their chief god. According to Mandan myth, this god divided the work of shaping the landscape between himself and the first man. The god diversified the west bank of the Missouri with hills, valleys, and stands of trees, but the first man left the east bank flat and featureless. When they met after finishing their labors, the god expressed his disappointment in the man's work, saying, "all is level, so that it will be impossible to surprise buffaloes or deer, and approach

---

[1] A biome is a terrestrial region "characterized throughout its extent by similar plants, animals, and soil type." Donald D. Chiras, *Environmental Science: Action for a Sustainable Future*, 4th ed. (Redwood City, Cal.: Benjamin/Cummings, 1994), 576.

[2] Donald E. Trimble, *The Geologic Story of the Great Plains* (Medora, N.D.: Theodore Roosevelt Nature and History Association, 1990; reprint of U.S. Geological Survey Bulletin 1493), 1–2, 10–22, 32. See also Edwin Thompson Denig, *Five Indian Tribes of the Upper Missouri: Sioux, Arikaras, Assiniboines, Crees, Crows*, ed. John C. Ewers (Norman: University of Oklahoma Press, 1961), 4, 10; Preston Holder, *The Hoe and the Horse on the Plains: A Study of Cultural Development among North American Indians* (Lincoln: University of Nebraska Press, 1970), 2–3.

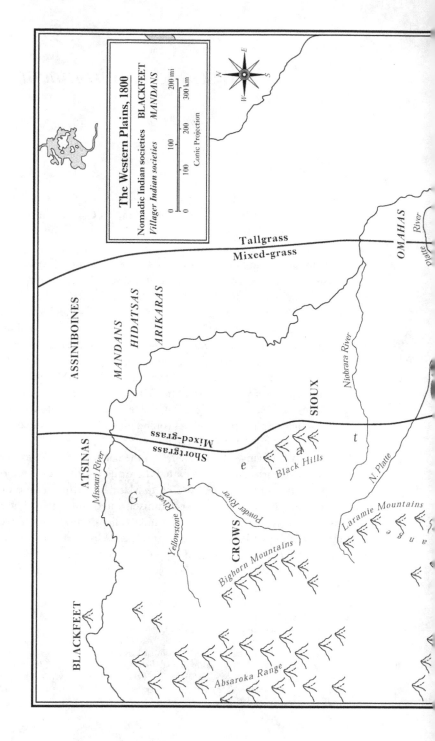

The Western Plains, 1800

Nomadic Indian societies **BLACKFEET**
Villager Indian societies *MANDANS*

200 mi
300 km
100   200
Conic Projection
100   200
0
0

Tallgrass
Mixed-grass

OMAHAS

Platte River

ASSINIBOINES

MANDANS
HIDATSAS
ARIKARAS

SIOUX

Niobrara River

Shortgrass
Mixed-grass

ATSINAS

Missouri River

e
a
t
Black Hills

G
r
Yellowstone River

Powder River

N. Platte

BLACKFEET

CROWS

Bighorn Mountains

Laramie Mountains

n g e

Absaroka Range

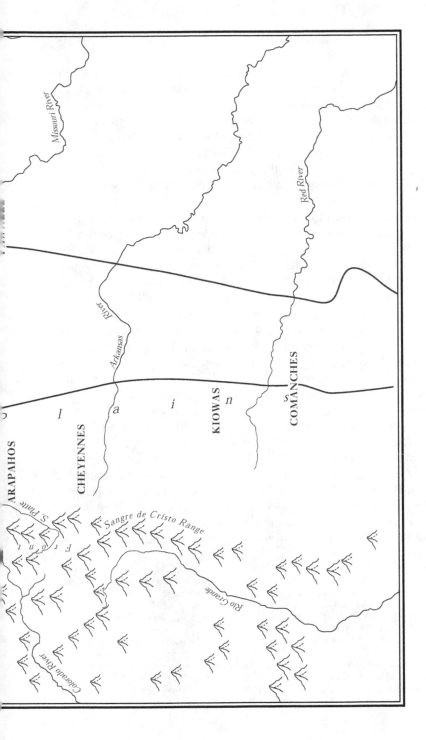

ARAPAHOS

CHEYENNES

Missouri River

S. Platte

Front

Colorado River

Sangre de Cristo Range

Rio Grande

Arkansas River

P l a i n s

KIOWAS

COMANCHES

Red River

them unperceived. Men will not be able to live there. See here, I have made springs and streams in sufficient abundance, and hills and valleys, and added all kinds of animals and fine wood. Here men will be able to live by the chase, and feed on the flesh of those animals."[3] Bison did indeed thrive on the diversity of the Great Plains environment. Although they subsisted primarily on the short-grasses of the high plains they also sought the shelter of river valleys in the winter. Hunters, who subsisted in the western plains for approximately 12,000 years, from the end of the last Ice Age to the nineteenth century, also relied on the diversity of the landscape. Like the bison, they took to the valleys in the winter. They drove bison and other animals to their deaths over the escarpments of the western Great Plains.[4]

The definitive characteristic of the Great Plains is not flatness but aridity. Between the Rocky Mountains and the ninety-eighth meridian, which divides North Dakota, South Dakota, Nebraska, Kansas, Oklahoma, and Texas, the average annual rainfall is less than 24 inches. Most of the region receives less than 16 inches of rainfall each year.[5] Except in river valleys, the sparse precipitation is insufficient to support trees or the tall grasses of the Iowa and Illinois prairies. John Bradbury, a naturalist who accompanied a fur trading expedition up the Missouri in 1811, described the striking difference between the river valley and the surrounding plains. After ascending a bluff along the river, Bradbury "found that the face of the country, soil, &c. were entirely changed. As far as the eye could reach, not a single tree or shrub was visible. The whole of the stratum immediately below the vegetable mould is a vast bed of exceedingly hard yellow clay."[6] Thomas Farnham, who crossed this "Great American Desert" in 1839, lamented that as he ascended into the high plains, both trees and the "green, tall prairie grass" gave place to "a dry, wiry species, two inches in height."[7]

Outside of the river valleys, which constitute approximately seven percent of the region, the semi-arid climate dictated that Farnham would find primarily shortgrasses. Annual precipitation minus evaporation – the effective precipitation – determines a region's vegetation. The forests of eastern North America and the coastal Pacific Northwest grow where rainfall exceeds the drying capacity of the air. In desert climates, by contrast, effective precipitation is

---

[3] Maximilian, Prinz zu Wied-Neuwied, *Travels in the Interior of North America* (London: Ackermann, 1843), in *Early Western Travels, 1748–1846*, vol. 23, ed. Reuben Gold Thwaites (Cleveland: Clark, 1904), 306–307. Maximilian's *Reise in das innere Nord-Amerika in den Jahren 1832 bis 1834* was originally published in Koblenz in two volumes in 1839–1841.

[4] Waldo R. Wedel, "The Prehistoric Plains," in Jesse D. Jennings, ed., *Ancient Native Americans* (San Francisco: W. H. Freeman, 1978), 188–192.

[5] Trimble, *Geologic Story of the Great Plains*, 2; Walter Prescott Webb, *The Great Plains* (Boston: Ginn, 1931), 17.

[6] John Bradbury, *Travels in the Interior of America in the Years 1809, 1810, and 1811* (London: Sherwood, Neely, and Jones, 1817), in *Early Western Travels*, vol. 5, 70–71.

[7] Thomas Farnham, *Travels in the Great Western Prairies* (London: Bentley, 1843), in *Early Western Travels*, vol. 28, 93.

minimal. Rain often evaporates before it reaches the ground. The low available moisture in desert climates means sparse vegetation. In steppe regions such as the Great Plains, effective precipitation is higher than in the desert but considerable moisture is nonetheless lost to evaporation. In such regions, grasses and shrubs predominate.[8]

Geographical peculiarities that interrupt the flow of moisture-bearing air currents produce aridity. In central North America, the Rocky Mountains cast a "rain shadow" over the plains to create semi-arid conditions. Moisture-bearing air currents moving across the continent from the Pacific Ocean are trapped on the western slopes of the Rockies. In the tall-grass prairie of the upper Mississippi River watershed, the influence of the rain shadow wanes and precipitation and evaporation are evenly balanced. The mean annual precipitation in the tall-grass prairie is 100 centimeters or 40 inches, approximately the same amount of moisture that is lost to evaporation. Closer to the mountains, in the shortgrass plains, evaporation exceeds the amount of annual precipitation. Between the eastern tall-grass prairie and the western shortgrass plains, tall-grass and short-grass species compete for dominance in the so-called mixed-grass zone. South of the Great Plains in the arid Sonoran desert, latitude and remoteness from moisture-bearing winds conspire to create a region too harsh even for the durable grasses of the American steppes.[9]

Located in the center of the North American continent, in the shadow of the Rocky Mountains, the western plains climate is characterized by droughts of several years' duration interspersed with years of above-average rainfall.[10] Climatologists chart rainfall over the centuries by studying tree rings; narrow rings indicate past dry years. Scientists conducted a number of such dendrochronological studies in the plains in the wake of the prolonged drought of the 1930s. By studying the width of tree rings in river valleys, scientists plotted the precipitation history in the surrounding plains. A study of tree-ring growth in the vicinity of Havre, Montana, showed that between 1784 and 1949 precipitation varied from one-fourth of the average to two times the average. A similar tree-ring study published in 1946 found that between 1406 and 1940 the area near Bismarck, North Dakota, had 11 periods of low precipitation lasting ten

[8] Robert E. Gabler, Robert J. Sager, Sheila M. Brazier, and Daniel L. Wise., *Essentials of Physical Geography*, 3d ed. (Philadelphia: Saunders, 1987), 205.

[9] Paul Sears, *Lands Beyond the Forest* (Englewood Cliffs, N.J.: Prentice-Hall, 1969), 31, 58; Carl Friedrich Kraenzel, *The Great Plains in Transition* (Norman: University of Oklahoma Press, 1955), 12–13; Douglas B. Bamforth, *Ecology and Human Organization on the Great Plains* (New York: Plenum, 1988), 53; Tom McHugh, *The Time of the Buffalo* (Lincoln: University of Nebraska Press, 1972), 19.

[10] Drought may be defined as a year in which precipitation is 65 percent or less of average, although not all the studies cited adhere to this definition. Average temperature, evaporation, and wind speed are also higher during drought. See Robert T. Coupeland, "The Effects of Fluctuations in Weather upon the Grasslands of the Great Plains," *Botanical Review*, 24 (May 1958), 284–286.

years or longer, and nine wet periods lasting ten years or more. Another
tree-ring study surveying western Nebraska discovered six droughts lasting five
years or more between 1539 and 1939. These droughts lasted an average of 13
years. The average period between droughts was just over 20 years. A study that
measured rainfall in eastern Montana between 1878 and 1946 found that precipitation was low in 32 of those 69 years. The average annual rainfall over the entire
period surveyed was 8.2 inches. The study characterized three years between
1881 and 1904 and seven years between 1917 and 1939 as "killer years," during
which drought was so severe it killed grass on the range.[11]

However prone to drought these studies showed the northern and central
plains to be, the southern plains were still more subject to deficient rainfall. As
one moves from north to south in the Great Plains, the climate becomes increasingly hotter and drier. The change in climate is the result of both latitude and
prevailing southwesterly winds from arid Mexico and New Mexico. Greater
average wind velocity also contributes to the drier climate of the southern
plains.[12] In addition, precipitation in the northern plains tends to be more evenly
distributed throughout the year. The region south of the Arkansas River suffers
longer periods of less precipitation.[13] Overall, drought in the southern plains
tends to be both more frequent and more prolonged than in the north. When
drought struck the southern plains in the 1930s after farmers had plowed under
large swaths of native grasses to plant wheat, it created the infamous "dust
bowl." When the wheat withered, strong winds picked up the topsoil and carried
it as far as the Atlantic Ocean.[14]

Although the native vegetation of the western plains also suffered during the
1930s, it is better adapted to drought than exotic species such as wheat. The shortgrasses consist primarily of two species: *Bouteloua grácilis*, or blue grama, and
Buchloë dactyloides, or buffalo grass. Blue grama is the dominant species of the
shortgrass plains. It is a densely tufted perennial plant; its blades are one to two
millimeters wide and three to ten centimeters long. Its dense root structure is confined to the twenty centimeters of soil closest to the surface. *Buchloë dactyloides* is
the second most common species in the shortgrass plains. Its curly blades are one
to two millimeters wide and ten to twelve centimeters long. Like blue grama,
buffalo grass has a dense root structure close to the surface of the soil. Other
common species in the historic shortgrass plains were hairy grama (*Bouteloua hir-
suta*), black grama (*Bouteloua eripoda*), and galleta (*Hilaria jamesii*) in the southern plains and plains muhly (*Muhlenbergia cuspidata*) in the northern grasslands.[15]

---

[11] Kraenzel, *Great Plains in Transition*, 17–23.
[12] For wind velocity in the plains, see Webb, *Great Plains*, 23.
[13] Bamforth, *Ecology and Human Organization*, 53–54.
[14] Donald Worster, *Dust Bowl: The Southern Plains in the 1930s* (New York: Oxford University Press, 1979), 13.
[15] A. S. Hitchcock, *Manual of the Grasses of the United States* (Washington, D.C.: Government Print-ing Office, 1935), 519–527. J. E. Weaver, *North American Prairie* (Lincoln: University of Nebraska

These species share with blue grama and buffalo grass dense root structures and short blades.[16] In the nineteenth century, Euroamerican settlers relied on the dense root structures of these grasses to build their sod houses.

Grama and buffalo grasses are admirably adapted to the unpredictable, semi-arid climate of the plains. They can endure drought and take advantage of brief bursts of summer rain. Blue grama allocates up to 76 percent of its annual carbon budget to the construction and maintenance of below-ground structures. By increasing its extensive fibrous root system rather than its leafage, blue grama keeps its leaf area low and its transpirational water loss to a minimum. In years of above-average rainfall, shortgrasses translocate a greater amount of available carbon to above-ground shoots. In hot and dry years, shortgrasses allocate more carbon to below-ground biomass. During drought years, blue grama rolls its leaves and assumes a dormant state.[17]

Not adapted to the extreme heat, light, and dryness of the western plains, tall grasses such as big bluestem (*Andropogon gerardi*) and needlegrass (*Stipa spartea*) grow as high as seven feet in the eastern prairies but die out in most of the western plains. They survive only in creekbeds, depressions, and on the leeward sides of hills, where they catch runoff and are protected from extreme light and wind, or river valleys, where their deep roots tap the moist soil.

Blue grama concentrates 85 percent of its roots in the 20 centimeters closest to the surface because in the high plains little soil water is found below this point. The extensive root system close to the surface can take advantage of sudden rainfall before the water is lost to runoff. This ability is crucial to survival, because rainfall events in the plains are brief. The north-south axis of the Rocky Mountains facilitates the movement of cold and dry Arctic air south from Canada and tropical maritime air currents north from the Gulf of Mexico. The warm and moist air from the Gulf typically travels up the Mississippi River valley and then turns eastward, avoiding the Great Plains entirely. Occasionally the moist Gulf air veers into the plains and meets the cold air from the north to produce violent rainstorms. These sudden showers generally occur between April and September and provide most of the region's annual precipitation.[18] As much as one-third of average annual precipitation can fall in one hour. Apart from these brief storms, parts of the western plains may endure as long as four months without

Press, 1954), 66, 92; Victor E. Shelford, *The Ecology of North America* (Urbana: University of Illinois Press, 1963), 344; Bamforth, *Ecology and Human Organization*, 32.

[16] Lauren Brown, *Grasslands* (New York: Knopf, 1985), 54–61.

[17] James K. Detling, "Processes Controlling Blue Grama Production in the Shortgrass Prairie," in *Perspectives in Grassland Ecology,* ed. Norman R. French (New York: Springer-Verlag, 1979), 25–39; Shelford, *Ecology of North America*, 340; Philip L. Sims, J. S. Singh, and W. K. Lauenroth, "The Structure and Function of Ten Western North American Grasslands I: Abiotic and Vegetational Characteristics," *Journal of Ecology*, 66 (March 1978), 270; Sims and Singh, "The Structure and Function of Ten Western North American Grasslands II: Intra-Seasonal Dynamics in Primary Producer Compartments," *Journal of Ecology*, 66 (July 1978), 565.

[18] Kraenzel, *Great Plains in Transition*, 12–13.

rain.[19] Blue grama can utilize as little as five millimeters of rainfall. In the plains, rainfall events of ten millimeters or less account for 41 percent of the rainfall during the growing season and 83 percent of all precipitation, and events of five millimeters or less contribute 25 percent of the growing season rainfall and 70 percent of all precipitation. By concentrating their roots at the top of the soil, and keeping their leafage minimal, shortgrass species conserve their moisture and take advantage of scarce rainfall.[20]

The ability to utilize scarce water enables shortgrasses to recover rapidly from drought. Biologists made note of shortgrasses' durability during the droughts of the 1930s and early 1950s. In an ungrazed shortgrass community near Hays, Kansas, the basal cover decreased from 89 percent in 1934 to 22 percent in 1939. Buffalo grass in particular, however, recovers from drought quickly, spreading new stolons after slight rainfalls, and by 1943, the Hays shortgrass community had regained its original density, with buffalo grass comprising five-sixths of the community. Blue grama, which is initially more resistant to drought but spreads more slowly, reached parity with buffalo grass in 1951. Almost immediately thereafter, drought struck the western plains again. By 1954, the basal cover had declined to 28 percent. At a moderately grazed grassland near Quinter, Kansas, buffalo grass and blue grama increased from a combined 8 percent of the basal cover in 1940 to 95 percent in 1943. Most of the recovery was made by the fast-growing buffalo grass.[21]

Though drought kills shortgrasses in the western plains, it opens niches for buffalo grass and blue grama in the mixed-grass zone. Adapted to moisture-deficient conditions, blue grama and other shortgrasses grow taller in the subhumid mixed-grass plains, but in wet years the taller species that are better adapted to the moist conditions eventually choke them out. The dominant species of the mixed-grass plains is little bluestem (*Andropogon scoparius*), a smaller version of the tall-grass bluestem. Also common is needle-and-thread (*Stipa comata*), a smaller relative of needlegrass. Little bluestem and needle-and-thread reach heights of between one and two feet. To label any species dominant in the changeable mixed-grass plains is something of a misnomer, however; the constituency of the mixed-grass plains changes annually, epitomizing the volatility of the grasslands. In wetter years, tall-grass species dominate; in drought years, the shortgrass species replace the tall grasses.[22] Between 1932 and 1937, for instance, drought reduced a little bluestem community in the mixed-grass plains from five-sixths of the total grass cover to a mere 4 percent. Shortgrasses, an insignificant presence in the area in 1932, comprised 90 percent of the

[19] Coupeland, "Effects of Fluctuations," 283.
[20] O. E. Sala and W. K. Lauenroth, "Small Rainfall Events: An Ecological Role in Semiarid Regions," *Oecologia*, 53 (June 1982), 301–304.
[21] Coupeland, "Effects of Changes in Weather Conditions upon Grasslands in the Northern Plains," in Howard B. Sprague, ed., *Grasslands* (Washington, D.C.: American Association for the Advancement of Science, 1959), 292–293; Coupeland, "Effects of Fluctuations," 288–307.
[22] Shelford, *Ecology of North America*, 335, 340.

community in 1937.[23] Changes in the constitution of the mixed-grass zone likely occurred in the nineteenth century, as shortgrasses invaded the area during drought years. In his geological survey for 1867–69, a dry period in the plains, Ferdinand Hayden listed only buffalo and grama grasses as the important grasses west of the one-hundredth meridian. The one-hundredth meridian now cuts through the middle of the mixed-grass zone.[24] "Herein lies the major problem of steppe regions," wrote one geographer. They "seem like better-watered deserts at one time and like slightly subhumid versions of their humid climate neighbors at another."[25]

Early Euroamerican explorers of the Great Plains found the desiccated grassland mysterious and exotic. To Henry Brackenridge, an American fur trader who ascended the Missouri River in 1811, the plains seemed especially foreign. He compared the grassland to "the Steppes of Tartary or the Saharas of Africa."[26] To other early observers, the landscape seemed cheerless. Farnham called the plains an "arid waste" and "a scene of desolation scarcely equalled."[27] The impressions of Brackenridge and Farnham were typical of nineteenth-century characterizations of the plains; Euroamericans generally saw the region as a desolate wilderness.[28] Yet in one seemingly incongruous sense the shortgrass plains were abundant: the region teemed with animal life. Stephen Long, a New Hampshire native and Dartmouth College graduate who explored the southern plains in 1819 and 1820 at the head of an Army expedition, remarked that although the plains were "wholly unfit for cultivation, and of course uninhabitable by a people depending upon agriculture for their subsistence," they were nonetheless "peculiarly adapted as a range for buffaloes, wild goats, and other wild game."[29] Josiah Gregg, who traveled through the southern plains in the 1830s, agreed that the plains were "all too dry to be cultivated. These great steppes seem only fitted for the haunts of the mustang, the buffalo, the antelope, and their migratory lord, the prairie Indian."[30]

[23] Coupeland, "Effects of Changes in Weather upon Grasslands," 293.

[24] F. V. Hayden, U.S. Geological Survey of the Territories for 1867, 1868, 1869, cited in Floyd Larson, "The Role of the Bison in Maintaining the Short Grass Plains," Ecology, 21 (April 1940), 113–121.

[25] Gabler, et al., Essentials of Physical Geography, 210.

[26] Henry M. Brackenridge, Journal of a Voyage up the River Missouri Performed in 1811 (Baltimore: Coale and Maxwell, 1816), in Early Western Travels, vol. 6, 153.

[27] Farnham, in Early Western Travels, vol. 28, 108–109.

[28] Roderick Nash, Wilderness and the American Mind, 3d ed. (New Haven: Yale University Press, 1982), 23–43. For an analysis of views of the Great Plains, see Brian W. Blouet and Merlin P. Lawson, eds., Images of the Plains: The Role of Human Nature in Settlement (Lincoln: University of Nebraska Press, 1975).

[29] Stephen H. Long, "A General Description of the Country Traversed by the Exploring Expedition," in Edwin James, Account of an Expedition from Pittsburgh to the Rocky Mountains, Performed in the Years 1819, 1820 (London: Longman, Hurst, Rees, Orme and Brown, 1823), in Early Western Travels, vol. 17, 147–148.

[30] Josiah Gregg, Commerce of the Prairies (New York: Langley, 1845), in Early Western Travels, vol. 20, 248.

Indeed, the shortgrass plains supported tens of millions of bison, the largest land animal in North America.[31] Subsisting largely on the stunted shortgrasses, an average full-grown bull nonetheless stands from five to six feet at his shoulder, is nine to ten feet long, and weighs sixteen hundred pounds. The average cow is five feet tall, seven feet long, and weighs from seven hundred to twelve hundred pounds. Given their size, bison are surprisingly swift; in quarter-mile stretches, they can reach speeds over 40 miles per hour, nearly as fast as racehorses.[32]

To survive, the shortgrasses and the bison adapted not only to the semi-arid climate but to each other. Bison concentrated in the western shortgrass and mixed-grass plains rather than in the tall-grass prairies not because the short-grasses were more nutritious. Indeed, by virtue of their greater size, tall grasses contain considerably more carbohydrates than shortgrasses, but a considerably smaller proportion of protein per unit of volume. The bison concentrated in the western plains and in the mixed-grass zone when and where shortgrasses could be found because their digestive system requires one part protein for every six parts carbohydrates. Shortgrasses offer a sufficiently high ratio of protein to carbohydrates. Even when they mature and dry out in the fall, shortgrasses contain 15 to 20 percent protein and 75 to 80 percent carbohydrates.[33]

The bison thrived on the forage of the historic western plains; shortgrasses, in turn, were well adapted to the bison. Although shortgrasses dominate the western plains primarily by virtue of their suitability to the semi-arid climate, the bison's presence helped select shortgrasses for dominance. Bison droppings returned fertilizers to the soil.[34] Buffalo grass responds to heavy grazing by increasing its uptake of nitrogen from the soil.[35] Grazing induces new growth to

---

[31] The American bison, or buffalo, like the European wisent belongs to the genus *Bison*. Scientists refer to the species as the bison rather than the buffalo to distinguish it from the African Cape buffalo, the wild Indian buffalo, the domesticated water buffalo, and other ruminants that belong to the *Bos* genus. The American bison once belonged to the *Bos* genus before being reclassified, the wisent (*bison bonasus*) was once classed not as a subspecies but as a different species altogether, and the *Bos* and *Bison* genera share similar chromosomal structures and blood types. To complicate nomenclature further, nineteenth-century naturalists classified two subspecies of the bison in North America: the plains bison (*bison bison*) and the less numerous wood bison (*bison athabascae*) in northern Canada. See McHugh, *Time of the Buffalo*, 27–38. A recent study suggests that the wood bison is an ecotype rather than a phenotype. See Valerius Geist, "Phantom Subspecies: The Wood Bison *Bison bison "athabascae"* Rhoads 1897 is Not a Valid Taxon, but an Ecotype," *Arctic*, 44 (December 1991), 283–300. Nineteenth-century observers consistently used the term "buffalo" to refer to both American subspecies (or ecotypes). For the purposes of this study, the terms bison and buffalo both refer to the plains bison unless otherwise noted.

[32] Martin S. Garretson, *The American Bison: The Story of Its Extermination as a Wild Species and Its Restoration Under Federal Protection* (New York: New York Zoological Society, 1938), 26; Francis Haines, *The Buffalo* (New York: Crowell, 1975), 29–30; McHugh, *Time of the Buffalo*, 171.

[33] Charles W. Johnson, "Protein As a Factor in the Distribution of the American Bison," *Geographical Review*, 41 (April 1951), 330–331.

[34] Shelford, *Ecology of North America*, 334.

[35] Detling, "Grasslands and Savannas: Regulation of Energy Flow and Nutrient Cycling by Herbivores," in Lawrence R. Pomeroy and James J. Alberts, eds., *Concepts of Ecosystem Analysis: A Comparative View* (New York: Springer-Verlag, 1988), 146–147.

restore the lost parts of the plant, producing a thick "grazing lawn."[36] Overgrazing, especially in combination with drought, could eventually degrade a range, but shortgrasses endure heavy grazing better than tall grasses.[37] Just as drought opens niches for shortgrasses in the eastern plains, when large herbivores graze in the mixed-grass plains, shortgrasses gradually replace tall grasses.[38]

The bison was so well adapted to the shortgrass plains that until the end of the nineteenth century, the species was ubiquitous in the region. While traveling on the Santa Fe Trail in 1839, Thomas Farnham reported seeing bison cover the whole country for three days. He calculated that the herd covered 1,350 square miles. Another traveler on the Santa Fe Trail in 1825 saw a herd that "could not have been less than 100,000." On the Arkansas River in 1871, Colonel Richard Irving Dodge wrote that "the whole country appeared one mass of buffalo." At the juncture of the Platte and Missouri rivers in the central plains, a member of Stephen H. Long's expedition reported "immense herds of bisons, grazing in undisturbed possession and obscuring with the density of their numbers the verdant plain; to the right and left as far as the eye was permitted to rove, the crowd seemed hardly to diminish, and it would be no exaggeration to say that at least ten thousand here burst on our sight in the instant." At the mouth of the White River in 1806, the American explorers Meriwether Lewis and William Clark saw a herd they estimated to be 20,000 strong. At the juncture of the Heart and Missouri rivers in the northern plains, John Bradbury ascended a bluff and counted 17 herds numbering more than 10,000 animals.[39] Sightings such as these prompted exaggerated estimates of the aggregate bison population. In the 1860s, the bison hunter Robert M. Wright and General Philip Sheridan calculated that 100 million bison roamed the Great Plains. Wright and Sheridan thought the number to be a conservative guess.[40]

Such estimates failed to consider that enormous herds congregated only during the summer months for the rutting season. During the summer, the shortgrasses were at their thickest and most nutritious and could support large aggregations of bison. During the winter, the huge herds dispersed into small groups to search for forage and shelter from the elements.[41] Every one of the

---

[36] Bamforth, *Ecology and Human Organization*, 37–38.

[37] For a recent analysis of the problems of overgrazing, see Elliott West, *The Way to the West: Essays on the Central Plains* (Albuquerque: University of New Mexico Press, 1995), 34–35.

[38] Sims, et al., "The Structure and Function of Ten Western North American Grasslands I," 256; Shelford, *Ecology of North America*, 335, 340.

[39] Farnham, in *Early Western Travels*, vol. 28, 96; Doctor Willard, "Inland Trade with New Mexico," *Western Monthly Review*, 2 (April–May 1829), in *Early Western Travels*, vol. 18, 334; Richard J. Dodge, *The Plains of North America and Their Inhabitants* (Newark: University of Delaware Press, 1989), 140; James, in *Early Western Travels*, vol. 15, 239; Meriwether Lewis and William Clark, *The History of the Lewis and Clark Expedition*, ed. Elliott Coues (New York: Harper, 1893), vol. 3, 1196–1197; Bradbury, in *Early Western Travels*, vol. 5, 148–149.

[40] Robert M. Wright, *Dodge City: The Cowboy Capital* (Wichita, 1913), 75.

[41] Symmes C. Oliver, *Ecology and Cultural Continuity as Contributing Factors in the Social Organization*

foregoing sightings – and they are but a small sampling of such reports – occurred during the summer months. Reckoners such as Wright and Sheridan assumed large summer herds were spread throughout the plains throughout the year. Yet "the American buffalo is a migratory animal," the naturalist George Perkins Marsh wrote in 1864. Therefore, "at the season of his annual journeys, the whole stock of a vast extent of pasture ground is collected into a single army."[42] Marsh concluded that although reports of huge summer herds may have been accurate, they actually reveal little about the total number of bison that inhabited the plains.

A better way to approximate the number of bison in the historic plains is to establish the carrying capacity of the grassland. As estimates of range carrying capacity become more precise, and as historians and ecologists suggest more factors possibly limiting the bison population, estimates of the historic bison population have fallen considerably. In 1929, the naturalist Ernest Thompson Seton estimated that before 1800 there were 75 million bison in North America. Seton based his estimate on the Agricultural Census of 1900, which counted 24 million horses and cattle and six million sheep in the rangelands of North Dakota, South Dakota, Montana, Wyoming, Nebraska, Kansas, Colorado, Texas, and Oklahoma. Considering that in 1900 the richest bottomlands were fenced in, and that bison are more effective grazers than domestic livestock, Seton estimated that if the western grasslands supported 30 million domestic livestock in 1900 it must have sustained 40 million bison a century earlier. The tall-grass prairie, according to Seton, was only one-third as large but four times as fertile as the shortgrass plains, so he set the bison population there at 30 million. The pre-Columbian forests, Seton figured, supported a further 5 million bison.[43]

Not only did Seton not account for the bison's preference for shortgrasses, or competition from other grazers, or thinning of the herd by fire, drought, severe winters, bovine diseases, and wolves, but he assumed that bison were found everywhere throughout North America even more densely than early twentieth-century ranchers stocked their ranges. The density of favored organisms in an artificial monoculture such as ranching is normally greater than the density of any single species in an unmanaged environment. Yet later writers have accepted Seton's calculations uncritically. As late as 1974, David Dary accepted Seton's calculation in his history of the bison. Frank Gilbert Roe, in a study published in 1951, implied that Seton's total was too low because, among other things, it underestimated the bison's prolific rate of natural increase.[44]

of the Plains Indians. University of California Publications in American Archaeology and Ethnology, vol. 48, no. 1 (Berkeley: University of California Press, 1962), 17.

[42] George Perkins Marsh, *Man and Nature: Or, Physical Geography as Modified by Human Action*, ed. David Lowenthal (Cambridge, Mass.: Belknap Press, 1965), 73–74.

[43] Ernest Thompson Seton, *Lives of Game Animals* (New York: Doubleday, 1929), vol. 3, pt. 2, 654–656.

[44] David A. Dary, *The Buffalo Book: The Full Saga of the American Animal* (Chicago: Swallow, 1974),

Recent studies that have taken more seriously the environmental limitations on the bison indicate that the semi-arid grassland could have supported no more than 30 million bison. According to the zoologist Tom McHugh, who observed bison in Yellowstone Park for several years, one bison could live for one year on 25 acres of grassland – provided that during that year those 25 acres received sufficient rainfall. That figure translates to 26 bison per square mile, or 32 million in the plains. Allowing for competition from other grazers, McHugh calculated that the nineteenth-century grasslands supported no more than 30 million bison.[45] The historian Dan Flores has arrived at a comparable figure by employing a similar methodology. According to the Census of 1910 – a year of median rainfall – the southern plains supported seven million cattle, horses, and mules. Bison are 18 percent more efficient grazers than these domestic animals; thus in a year of median precipitation the pre-horse southern plains could have supported just over eight million bison. The entire plains, according to this calculation, could have supported between 28 and 30 million bison.[46]

Evidence from a twentieth-century bison preserve indicates that the bison population at its highest may have been smaller still. In the mid-1920s, the 29-square-mile National Bison Range in Montana supported 550 bison and an equal number of elk (*Cervus elaphus canadensis*).[47] If the conditions at the Montana preserve were representative of the plains before its transformation by Euroamerican settlement, then the carrying capacity of the grassland was less than 24 million. The Montana preserve, however, did not exactly recreate the conditions of the western plains before the coming of Euroamericans; the number of elk did not equal the bison population in the historic plains.[48] A bison requires three times as much forage as an elk, so if the Montana range had stocked only bison, it might have supported 733. Based on this figure, the plains might have supported 27 million bison.

29; Frank Gilbert Roe, *The North American Buffalo: A Critical Study of the Species in Its Wild State* (Toronto: University of Toronto Press, 1951), 489–520.

[45] McHugh, *Time of the Buffalo*, 16–17.

[46] Dan Flores, "Bison Ecology and Bison Diplomacy: The Southern Plains from 1800 to 1850," *Journal of American History*, 78 (September 1991), 470–471. See also James H. Shaw, "How Many Bison Originally Populated Western Rangelands?" *Rangelands*, 17 (October 1995), 148–150.

[47] W. C. Henderson, Acting Chief of the Bureau of Biological Survey, Washington, D.C., to William T. Hornaday, New York Zoological Park, 20 November 1923; E. W. Nelson, Chief of the Bureau of Biological Survey, Washington, D.C., to Martin Garretson, Secretary, American Bison Society, Clifton, New Jersey, American Bison Society Papers, Box 272, File 27, Conservation Collection, Western History Department, Denver Public Library.

[48] James M. Peek, "Elk," in Joseph A. Chapman and George A. Feldhammer, eds., *Wild Mammals of North America: Biology, Management, and Economics* (Baltimore: The Johns Hopkins University Press, 1982), 851–852; Olaus J. Murie, *The Elk of North America* (Harrisburg, Penn.: Stackpole, 1951), 293–294. The North American elk (*Cervus elaphus canadensis*) is a large deer. (The European relative, *Cervus elaphus elaphus*, is known as the red deer.) The North American elk is perhaps more accurately called a wapiti, to distinguish it from the European elk (*Alces alces*), a smaller relative of the North American moose (*Alces americanus*).

The nineteenth-century bison population was not static but constantly in flux. Changing ecological factors exerted downward pressure on the bison's numbers. In the desiccated plains, lightning periodically ignited grass fires. Some fires gathered enough force and size to become fire storms that consumed every living thing over a broad area.[49] During the winter, many bison died attempting to cross rivers that had frozen over. At weak points in the ice, some bison broke through and drowned. In 1805, the fur trader Charles McKenzie observed that, as a consequence, "in the Spring both sides of the [Missouri] River are in several places covered with rotten carcasses."[50]

In the early nineteenth century, perhaps 1.5 million plains wolves (*Canis lupus nubilis*) attended the bison. The wolves, wrote one fur trader, "follow in the wake of the buffalo in bands of several hundreds."[51] Wolves largely preyed on the aged, diseased, and very young; they may have killed as many as one-third of bison calves.[52] Even after their first year, juvenile bison are more liable to die than adults. During the course of a study of bison in Yellowstone Park, only one-half of the bison that survived their first year lived to 2.5 years of age.[53] At modern preserves in the Dakotas and Oklahoma, fire, drowning, falls, or inclement weather kill between 3 and 9 percent of the bison annually.

In the historic plains, horses, which have an 80 percent dietary overlap with bison, competed with the herds for forage. Equestrian Indian hunters watered their horses at the very places frequented by the bison. In the early nineteenth century, the estimated 60,000 Indians who inhabited the western plains maintained horse herds that ranged in size from six to fifteen horses per person. Thus, between 360,000 and 900,000 domesticated horses grazed in the early nineteenth-century plains. Furthermore, an additional two million wild horses grazed in the southern plains alone.[54] These horses consumed forage that might have supported between 1.9 and 2.3 million bison.

---

[49] Richard J. Vogl, "Effects of Fire on Grasslands," in *Fire and Ecosystems*, ed. T. T. Kozlowski and C. E. Ahlgren (New York: Academic Press, 1974), 145–146.

[50] "Charles McKenzie's Narratives," in W. Raymond Wood and Thomas D. Thiessen, eds., *Early Fur Traders on the Northern Plains: Canadian Traders Among the Mandan and Hidatsa Indians, 1738–1818* (Norman: University of Oklahoma Press), 239. For the drowning of bison during the winter, see Roe, *North American Buffalo*, 160–179.

[51] Denig, *Five Indian Tribes*, 119–120. The estimate of the wolf population in the plains is from John K. Townsend, *Narrative of a Journey Across the Rocky Mountains to the Columbia River* (Boston: Perkins and Marvin, 1839), in *Early Western Travels*, vol. 21, 170; and George Catlin, *North American Indians: Being Letters and Notes on Their Manners, Customs, and Conditions, Written During Eight Years' Travel Among the Wildest Tribes of Indians in North America, 1832–1839*, vol. 1 (Philadelphia: Leary, Stuart, 1913), 59.

[52] Flores, "Bison Ecology," 481–482.

[53] Margaret Mary Meagher, *The Bison of Yellowstone National Park*. National Park Service Scientific Monograph Series, 1 (Washington, D.C.: Government Printing Office, 1973), vi.

[54] Flores, "Bison Ecology," 481–482; James Sherow, "Workings of the Geodialectic: High Plains Indians and Their Horses in the Region of the Arkansas River Valley, 1800–1870," *Environmental History Review*, 16 (Summer 1992), 68.

The most destructive influence of the plains environment on the bison was the periodic visitation of drought. The central plains suffered droughts from 1761 to 1773, from 1798 to 1803, and from 1822 to 1832.[55] In the northern plains, there were nine dry years between 1752 and 1786; seven dry years between 1802 and 1830; and a 15-year drought between 1836 and 1851.[56] During extended dry periods, between 70 and 90 percent of plains vegetation dies, causing a significant decline in range carrying capacity.[57] In southeastern Montana, for instance, rainfall in 1934 was a mere 38 percent of the average. The drought reduced the carrying capacity of the range to 36 percent of its 1933 capacity.[58]

It is impossible to know precisely how many bison died during such dry periods in the eighteenth and nineteenth centuries. During the droughts of the 1880s, an estimated 15 percent of the cattle in the plains perished – although blizzards, fences, and overstocking of the range also contributed to the decline.[59] In past centuries, the loss of forage no doubt caused the numbers of bison to decline precipitously. This fluctuation of the population has probably persisted since the bison emerged as the dominant species in the plains at the end of the last Ice Age. Indeed, at sites in the southern plains where pedestrian hunters drove bison to their deaths there are two long periods – from 6000 to 2500 B.C.E. and from 500 to 1300 C.E. – when bison were absent from the kill sites. The absence of bison remains indicates a dramatic decline in the density of the herds.[60]

The bison's rate of increase was as volatile as its rate of mortality. On modern game preserves, the bison reproduces at an annual rate of 20 percent or higher. On preserves, approximately 35 percent of the bison are females between three and thirteen years old – the bison's prime breeding age. At one preserve near the Badlands of South Dakota, between 58 and 75 percent of cows between three and thirteen years old produced a calf every year.[61] If these figures are applicable to the historic grasslands, a population of 27 to 30 million bison included between 9.5 and 10.5 million cows of breeding age who produced between 5.5 and 7.9 million calves every year. These figures may be too high, however. At the Wichita Mountains Wildlife Refuge in Oklahoma, during a seven-year study between 1960 and 1966, calf production by cows older than one year varied between

[55] Harry E. Weakly, "A Tree-Ring Record of Precipitation in Western Nebraska," *Journal of Forestry*, 41 (November 1943), 819; Merlin P. Lawson, *The Climate of the Great American Desert: Reconstruction of the Climate of the Western Interior United States, 1800–1850*. University of Nebraska Studies, New Series no. 46 (Lincoln: University of Nebraska Press, 1974).

[56] Kraenzel, *Great Plains in Transition*, 19.

[57] Charles Rehr, "Buffalo Population and Other Deterministic Factors in a Model of Adaptive Processes on the Shortgrass Plains," *Plains Anthropologist*, 23 (November 1978), 23–39.

[58] Coupeland, "Effects of Fluctuations," 288, 292.

[59] Richard White, "Animals and Enterprise," in *The Oxford History of the American West*, ed. Clyde A. Milner II, et al. (New York: Oxford University Press, 1994), 266.

[60] Tom D. Dillehay, "Late Quaternary Bison Population Changes in the Southern Plains," *Plains Anthropologist*, 19 (August 1974), 180–196.

[61] Joel Berger and Carol Cunningham, *Bison: Mating and Conservation in Small Populations* (New York: Columbia University Press, 1994), 99–101, 132–135, 145–148; Flores, "Bison Ecology," 476.

47 and 60 percent. The average during the period was 52 percent.[62] That figure accords with a study, conducted between 1963 and 1969, of the Yellowstone Park bison, where the pregnancy rate for all cows 2.5 years and older was also 52 percent.[63] Delayed puberty – most females did not reach sexual maturity until four years old – and lower fecundity at Yellowstone are likely a response to the environment's severe winters and sub-optimal forage. Generously assuming that the historic bison's rate of increase was the higher rate of 58 to 75 percent of adult cows observed in South Dakota, from between 5.5 and 7.9 million calves would have been born each year. Wolf predation likely reduced the number of surviving calves by one-third, to between 3.7 and 5.3 million. The annual increase of the bison herd was, as a result, probably between 13.6 and 17.6 percent. Each year, natural mortality and competition from other grazers might have eliminated between 2.6 and 4.5 million bison, a decrease of between 10 and 15 percent. The combination of wolf predation, competition from other grazers, and accidents raised the natural mortality of the bison to the point that in some years it may have exceeded its natural increase.

When drought struck the grassland, it probably exceeded in severity all other causes of bison mortality, causing an acute decline in the population. A drought's effect on the bison was not limited to the number who died as a result of reduced forage. Bison assembled as large breeding groups in the summer, when relatively heavy rainfall produced thick, nutritious shortgrasses that could support large aggregations. Mammals and birds that rely on such communal breeding systems require a sufficiently large breeding group to insure reproductive success. When drought prevented the congregation of summer breeding groups, it threatened population stability. An extended drought could cause a long-term population decline.[64]

Paradoxically, the absence of drought, severe winters, competition from other grazers, and wolf predation could have similarly destabilized the bison population. Without these limitations on the bison's numbers, the herds were liable to increase beyond the capacity of the shortgrass plains to sustain them. Such eruptions of ungulate populations are almost always followed by sharp declines, as increased numbers are unable to find forage. Because they are so prolific in the absence of predators, ungulate populations seem to be particularly liable to such eruptions and crashes. One ecologist has argued that at any given time, it is likely that the biomass of an ungulate population and the biomass of forage are at disequilibrium with each other. Such fluctuations can be relatively minor: There

---

[62] Arthur F. Halloran, "Bison (Bovidae) Productivity on the Wichita Mountains Wildlife Refuge, Oklahoma," *Southwestern Naturalist*, 13 (May 1968), 23–26.

[63] Meagher, *Bison of Yellowstone*, v.

[64] See H. Ronald Pulliam and Thomas Caraco, "Living in Groups: Is There an Optimal Group Size?" in J. R. Krebs and N. B. Davies, eds., *Behavioral Ecology: An Evolutionary Approach*, 2d ed. (Sunderland, Mass.: Sinauer, 1984).

were over 100 suberuptions of deer populations in the United States between 1900 and 1945. They can also be catastrophic. A population of 29 reindeer (*Rangifer tarandus*) introduced in 1944 to St. Matthew Island in the Bering Sea had increased to 6,000 by the summer of 1963 before crashing to fewer than 60 the following winter.[65] Similarly, the generally favorable conditions for bison from the mid-eighteenth to the mid-nineteenth centuries may have raised the population to an unsustainably high level, increasing the severity of the late-nineteenth-century decline.

In general, the greater the number of variables affecting a population – predation, competition from other grazers, and availability of forage being the most important – the more likely it is that the population will be prone to unpredictable upward and downward fluctuations.[66] In the western plains, the variables affecting the bison were numerous. Thus, whereas the maximum possible sustainable bison population was probably between 27 and 30 million, the population was not static. Eruptions could have briefly increased the population to well above the sustainable maximum. Severe drought in combination with other factors could have depressed the population to far lower levels. The bison's dominance of the plains was as subject to change as the plains environment itself.

The volatility of the bison population is the key to understanding its near-extinction in the nineteenth century. Ecologists once generally agreed that ecosystems were characterized by equilibrium. The extinction of a species – especially one so dominant in its biome as was the bison in the Great Plains – was unlikely to result from drought or other environmental shocks. Disruptions occurred, but they were temporary aberrations; the stability of an ecological community was threatened less by natural disaster than by humanity's destructiveness. There is a certain validity to this perspective. Until the nineteenth century, although environmental changes periodically decimated the plant and animal species in the Great Plains, the durable shortgrasses and resilient bison always recovered and reestablished their dominance in the region.[67] In recent

---

[65] See Graeme Caughley, "Wildlife Management and the Dynamics of Ungulate Populations," in T. H. Coaker, ed., *Applied Biology*, vol. 1 (London: Academic Press, 1976), 189, 240. And Caughley, "Plant-Herbivore Systems," in Robert M. May, ed., *Theoretical Ecology: Principles and Applications* (Philadelphia: W. B. Saunders, 1976). For suberuptions in deer populations, see A. Leopold, L. K. Sowls, and D. K. Spencer, "A Survey of Over-Populated Deer Ranges in the United States," *Journal of Wildlife Management*, 11 (1947), 162–177; for the reindeer, see David R. Klein, "The Introduction, Increase, and Crash of Reindeer on St. Matthew Island," Ibid., 32 (April 1968), 350–367.

[66] To survive random environmental change, a population must be very large. The historic bison population, although quite large, was thus liable to acute decline in the stochastic environment of the plains. See Michael E. Soulé, ed., *Viable Populations for Conservation Biology* (Cambridge: Cambridge University Press, 1987).

[67] Such views were advanced in the early twentieth century by plant ecologists such as Frederic Clements and John Weaver. See Ronald C. Tobey, *Saving the Prairies: The Life Cycle of the Founding School of American Plant Ecology, 1895–1955* (Berkeley: University of California Press, 1981), 76–109, and Donald Worster, "The Ecology of Order and Chaos," in *The Wealth of Nature:*

years, however, many ecologists have come to believe that nature does not tend toward equilibrium. Although not diminishing the role of human beings in altering the environment, the new ecology of dynamism argues that rather than tending toward self-regulating equilibrium, nonhuman nature is characterized by change.[68] Some parts of the environment are more volatile than others. Studies of environmental dynamism focus particularly on climate and wildlife population, which in the Great Plains are characteristically volatile.

The complex and constant changes inherent in the Great Plains environment played fundamental roles in the decline of the bison in the nineteenth century. The near-extinction of the species cannot be understood simply as the result of hunting. It was surely also the consequence of less direct human alteration of the bison's habitat: displacement of bison from river valleys by Indians' horses and the livestock of Euroamerican emigrants; and the introduction of cattle to the bison's range. More important, however, the volatile plains environment itself contributed to the near-extinction of the herds. The pressures of drought, fires, blizzards, and other animals chronically depressed the bison's numbers. Favorable conditions – rain, abundant forage, and mild winters – could also ultimately be disastrous, as an eruption of the population could lead to overgrazing and a population crash. Human hunters pressured the bison in combination with these unpredictable environmental forces. Thus, the destruction of the bison was not merely the result of human agency, but the consequence of the interactions of human societies with a dynamic environment.

Environmental History and the Ecological Imagination (New York: Oxford University Press, 1993), 156–170.

[68] For a summary of these new perspectives, see James Gleick, *Chaos: Making a New Science* (New York: Penguin, 1987). See also Daniel B. Botkin, *Discordant Harmonies: A New Ecology for the Twenty-first Century* (New York: Oxford University Press, 1990).

2

The Genesis of the Nomads

In 1811, the naturalist John Bradbury paused near the juncture of the Grand and Missouri rivers and remarked upon the abundance of honeybees there. Bradbury, an English botanist accompanying a group of American fur traders up the Missouri, was astounded that a European insect could be found in great numbers in the trans-Mississippi West. He wrote, "Even if it be admitted that they were brought over soon after the first settlement took place" – indeed, bees arrived in Virginia in the 1620s – "their increase since appears astonishing, as bees are found in all parts of the United States; and since they have entered upon the fine countries of the Illinois and Upper Louisiana, their progress westward has been surprisingly rapid." Bradbury believed that bees had not crossed the Mississippi River until 1797, although later in the nineteenth century some writers claimed that Madame Marie Thérèse Chouteau kept bees in her St. Louis garden in 1792. In any event, as Bradbury wrote, "They are now found as high up the Missouri as the Maha nation, having moved westward to the distance of 600 miles in fourteen years."[1]

Indians of the Missouri watershed such as the Omahas, or the Mahas as Bradbury called them, regarded honeybees as the vanguard of European expansion. Bradbury wrote, "Bees have spread over this continent in a degree, and with a celerity so nearly corresponding with that of the Anglo-Americans, that it has given rise to a belief, both amongst the Indians and the Whites, that bees are their precursors, and that to whatever part they go the white people will follow."[2] Washington Irving reiterated that idea in his 1835 travel book, *A Tour on the Prairie.* Irving wrote, "It is surprising in what countless swarms the bees have overspread the Far West, within but a moderate number of years. The Indians consider them harbingers of the white man, as the buffalo is of the red man; and say that, in proportion as the bee advances, the Indian and the buffalo retire."[3]

[1] John Bradbury, *Travels in the Interior of America in the Years 1809, 1810, and 1811* (London: Sherwood, Neely, and Jones, 1819), in *Early Western Travels, 1748–1846*, vol. 5, ed. Reuben Gold Thwaites (Cleveland: Clark, 1904), 58. Richard Edwards and Menra Hopewell, *The Great West and Her Commercial Metropolis* (St. Louis, 1860) claimed that the first bees west of the Mississippi were found in Mme. Chouteau's garden.
[2] Bradbury, in *Early Western Travels*, vol. 5, 58–59.
[3] Washington Irving, *A Tour on the Prairie*, ed. John Francis McDermott (Norman: University of Oklahoma Press, 1956), 50.

The honeybee's conquest of the plains was a small part of the remarkably rapid and complete expansion of European plants, animals, and microbes in North America. This European ecological invasion, carried by the expanding European market economy, largely shaped the first four hundred years of inter-action between Indians and Euroamericans. When Europeans brought to North America their ecological and economic complex of large draft animals, intensive agriculture, and communicable diseases bred in crowded Old World cities, they forever altered the indigenous environment and Native American land use. The rise of the nomadic, equestrian, bison-hunting Indian societies of the west-ern plains was largely a response to this European ecological and economic incursion.

Irving scoffed at the Indians' apprehension of the honeybee. Yet their belief that a causal relationship existed between the advance of European biota and the advance of Europeans themselves was quite correct. Beginning in the early six-teenth century, European plants, animals, and germs invaded and often largely displaced indigenous ecological communities, helping colonists gain rapid and thorough control of the temperate regions of the New World. Old World biota was not universally successful in North America. Several attempts to introduce camels to the Southwest in the nineteenth century ended in failure, for instance.[4] More often, however, Old World plants and animals prospered in North Amer-ica. The salient characteristic of this invasion, which the historian Alfred W. Crosby has called "ecological imperialism," was that Old World microbes, plants, animals, and people often accomplished their conquests in concert. Eurasian diseases such as smallpox and measles devastated the indigenous popu-lation of North America, clearing the way for European settlers. Those settlers felled trees to clear the land for agriculture, while their livestock overgrazed the indigenous grasses, opening niches for European plants. Even the honeybee participated, pollinating both European crops and weeds.[5]

The cooperative character of European expansion included both ecology and economy. European biota and the European economy each facilitated the expan-sion of the other, although Europeans themselves were not always aware of the synergy. The dual expansion of European biota and the European economy was a curse to most Native Americans because it abetted the European political conquest of North America.[6] Contrary to Irving's assertion, however, that all Indians feared the proliferation of European biota, some Indian societies initially thrived on the European economic and ecological conquests. The nomads of the

[4] Eva Jolene Boyd, *Noble Brutes: Camels on the American Frontier* (Plano: Republic of Texas Press, 1995).

[5] Alfred W. Crosby, *Ecological Imperialism: The Biological Expansion of Europe, 900–1900* (New York: Cambridge University Press, 1986).

[6] William Cronon, *Changes in the Land: Indians, Colonists, and the Ecology of New England* (New York: Hill and Wang, 1983), 6.

western plains improvised their social structures and resource strategies in response to the introduction of the horse, crowd diseases, and the fur trade. So new was the effect of the European ecology and economy that the Arapahos, Assiniboines, Atsinas, Blackfeet, Cheyennes, Comanches, Crows, Kiowas, and Sioux did not become exclusively equestrian bison hunters until the late eighteenth century, after European diseases had weakened Missouri River horticultural societies, and European horses and commerce had reached the grasslands. The improvisational nature of these societies was evident in their singular land use strategy. Most North American Indians diversified their resource use and followed seasonal cycles: planting in the spring, hunting and gathering in the summer, harvesting in the fall, and hunting again in the winter. By contrast, as the utility of the horse, the lure of the fur trade, and the fear of disease drove the Indians to the grasslands, they came to rely primarily on one resource, the bison. The migration of many of the nomadic societies from the fertile and diverse woodlands to the semi-arid high plains was typical of hunter-gatherers worldwide, who often moved to marginal lands in reaction to the expansion of Europeans.[7] By the end of the nineteenth century, the nomads' reliance on the bison had become a liability for them and a disaster for the herds.

I

"Without horses Indians cannot support their families by a hunter's life," wrote the American fur trader Edwin Thompson Denig in 1855. "They must have them or starve."[8] The horse was indeed essential to the nomadic societies. It was the primary means of travel, vital to bison hunting, and the object of intertribal raiding and trading. Yet just a century and a half earlier the animal was a rarity in the grasslands. The horse did not reach the plains until the late seventeenth century, nearly two centuries after Europeans had introduced it to North America – or, rather, re-introduced it. Horses were native to the Americas. During the Pleistocene epoch, as the ancestors of Native Americans crossed the Bering Strait land bridge from Siberia to Alaska, horses migrated in the opposite direction from America to Asia. Horses flourished in Eurasia but eventually became extinct in the Americas. When semisedentary Native Americans on the fringes of the plains acquired horses in the eighteenth century, they began to transform themselves into equestrian nomads. That transformation necessitated an almost total reliance on the bison, a new dependence on trade, and the adoption of a decentralized social structure.

---

[7] Richard B. Lee and Irven DeVore, "Problems in the Study of Hunters and Gatherers," in Lee and DeVore, eds., *Man the Hunter* (Chicago: Aldine, 1968), 5.

[8] Edwin Thompson Denig, *Five Indian Tribes of the Upper Missouri: Sioux, Arikaras, Assiniboines, Crees, Crows*, ed. John C. Ewers (Norman: University of Oklahoma Press, 1961), 147.

When Europeans established their first colonies in North America, the societies that Euroamericans would come to know in the eighteenth and nineteenth centuries as the western plains nomads – the Arapahos, Assiniboines, Atsinas, Blackfeet, Cheyennes, Comanches, Crows, Kiowas, and Sioux – hunted game, gathered fruits and vegetables, and in some cases planted crops, primarily on the fringes of the plains. The Comanches and Kiowas inhabited the Rocky Mountains and the Great Basin, while the Arapahos, Assiniboines, Atsinas, Blackfeet, Cheyennes, and Sioux resided in the woodland-prairie border region of the Great Lakes and Mississippi River valley. In the seventeenth century, the Crows did not yet exist as a discrete group. They did not break off from the Hidatsas, village-dwelling horticulturists on the upper Missouri River, until the end of the century.

In the seventeenth century, these societies ranged over a broad area, gleaning their subsistence from two or more environments. Until the eighteenth century, the Comanches spent much of the year eking out an existence between the Colorado Front Range and the Sawatch Mountains. In this region, from the San Luis Valley in the south to the Laramie Basin in the north, the Comanches and their Ute allies snared jack rabbits and other small mammals, fished, and gathered wild seeds, nuts, and berries. On the slopes of the Yampa River valley, the Comanches dug for the roots of the *yampa* plant. During the summer and fall the Comanches and Utes traveled east to the plains to hunt bison on foot, and south to the Pueblos to raid or trade for corn. Spanish documents first record the coming of the Comanches to New Mexico in 1716.[9] So all-consuming was the search for food that the three primary divisions of the Comanches were known as the Yampa Diggers (Yamparikas), Antelope Eaters (Kwahari), and Buffalo Eaters (Kotsoteka).[10]

Like the Comanches, the seventeenth-century ancestors of the Kiowas combined hunting and gathering in the northern Rockies, near the sources of the Missouri and Yellowstone rivers, with pedestrian bison hunting in the northwestern plains. Among their most important resources were deer, bighorn sheep, pronghorn, jackrabbits, gophers, ground squirrels, acorns, and pine nuts.[11] As in the case of the Comanches, the search for food was all important; it could even cause social division. According to Kiowa folklore, the ancestors of the plains Kiowas broke off from the parent group and migrated southeast following a

[9] James H. Gunnerson and Dolores A. Gunnerson, *Ethnohistory of the High Plains* (Denver: Colorado State Bureau of Land Management, 1988), 29.

[10] George E. Hyde, *Indians of the High Plains: From the Prehistoric Period to the Coming of Europeans* (Norman: University of Oklahoma Press, 1959), 52–60, 118; Dan Flores, "Bison Ecology and Bison Diplomacy: The Southern Plains from 1800 to 1850," *Journal of American History*, 78 (September 1991), 468. The Comanche divisions were ephemeral. See Thomas Kavanaugh, *Comanche Political History: An Ethnohistorical Perspective, 1706–1875* (University of Nebraska Press, 1996), 21.

[11] Steven R. Simms, *Behavioral Ecology and Hunter-Gatherer Foraging: An Example From the Great Basin*, B.A.R. International Series 381 (Oxford: B.A.R., 1987), 46–47.

dispute between two women over the division of a pronghorn.[12] Yet following the pattern of fission and fusion that would characterize plains social organization in the eighteenth and nineteenth centuries, the Kiowas also joined with other groups in the search for food. Early in the eighteenth century, as the Kiowas established themselves in the central plains, they associated themselves with a group of Jicarilla Apaches. In the nineteenth century, these Apaches functioned essentially as a band within the larger Kiowa society, maintaining their own language and ethnic identity. The Kiowas were highly mobile, a further characteristic of high plains societies. In 1804, the explorers Meriwether Lewis and William Clark wrote that the Kiowas lived southwest of the Black Hills.[13] Devil's Tower northwest of the Black Hills continued to figure prominently in Kiowa folklore despite the Kiowas' eventual migration farther south to the Arkansas River.

Unlike the Comanches and Kiowas, who came to the plains from the west, the seventeenth-century Blackfeet came to the grasslands from the northeast. Their confederation consisted of three divisions: the largest group was the Piegans or Pikunis; the second division was the Kainahs or Bloods; and the third was the Siksikas.[14] When the English fur trader David Thompson wintered with the Piegans near the Bow River in Alberta in 1787–88, he learned that before 1730 they had inhabited the region near the Eagle Hills in Saskatchewan.[15] In the late seventeenth century they had probably been farther east, along the Red River and in southern Manitoba. In this transitional region between the Eastern woodlands and the plains, the Blackfeet hunted small game and gathered wild roots and berries. Yet by 1690, according to the diary of the fur trader Henry Kelsey, the Blackfeet also migrated to the plains every summer to hunt bison on foot.[16]

The Sioux – the largest and most powerful society in the plains in the nineteenth century – were formerly centered at Mille Lacs in Minnesota, to the southeast of the Blackfeet. In the woodland-prairie border zone of the upper Mississippi, the Sioux probably planted little corn and rather relied heavily on gathering and hunting a diverse variety of plants and animals. This resource

---

[12] James Mooney, "Calendar History of the Kiowa Indians," *Seventeenth Annual Report of the Bureau of American Ethnology* (Washington: Government Printing Office, 1898), 153.

[13] Meriwether Lewis and William Clark, *The History of the Lewis and Clark Expedition*, ed., Elliot Coues, vol. 1 (New York: Harper, 1893), 57–60; Gunnerson and Gunnerson, *Ethnohistory*, 7. Hereafter, "Kiowa" refers to both the Kiowas and Kiowa-Apaches, unless otherwise noted.

[14] Siksika means "Blackfoot"; it was from this band that the Blackfoot confederation took its name. One of the seven bands of the Teton Sioux was known as the Sihasapa, which also means "Blackfoot." There is, however, no linguistic relationship between the Siouan Tetons and the Algonquian Blackfeet.

[15] *David Thompson's Narrative of His Explorations in Western America, 1784–1812*, Publications of the Champlain Society XII (Toronto: Champlain Society, 1916), 328–344.

[16] Oscar Lewis, *The Effects of White Contact on Blackfoot Culture with Special Reference to the Role of the Fur Trade*, Monographs of the American Ethnological Society, vol. 6 (New York: Augustin, 1942), 7–15; Hyde, *Indians of the High Plains*, 119–120, 127, 140.

strategy was typical of the woodland Indians of eastern North America.[17] In the early summer they gathered wild berries, plums, and nuts. Sioux women dug the roots of the *psincha* and *psinchincha*, which grew in shallow lakebeds, the *mdo*, a potatolike plant, and the wild turnip. In the fall, Sioux women harvested the wild rice that grew in abundance in Minnesota's lakes by bending the heads of the rice plants over their canoes and beating the seeds into the vessels with paddles. In the Minnesota forests the staple game animals of the Sioux were deer, ducks, and geese. In the spring the Sioux harvested large quantities of fish that came upstream to spawn. In the winter they cut holes in the ice and fished with hooks and lines or with spears or arrows attached to strings. In the summer and early fall, the Sioux migrated to the plains to hunt bison.[18] According to the "winter count" pictographic calendar of the Brulé Sioux Battiste Good, migrations to the plains to procure bison meat occurred as early as 1716.[19] In the bountiful prairie–forest border region, the Sioux were already a populous and powerful society in the seventeenth century.

The Assiniboines, another group from the woodland – prairie border region northwest of Lake Superior, similarly divided their time between the forest and the prairie. The Assiniboines hunted game in the Eastern woodlands in the fall and winter and migrated to the plains in the summer to hunt bison. They also cultivated tobacco, according to the eighteenth-century French explorer Pierre Gaultier de Varennes de la Vérendrye.[20] The Assiniboines belonged to the Sioux confederation until the middle of the seventeenth century. According to the French missionary Pierre-Jean De Smet, the Assiniboines broke off from the Sioux when, during a hunting expedition to the plains, two women quarreled over the apportionment of a bison, a tale similar to the story of the Kiowa genesis and a further indication of the centrality of food procurement and apportionment among the pre-equestrian Indians.[21] Like those of the Blackfeet, the Assiniboines' migrations to the plains to hunt bison from foot gradually drew them westward. The Assiniboines followed the Blackfeet – or perhaps spurred them forward with firearms they had obtained from the Hudson's Bay trading post.[22]

Like the Assiniboines, the seventeenth-century Cheyennes hunted and planted in the region of the Great Lakes and the upper Mississippi River drainage. In 1680, a delegation of "Chaa" Indians visited the French explorer

[17] See Cronon, *Changes in the Land*, 34–53.
[18] Samuel W. Pond, *The Dakota or Sioux in Minnesota As They Were in 1834* (St. Paul: Minnesota Historical Society Press, 1986), 26–31.
[19] Garrick Mallery, "Picture-Writing of the American Indians," *Tenth Annual Report of the Bureau of American Ethnology* (Washington , D.C.: Government Printing Office, 1889), 296.
[20] *Journals and Letters of Pierre Gaultier de Varennes de la Vérendrye and His Sons*, ed. Lawrence J. Burpee (Toronto: The Champlain Society, 1927), 318–319.
[21] *Life, Letters and Travels of Father Pierre-Jean De Smet, S.J., 1801–1873*, vol. 4, ed. Hiram M. Chittenden (New York: Harper, 1905), 1382.
[22] Royal Hassrick, "Assiniboine Succession," *North Dakota History*, 14 (April 1947), 148; Hyde, *Indians of the High Plains*, 127.

Robert Cavelier, the Sieur de la Salle, on the Illinois River. They urged him to come to their village on the upper Mississippi to trade. In 1684 the map of the French cartographer Jean Baptiste Louis Franquelin placed the Cheyennes on the Minnesota River. There they lived in earth-lodge villages and subsisted on planting, hunting, and gathering. When Francis Parkman visited an abandoned village on a tributary of the Minnesota in the 1850s, the old earth lodges were still visible. By the end of the seventeenth century, however, the more numerous Sioux had pushed the Cheyennes from the Minnesota to the Sheyenne River in North Dakota, where the Cheyennes constructed new earth-lodge villages and subsisted on corn agriculture and pedestrian bison hunting.[23] The French fur trader Jean Baptiste Truteau wrote in 1796 that "the Cheyenne built there some permanent huts, around which they cultivated little fields of maize or tobacco."[24]

Near the Red River of Lake Winnipeg, the Algonquian parent group of the Arapahos and Atsinas hunted, gathered, and perhaps cultivated corn. These Algonquians were sometime allies of their neighbors and linguistic relatives, the Cheyennes. In the late seventeenth or early eighteenth century, the Atsinas broke off from the Arapahos and moved northwest to the Eagle Hills, perhaps, like the Blackfeet, spurred by the Assiniboines or other groups who had acquired firearms from the English or French. There, the Atsinas probably subsisted by gathering and pedestrian bison hunting, although they also planted tobacco. The Arapahos probably followed the Cheyennes from Minnesota to the Sheyenne River at the end of the seventeenth century. They broke from the Cheyennes at the end of the eighteenth century.[25] Euroamericans, who had little direct contact with the remote Arapahos before 1800, placed them variously at the headwaters of the Arkansas, the Yellowstone, the Platte, and the Bighorn rivers. Though the Arapahos may have traveled widely to trade or hunt, they eventually came to inhabit the upper Arkansas, where Euroamerican traders wintered with them in the 1810s.[26]

Seven centuries before the horse reached the grasslands, the Hidatsas lived in earth-lodge villages along the Missouri in the northern plains. There, they relied

---

[23] Donald J. Berthrong, *The Southern Cheyennes* (Norman: University of Oklahoma Press, 1963), 3–26; E. Adamson Hoebel, *The Cheyennes: Indians of the Great Plains*, 2d ed. (New York: Holt, Rinehart & Winston, 1978), 4–11

[24] "Truteau's Description of the Upper Missouri," in *Before Lewis and Clark: Documents Illustrating the History of the Missouri, 1785–1804*, vol. 2, ed. A. P. Nasatir (Lincoln: University of Nebraska Press, 1990), 379.

[25] Preston Holder, *The Hoe and the Horse on the Plains: A Study of Cultural Development Among North American Indians* (Lincoln: University of Nebraska Press, 1970), 90–109; Hyde, *Indians of the High Plains*, 47–48, 140–142. Nineteenth-century writers often referred to the Atsinas, an Algonquian-speaking, nomadic society, as the Gros Ventres. They also called the Hidatsas, a Siouan-speaking, village society of the Missouri River valley, the Gros Ventres. In order to avoid confusion, this study consistently refers to the "Gros Ventres of the Prairie" as the Atsinas, and the "Gros Ventres of the Missouri" as the Hidatsas.

[26] Gunnerson and Gunnerson, *Ethnohistory*, 37–38.

on a diversity of resources at different seasons of the year: planting corn, beans, and squash in the spring, hunting bison in the high plains in the summer, and returning to their villages in the fall to harvest their crops. Along the Missouri River, they caught catfish with traps made of willow branches.[27] As early as the late sixteenth century a division of the Hidatsas spent much time hunting in the Powder River valley, but it was probably not until the introduction of the horse in the eighteenth century that this division broke with the other Hidatsas entirely to become the nomadic Crows.

Thus, before the arrival of the horse, the immense bison herds of the plains served many societies as a partial source of subsistence. In addition to the groups that migrated to the grasslands from nearby regions, the horticulturists of the Missouri River valley supplemented their corn production with bison hunting. The village Indians who hunted in the grasslands included the Arikaras, Poncas, Omahas, Pawnees, Osages, Kansas, and Wichitas. At the beginning of the eighteenth century, the villagers were both more numerous and more powerful than the nomads.

The villagers organized their societies into hierarchical clans in part because pedestrian bison hunting demanded cooperation. In his memoir, the seventeenth-century French fur trader Nicolas Perrot described the organization necessary to a successful pedestrian bison hunt. According to Perrot, a village – or several villages together if it were necessary to muster more people – assembled in the plains during the bison's summer rutting season and selected a leader of the hunting expedition. Until the successful completion of the hunt, everyone in the community accorded this leader absolute obedience. Strict order dissuaded anyone from breaking from the group and hunting alone, thereby frightening the entire herd away. The leader organized all members of the village(s) to form a large circle around the herd. On cue, the hunters slowly closed the circle, careful not to alarm the animals. Once they had closed the circle, they fired the prairie grass, enclosing the herd, and proceeded to shoot the trapped animals with arrows. Perrot wrote that by employing this method, "there are some villages which have secured as many as fifteen hundred buffaloes."[28] Other pedestrian hunters started fires in order to stampede the bison over a bluff or into a cul-de-sac.[29] This strategy, like the surround, required the cooperation of large numbers of people.

---

[27] Bella Weitzner, *Notes on the Hidatsa Indians Based on Data Recorded by the Late Gilbert H. Wilson*, Anthropological Papers of the American Museum of Natural History, vol. 56, pt. 2 (New York: American Museum of Natural History, 1979), 189–209.

[28] Emma Helen Blair, ed., *The Indian Tribes of the Upper Mississippi and Region of the Great Lakes*, vol. 1, (Cleveland: Clark, 1912), 119–126. See also Henry Kelsey, *The Kelsey Papers* (Ottawa: Public Archives of Canada, 1929), 13.

[29] The Blackfeet, for instance. See Lawrence J. Burpee, ed., "Journal of Matthew Cocking, from York Factory to the Blackfeet Country, 1772–73," *Proceedings and Transactions of the Royal Society of Canada* (Ottawa: Hope and Sons, 1908), 109. See also Robert H. Lowie, *Indians of the Plains* (Lincoln: University of Nebraska Press, 1982), 13–16.

Before the eighteenth century, the Indians of the plains diversified their resource use, relying on the production of the prairie, the forest, and the garden. The village Indians from the Missouri River valley combined corn agriculture with cooperative summer bison hunting. The Indians from the fringes of the plains combined bison hunting in the grasslands with hunting, gathering, and perhaps planting outside of the region. The Indians' resource diversity was a conscious land use strategy, which the environmental historians William Cronon and Richard White have called a system of ecological "safety nets." Economic specialization was dangerous, but Indians who gathered a variety of plants and hunted several species of animals as well as planted crops could survive droughts, the unpredictability of wildlife population dynamics, or agricultural failures. Furthermore, by varying their production the Indians reduced the likelihood that they would overexploit any one resource.[30] The Indians' land use strategy protected them from both random environmental shock and overexploitation.

In the eighteenth century, the societies that would become the nomadic Indians of the western plains abandoned their ecological safety nets in order to concentrate year-round on bison hunting. The catalyst for this change was the horse, which Europeans had introduced to North America in the sixteenth century. Hernando Cortés first brought horses to mainland America in 1519. Aided by a propitious outbreak of smallpox, Cortés's small cavalry unit had conquered Mexico by 1521. Thereafter, European livestock thrived in New Spain. By the third quarter of the sixteenth century, herds of cattle numbering over 100,000 were not uncommon in northern Mexico, and sheep herds of similar size grazed in the central highlands. By the middle of the sixteenth century, the number of horses in Mexico had multiplied into the tens of thousands.[31] Thus in Mexico, livestock populations erupted as Europeans replicated Old World land use strategies. These domesticated ungulates would eventually replace the bison in the western plains.

At the end of the sixteenth century, Spaniards in Mexico initiated the process that eventually brought the horse to the plains. In 1598, Don Juan de Oñate, a Spanish encomendero, gathered together some soldiers, missionaries, seeds, and livestock, and set out to establish Spanish control over the Pueblo Indians of what is now New Mexico. Oñate stayed in New Mexico until 1607. His colony

---

[30] "Indians in the Land: A Conversation between William Cronon and Richard White," *American Heritage*, 37 (August–September 1986), 21; also see Cronon, *Changes in the Land*, 34–53; Richard White, *The Roots of Dependency: Subsistence, Environment, and Social Change among the Choctaws, Pawnees, and Navajos* (Lincoln: University of Nebraska Press, 1983), 1–33, 147–177; Arthur F. McEvoy, *The Fisherman's Problem: Ecology and Law in the California Fisheries, 1850–1980* (New York: Cambridge University Press, 1986), 19–40; Barbara Leibhardt, "Law, Environment, and Social Change in the Columbia River Basin: The Yakima Indian Nation as a Case Study, 1840–1933" (Ph.D. dissertation, University of California-Berkeley, 1991).

[31] Alfred W. Crosby, *The Columbian Exchange: Biological and Cultural Consequences of 1492* (Westport: Greenwood Press, 1972), 35–121. See also Elinor G. K. Melville, *A Plague of Sheep: Environmental Consequences of the Conquest of Mexico* (New York: Cambridge University Press, 1994).

was distinguished for its cruel treatment of the Pueblos and in 1680, the Indians rebelled. The rebels killed several hundred Spanish settlers, seized their livestock, and forced about 2,000 Spaniards to flee.[32]

By the end of the century, when the Spaniards had reestablished their control over New Mexico, the Pueblos had already opened an intertribal trade in horses. In the first decade of the eighteenth century, the Comanches acquired their first horses from the Pueblos or commercial intermediaries.[33] Given the horse's superiority over the dog for traction and transport, and the greater ease of equestrian over pedestrian bison hunting, horses proliferated throughout the southern plains.[34] Horses were not uncommon along the Red River by 1690, and had reached the Arkansas River by 1719. An equestrian pictograph on a rock wall near the White River in western Arkansas dates from around 1700.[35]

The Navajos to the northwest of the Pueblos also acquired horses in the aftermath of the 1680 revolt. The Navajos initiated an intertribal equestrian trade that spread rapidly along the western slopes of the Rocky Mountains, bringing horses to the Nez Percé and Shoshones in the northern Rocky Mountains in the early eighteenth century. According to David Thompson, the Blackfeet acquired their first horses from the Shoshones in the 1730s.[36] Crow tradition maintains that their first horses came from the Nez Percé around the same time. A Sioux winter count records the acquisition of horses from the Omahas as early as 1708–09. The acquisition of horses from other groups – the Omahas, Assiniboines, Hidatsas, and Pawnees – was regarded as important enough to be recorded in nine winters between 1708–09 and 1766–67.[37] Horses thus diffused into the plains from the southwest and the northwest between 1700 and 1750, reaching the northeastern plains by mid-century.[38]

---

[32] Edward H. Spicer, *Cycles of Conquest: The Impact of Spain, Mexico, and the United States on the Indians of the Southwest, 1533–1960* (Tucson: University of Arizona Press, 1962), 162; Elizabeth A. H. John, *Storms Brewed in Other Men's Worlds: The Confrontation of Indians, Spanish, and French in the Southwest, 1540–1795* (College Station: Texas A & M Press, 1975), 98–103; Charles L. Kenner, *A History of New Mexico-Plains Indian Relations* (Norman: University of Oklahoma Press, 1969), 3–19.

[33] According to Comanche folklore, they stole their first horses directly from the Europeans after observing the Spaniards in New Mexico for some time and taking note of the proper care and feeding of the "magic dogs." It is more likely that the Comanches and their Ute allies stole or bartered for horses from the Pueblos after the 1680 rebellion. Alice Marriott and Carol K. Rachlin, *Plains Indian Mythology* (New York: Crowell, 1975), 89–93.

[34] R. Brooke Jacobsen and Jeffrey L. Eighny, "A Mathematical Theory of Horse Adaptation on the North American Plains," *Plains Anthropologist*, 25 (November 1980), 333–341.

[35] Jerry Hilliard, "An Equestrian Pictograph in Western Arkansas," *Plains Anthropologist*, 34 (November 1989), 327–330.

[36] *Thompson's Narrative*, 330–334.

[37] Mallery, "Picture-Writing," 295–305.

[38] For the diffusion of horses into the plains, see Francis Haines, "The Northward Spread of Horses Among the Plains Indians," *American Anthropologist*, 40 (July-September 1938), 429–437; Frank R. Secoy, *Changing Military Patterns in the Great Plains*, Monographs of the American Ethnological Society, vol. 21 (Locust Valley: Augustin, 1953), 6–38. For the acquisition of horses by the

It is popularly assumed that many Indians of the western plains first acquired horses not through trade but by capturing them in the wild. This method is unlikely for two reasons. First, although there might have been wild horses in the southern plains early in the eighteenth century, there were none in the northern plains until much later – long after the northern plains nomads had acquired horses through trade. Sioux pictographic winter counts record the first capture of wild horses only in 1781 (according to the Oglala division of the Sioux), 1811–12 (according to the Brulé division), and 1812–13 (according to the Yancton division).[39] Second, intertribal trade diffused not only horses but the techniques, equipment, and knowledge of riding and caring for them. The nomads' acquisition and use of domesticated horses depended as much on this information as it did on the horses themselves. Wild horses may have diffused into the plains, but equestrianism spread by trade.

According to Cheyenne folklore, the Comanches brought horses to the Cheyennes while the latter still lived in earth-lodge villages in the northern plains. The Comanches offered to trade horses to the Cheyennes, and invited them to come on a horse raid to the Pueblos. After the Cheyenne priests fasted and prayed for four days over the decision, the Cheyenne's chief god, Maheo, told them through the oldest priest, "If you have horses everything will be changed for you forever."

> You will have to move around a lot to find pasture for your horses. You will have to give up gardening and live by hunting and gathering, like the Comanches. And you will have to come out of your earth houses and live in tents.... You will have to have fights with other tribes, who will want your pasture land or the places where you hunt. You will have to have real soldiers, who can protect the people. Think, before you decide.[40]

The Cheyennes probably created this story long after the transition to nomadism; they were too far north of the Comanches in the eighteenth century to have had much contact with them. Nonetheless, the tale is an indication that the plains nomads understood that the characteristics of nomadism – migrating in search of forage and bison, fighting with other groups for horses and hunting territory, and relying primarily on the bison – were due largely to the adoption of the horse.

Comanches, Kiowas, Assiniboines, and Crows, see Hyde, *Indians of the High Plains*, 128–139; for the Blackfoot acquisition of horses, see Lewis, *Blackfoot Culture*, 11; for the acquisition of horses by the Sioux, see White, "The Winning of the West: The Expansion of the Western Sioux in the Eighteenth and Nineteenth Centuries," *Journal of American History*, 65 (September 1978), 323; for the acquisition of horses by the Cheyennes, see Joseph Jablow, *The Cheyenne in Plains Trade Relations, 1795–1840*, Monographs of the American Ethnological Society, vol. 19 (New York: Augustin, 1951), 10.

[39] Martha Warren Beckwith, "Mythology of the Oglala Dakota," *Journal of American Folklore*, 43 (October–December 1930), 353; Mallery, "Pictographs of the North American Indians," *Fourth Annual Report of the Bureau of American Ethnology, 1882–83* (Washington, D.C.: Government Printing Office, 1886), 108; Mallery, "Picture-Writing," 315.

[40] Marriott and Rachlin, *Plains Indian Mythology*, 94–98.

The acquisition of the horse initiated the long transformation of the Arapa-hos, Assiniboines, Atsinas, Blackfeet, Cheyennes, Comanches, Crows, Kiowas, and the western divisions of the Sioux from life on the fringes of the plains and partial dependence on the bison for subsistence to nomadism and primary dependence on the bison. The Comanches had staked out their hunting territory in the southern plains by the second decade of the eighteenth century. In the northwestern plains, the Blackfeet and Crows had made the transition to nomadism by the 1730s. The Assiniboines and Atsinas established themselves in the north-central plains by mid-century. The western Sioux reached the Black Hills in the 1770s, and the Cheyennes and Arapahos had migrated to the upper Platte River in the central plains by the 1780s.

The western plains were by no means uninhabited when the equestrian nomads arrived. Wielding dominant power in the northwestern plains in the mid-eighteenth century were the Eastern Shoshones, or Snakes. In the 1780s, the Blackfeet, supplied with guns by English fur traders, forced the Eastern Shoshones to retreat into the Rocky Mountains.[41] The Apaches, who had domi-nated the southern plains at least since the time of Francisco de Vasquez de Coronado's explorations in the early sixteenth century, resisted the Comanche incursion into their territory until the late eighteenth century.[42] The equestrian nomads also jostled for territory; the Sioux forced the Kiowas out of the Black Hills region at the end of the eighteenth century.[43] In Battiste Good's winter count, forty-four of the annual pictographs from the eighteenth century refer to raids or attacks; the Pawnees and Arikaras, both of whom are represented by an ear of corn in the Sioux calendars, were the Sioux's primary enemies.[44]

In the first half of the eighteenth century, the transformation to nomadism was slow and halting. The nomadic societies became increasingly divided as they adapted to the horse and the bison. Some bands embraced equestrian bison hunting readily while others continued to return to the fringes of the plains for planting, hunting, and gathering. The Hidatsa-Crows, for instance, splintered into three groups. The Mountain Crows moved from the Missouri to the tribu-taries of the Yellowstone, a region thick with bison and near their allies in the horse trade, the Nez Percé. The River Crows moved to the confluence of the Yellowstone and Powder rivers. The Hidatsas remained planters along the Mis-souri.[45] Other societies were similarly divided. The Piegan were at the fore-front of the Blackfoot migration, while the Kainahs and Siksikas lagged behind. By the middle of the eighteenth century the Assiniboines had split into two recognizable groups: the Assiniboines of the Woods and the Assiniboines of the

[41] Colin G. Calloway, "Snake Frontiers: The Eastern Shoshones in the Eighteenth Century," *Annals of Wyoming*, 63 (Summer 1991), 83–92.
[42] Gunnerson and Gunnerson, *Ethnohistory of the High Plains*, 1–16.
[43] White, "Winning of the West," 320, 327.
[44] Mallery, "Picture-Writing," 293–313.
[45] Denig, *Five Indian Tribes*, 142–143.

Meadows.[46] As late as 1776, the Yamparika Comanches still periodically returned to the Uinta Mountains in eastern Utah to hunt and gather.[47] The Sioux divisions which migrated to the western plains – the Oglala, Brulé, Hunkpapa, Sans Arcs, Two Kettles, Minneconjou, and Blackfeet – came to be known as the Tetons, from *tetonwan*, meaning dwellers of the prairie. Four Sioux bands remained in Minnesota, and two – the Yancton and Yanctonnai – were suspended in the eastern prairies midway between the woodlands and the western plains.[48] Fragmentation undermined social authority. The Teton bands were effectively autonomous. When Jean Baptiste Truteau encountered some Tetons on the Missouri in 1794, he asked to meet with the notable chiefs. "They replied to me that the Tetons did not have one great chief greater than all the others. That each man was chief of his cabin."[49] Gradually, as the groups that would become equestrian nomads were drawn to the plains, toward the bison and the sources of horses, their social structures became increasingly decentralized.

The social segmentation of the groups that migrated to the plains was a direct consequence of the nature of mounted bison hunting. In the semi-arid plains, the shortgrasses were thick enough to support large aggregations of bison only during the summer. During the rest of the year, small congregations of bison searched for forage and water in the unpredictable environment. Bison changed their location in response to local conditions of drought, fire, or cold. If they were too densely concentrated, they were apt to overgraze an area and disperse further. The Indians broke into small bands in the winter, mirroring the actions of the herds.[50] The pattern of aggregation and dispersal was typical of groups that relied primarily on hunting or fishing. Eskimos in the Canadian Arctic assembled in large camps only in the winter and spring to hunt seals. In Alaska, Eskimos similarly assembled in large groups only in the winter and spring to hunt the migrating bowhead whale. In the Canadian sub-Arctic, large groups assembled only in the summer around productive fishing sites.[51]

The number of Indian winter bands changed in response to environmental conditions. The *wicotipi*, or winter camps, of the Hunkpapa Sioux varied between

---

[46] Lewis, *Blackfoot Culture*, 7–15; Hassrick, "Assiniboine Succession," 147.

[47] Hyde, *Indians of the High Plains*, 59.

[48] There were seven divisions of the Tetons. The two largest were the Oglala ("they scatter their own"), and the Siçangu or Brulé ("burnt thigh"). The five smaller divisions were the Hunkpapa ("those who camp at the entrance"), Sihasapa ("blackfeet"), Itazipco or Sans Arcs ("without bows"), Oohemonpa or Two Kettles, and Minneconjou ("those who plant by the stream"). The latter five divisions were together known as the Saone ("whitish people") for their bleached bisonhide tepees. See Elizabeth Grobsmith, *Lakota of the Rosebud: A Contemporary Ethnography* (New York: Holt, Rinehart & Winston, 1981), 7.

[49] "Journal of Truteau on the Missouri River, 1794–1795," in *Before Lewis and Clark*, vol. 1, 270.

[50] Symmes Oliver, *Ecology and Cultural Continuity as Contributing Factors in the Social Organization of the Plains Indians*, University of California Publications in American Archaeology and Ethnology, vol. 48, no. 1 (Berkeley: University of California Press, 1962), 6–18.

[51] David Riches, *Northern Nomadic Hunter-Gatherers: A Humanistic Approach* (London: Academic Press, 1982), 15–17.

four and seven. Euroamericans counted four Comanche bands in the mid-eighteenth century and as many as nine in the mid-nineteenth century during a drought. The various names and number of Comanche bands indicates not only the unreliability of some Euroamerican accounts, but the shifting constituency, size, and number of the bands as the Indians continually adapted and re-adapted to the migrations and population dynamics of the bison.[52] The equestrian nomads found that year-round bison hunting demanded a flexible social organization.

Despite the social pressures attendant on bison hunting, once they had acquired horses, the nomads' subsistence was more facile even than that of the villagers of the river valleys – the Hidatsas, Mandans, Arikaras, and Pawnees – who combined planting with bison hunting. The eighteenth-century entries in Battiste Good's winter count are replete with references to the abundance of meat the Sioux produced. By contrast, an early nineteenth-century observer noted that bison "are a sort of roaming creatures, congregating occasionally in huge masses, and strolling away about the country from east to west, or from north to south, or just where their whims or strange fancies may lead them; and the Mandans are sometimes by this means most unceremoniously left without anything to eat." The same observer wrote that when the bison were far from the Hidatsa villages, "there was great danger of their actual starvation."[53] Similarly, the French fur trader Pierre-Antoine Tabeau, who lived among the Arikaras from 1803 to 1805, wrote, "When the Ricaras lack maize, which happens very often, they find that the buffalo cow is also a very uncertain resource."[54] The equestrian nomads mitigated such uncertainty by using the horse to adapt their movements to the migrations of the herds. In essence, the horse regularized food procurement in the unpredictable environment of the western plains. This new resource strategy demanded social decentralization, but the diffusion of the horse into the plains made nomadic bison hunting a more secure land-use strategy than the combination of hunting and sedentary horticulture – at least in the short term.

II

According to Battiste Good's winter count, the Brulé Sioux first encountered European manufactured articles in 1707. An unlikely series of events led to this introduction to trade goods, beginning with the murder of a Brulé woman by her

---

[52] Kavanaugh, *Comanche Political History*, 1–21.
[53] George Catlin, *North American Indians: Being Letters and Notes on Their Manners, Customs, and Conditions, Written During Eight Years' Travel Amongst the Wildest Tribes of Indians in North America, 1832–1839*, vol. 1 (Philadelphia: Leary, Stuart, 1913), 143.
[54] Pierre-Antoine Tabeau, *Narrative of Loisel's Expedition to the Upper Missouri*, ed. Annie Heloise Abel (Norman: University of Oklahoma Press, 1939), 74.

husband, a man named Corn. Facing certain exile from Brulé society, Corn fled to the east. He returned to the Brulés a year after the killing, however, bringing with him three guns obtained from the English. Good's pictographic calendar does not indicate whether Corn sought to atone for his crime by bringing such valuable items to the Brulés, but he does say that Corn subsequently led a Brulé party to the English, from whom they acquired many kettles.[55] Thus, trade goods, which would further the atomization of Brulé and other plains nomadic societies in the nineteenth century, first came to the Brulés from a social outcast.

The few guns and kettles the Brulés acquired in 1707 presaged a flood of manufactured goods into the plains in the eighteenth century. This emerging trade network encouraged the nomads to specialize as hunters. Euroamericans were latecomers to trade in the grasslands, where, by the mid-eighteenth century, extensive intertribal exchanges were already centered on the leading edge of the European biotic invasion, the horse. In order to acquire horses and to supplement their reliance on the bison, the nomads developed a widespread intertribal trade network in horses and foodstuffs. Trading – or raiding, when terms were not to their liking – furthered the rise of decentralized bands and kinship groups. When European fur traders came to the plains in the mid-eighteenth century in search of beaver pelts, they found the nomads already socially divided and dependent on hunting and trading. The fur trade in the western plains emerged from the spread of horses and furthered the primacy of hunting among the nomads.

Horses remained a foreign ecological element in the northern and central plains throughout the eighteenth and nineteenth centuries. Many Indian horses died in the winter months when they were unable to find sufficient forage. In 1776, the fur trader Alexander Henry noted that the Assiniboines abandoned their horses in wooded areas at the beginning of the winter, and returned to claim the survivors in the spring.[56] In 1800, Henry's nephew and namesake – Alexander Henry the Younger – remarked on the generally poor conditions of the horses of the northern plains: "The greater part of the Horses which belong to these Indians have very sore backs. . . . The poor brutes are in a shocking condition. . . . No particular care is taken of them. When they have performed their days journey their two forefeet are tied together, and they are sent away to look out for themselves, and seldom stray far from the Camps."[57] In 1809, the naturalist Bradbury noted that the only winter provisions the Missouri River Indians supplied to their horses were the twigs and bark of cottonwood, elm, and mulberry trees.[58] A

[55] Mallery, "Picture-Writing," 295.
[56] Alexander Henry, *Travels and Adventures in Canada and the Indian Territories Between the Years 1760 and 1776*, ed. James Bain (Rutland,: Charles E. Tuttle, 1969), 316.
[57] Barry M. Gough, ed., *The Journal of Alexander Henry the Younger, 1799–1814, Volume I: Red River and the Journey to the Missouri* (Toronto: The Champlain Society, 1988), 21.
[58] Bradbury, in *Early Western Travels*, vol. 5, 42–43, 175.

poor winter diet and the constant pursuit of bison meant that the nomads' mares bore few colts.[59] Most of the northern plains nomads therefore relied on intertribal raid and trade for continual infusions of horses from New Mexico and the Northwest.[60]

South of the Arkansas River, however, milder winters allowed the Comanches and Kiowas to raise large herds of horses. Although the pursuit of the bison remained their primary means of subsistence, the southern plains nomads eventually became as much horse pastoralists as hunters. By the end of the eighteenth century the Comanches and Kiowas had become expert at stealing the horses of the Pueblos and of the mestizo settlers on the Mexican frontier. The Cheyennes found a trade niche shuttling those horses from the Comanches and Kiowas to the Indians in the northeastern grasslands.[61] The Cheyennes often brought their horses to the trade fairs at the Arikara villages on the Missouri. A good horse, which in 1805 Tabeau called "the most important article" of the Cheyennes' trade with the Arikaras, was worth a gun and 100 balls and charges of powder.[62] Similarly, the Crows maintained large herds for trade. In 1822, a trader for the Missouri Fur Company counted ten thousand horses in the Crow herd.[63] The Crows brought horses from the Nez Percé in the Rocky Mountains to the Hidatsa trade centers on the Missouri. The Blackfeet regularly raided the Crows for their horses. Indeed, northern plains groups often supplied themselves with horses by stealing from neighbors. Denig wrote, "The Assiniboines supply themselves with horses by stealing from the Blackfeet, and the Sioux in their turn take them from the Assiniboines." Horse raiding, in short, was "one of the principal causes of personal warfare existing among the tribes," and "a great portion of the time of each nation is occupied either in guarding their own horses or in attempts to take those of their enemies."[64]

The nomads also depended on intertribal exchange to supplement their singular reliance on the bison. The northern plains nomads came each fall to the Missouri River villages, where they exchanged the products of the hunt – hides, robes, and dried meat – for the products of the garden – corn, beans, and squash.[65]

---

[59] Frank Norwall, *Bourgmont, Explorer of the Missouri, 1698–1725* (Lincoln: University of Nebraska Press, 1988), 159.

[60] Alan J. Osborn, "Ecological Aspects of Equestrian Adaptations in Aboriginal North America," *American Anthropologist*, 85 (September 1983), 563–591.

[61] Bradbury, *Early Western Travels*, vol. 5, 176; Jablow, *The Cheyenne in Plains Trade Relations*, 58–60; Catlin, *North American Indians*, vol. 2, 2; Kenner, *New Mexican-Plains Indian Relations*, 3–77.

[62] Tabeau, *Narrative of Loisel's Expedition*, 158.

[63] William Gordon to Lewis Cass, 3 October 1831, Fur Trade Collection, Box 1, Missouri Historical Society, St. Louis, Missouri.

[64] Denig, *Five Indian Tribes*, 145–147.

[65] W. Raymond Wood, "Plains Trade in Prehistoric and Protohistoric Intertribal Relations," in *Anthropology on the Great Plains*, ed. Wood and Margot Liberty (Lincoln: University of Nebraska Press, 1980), 99.

"In the beginning of June, there arrive at the great fort on the bank of the river of the Mandan, several savage tribes which use horses and carry on trade with them," wrote la Vérendrye in 1739. "They bring dressed skins trimmed and ornamented with plumage and porcupine quills, painted in various colors, also white buffalo-skins, and the Mandan give them in exchange grain and beans, of which they have an ample supply."[66] As early as the 1720s, the southern plains nomads traveled to the Pueblos to exchange bison products for corn. Revilla Gigedo, a Spanish official, wrote in 1753 that the Comanches "have the custom of coming to the capital [of New Mexico], Santa Fe, each year to hold a fair to trade their pelts."[67] In this way, the Indians of the plains – both the villagers and the nomads – continued to rely indirectly on both hunting and gardening. The exchange of meat for corn diversified the resource reliance of both the nomads and the villagers. For the villagers, trade with the nomads was a means of access to the unpredictably migrating bison. For the nomads, trade with the villagers served to replace the ecological safety nets that they had abandoned by specializing as bison hunters.

Thus, during the eighteenth century the nomads' division of labor and relationships with technology and resources were startlingly transformed. By mid-century, the nomads had abandoned their ecological safety nets to become bison hunters, economic specialists. In order to effect this transformation, they adopted a new technology, the horse. They devised a new gender division of labor: women's primary economic responsibility, once horticulture or gathering or both, became the dressing of meat and the tanning of hides. In order to compensate for the abandonment of their resource diversity, the nomads exchanged the products of the hunt with Missouri River villagers who produced a surplus of corn.

In one sense, the increased importance of intertribal exchange was merely a new form of ecological safety net: the Indians depended on trade rather than on their own labor to insure a diversity of resources. In another sense, the transition to nomadism was a rational economic adjustment: equestrian bison hunting yielded greater wealth at less expense than a combination of hunting, gathering, and planting. At any rate, once the plains nomads had become decentralized bands of economic specialists who produced a surplus for the purpose of intertribal exchange – all elements of the protohistoric transition to nomadism – it was a comparatively small step to commercial exchange with Euroamerican beaver pelt traders. Eighteenth-century European fur traders simply grafted their commerce onto the existing intertribal trade network, centering their activities at or near the villages to which the nomads brought the products of the hunt.

[66] *Journals and Letters of la Vérendrye*, 366.
[67] Alfred Barnaby Thomas, *The Plains Indians and New Mexico, 1751–1778: A Collection of Documents Illustrative of the History of the Eastern Frontier of New Mexico* (Albuquerque: University of New Mexico Press, 1940) 111.

The social and economic changes in the period between Indian prehistory and the onset of recorded contact with Euroamericans – the protohistoric era – made possible the plains nomads' remarkably thorough integration into the emerging Euroamerican market system. Foremost among those changes was social decentralization. The divisions of the nomadic societies were necessary to the pursuit of the wandering bison. As the equestrian nomads sought out the bison, bands centered around kinship groups gradually assumed increased authority. However flexible and adaptable bands and kinship groups may have been to the demands of bison hunting, native societies organized around kinship groups proved to be too decentralized to withstand the blandishments of European trade. David Thompson wrote of the ultimately unsustainable late eighteenth-century trade in beaver pelts in the northern plains: "Every intelligent Man saw the poverty that would follow the destruction of the Beaver, but there were no Chiefs to controul it; all was perfect libertie and equality."[68] Among societies already leveled by social segmentation and intertribal trade, European commerce spread rapidly.

The effects of social segmentation were manifested in the different experiences of the nomads and the village-dwelling Pawnees. Pawnee society was integrated and hierarchical. Lower-ranking Pawnees presented gifts – products of the garden and of the hunt – to chiefs and priests, who in turn redistributed goods down the social pyramid. Goods were thus channeled first upward and then shared, although not equally, by all. Elders restricted traders' access to lower-ranking members of Pawnee society. Pawnee leaders thus were able to prevent the growth of a trade in bison robes that later debilitated many nomadic societies.[69] Leaders of the nomadic groups tried to exercise the same control over trade, but with less success. When Peter Fidler, a Hudson's Bay Company trader, wintered with a Piegan group in 1792–93, the leader of the group sought to control Fidler's access to young men in his band. Such interactions would have undercut the leader's position as broker with the Euroamerican trader, and ended his control over trade goods, which he redistributed to his followers. Such redistribution was essential to maintain his status and influence in the group.[70]

The authority of Pawnee leaders was grounded in the rituals of reciprocal giving surrounding agricultural production and communal bison hunting. Pawnee leaders defused the potentially explosive effect of trade by incorporating trade goods into the existing flow of goods through the social hierarchy. By contrast, the nomads' social organization, based not on agriculture but on hunting,

[68] Thompson's Narrative, 205.
[69] Richard White, Roots of Dependency, 173–177, 189–192.
[70] Eric R. Wolf, Europe and the People without History (Berkeley: University of California Press, 1982), 193; Loretta Fowler, Shared Symbols, Contested Meanings: Gros Ventre Culture and History, 1778–1984 (Ithaca: Cornell University Press, 1987), 35–39.

was too fluid to allow leaders to restrict access to Euroamerican traders. When divided into small hunting groups, there were few social restraints on individual economic behavior. Ambitious young men who sought to establish their own credentials for leadership hunted and trapped for traders in return for rare and prestigious European manufactured goods: guns, knives, woven cloth, and alcohol. The traders were only too happy to oblige this enthusiasm. Fidler and other Hudson's Bay and Northwest Company traders "rigged" ambitious young hunters with goods, increasing competition for band leadership.[71]

In the eighteenth century, the beaver (*Castor canadensis*) was the primary object of fur traders in the plains. While there were once tens of millions of beaver throughout North America, in the plains they were limited to the narrow confines of the river valleys. Many of the meandering rivers of the plains are ideally suited to beavers, and the animals, in turn, existed in close proximity to the rivers. Beavers construct dens made of mud and tree branches, and subsist on the bark and twigs of cottonwood and willow trees that grow close to the rivers. The beaver's well-defined environment made it easy to trap, and its slow-growing population left the species vulnerable to depletion.[72]

As late as the middle of the eighteenth century, the plains nomads had not yet become thoroughly engaged in the beaver pelt trade. La Vérendrye wrote in 1730 that near the Saskatchewan River, the "beaver is so plentiful that the savages place little value on it."[73] In the northwestern plains, the fur trade made few inroads. In 1754, the Hudson's Bay Company agent Anthony Hendry visited the Blackfeet to induce them to hunt beaver for trade. A Blackfoot leader refused Hendry's entreaties, telling him that "they never wanted food, as they followed the Buffalo & killed them with the Bows and Arrows; and he was informed the Natives that frequented the Settlements [to trade pelts] were oftentimes starved on their journey." Hendry reflected: "Such remarks I thought exceedingly true."[74] As late as 1804, Charles McKenzie wrote that the beaver pelts of the Crows "were badly dressed and split upon the back in place of the belly – a sign that they were not much acquainted with that favourite article of commerce."[75]

The Blackfeet and Crows in the northwestern plains were only on the fringes of the late eighteenth-century beaver trade, but in the northeastern grasslands commerce with Euroamericans flourished. As early as 1714, according to Etienne

[71] Fowler, *Shared Symbols*, 39.

[72] David J. Wishart, *The Fur Trade of the American West, 1807–1840: A Geographical Synthesis* (Lincoln: University of Nebraska Press, 1979), 27–33.

[73] *Journals and Letters of la Vérendrye*, 59.

[74] Lawrence J. Burpee, ed., "York Factory to the Blackfeet Country: The Journal of Anthony Hendry, 1754–1755," *Proceedings and Transactions of the Royal Society of Canada*, 3d ser., 1 (Ottawa: Hope, 1907), 338.

[75] "Charles McKenzie's Narratives," in W. Raymond Wood and Thomas D. Thiessen, eds., *Early Fur Trade on the Northern Plains: Canadian Traders Among the Mandan and Hidatsa Indians, 1738–1818* (Norman: University of Oklahoma Press, 1985), 246.

de Véniard, Sieur de Bourgmont, the Sioux traded beaver pelts to the French.[76] After the Tetons migrated west to the plains, they continued to trade pelts to the French through their kinspeople in Minnesota. By the last quarter of the eighteenth century, as the plains nomads accumulated beaver pelts for trade with Europeans, they steadily exterminated the beaver. In 1796, the French fur trader Truteau wrote that the Sioux "hunt most for the beaver and other good peltries of the Upper Missouri. They scour all the rivers and streams without fearing anyone. They carry away every springtime, from out of our territory, a great number of them, which they exchange for merchandise." The Cheyennes, Truteau wrote, "know very well how to hunt the beaver, the skins of which they barter with the Sioux for merchandise." He noted that the Assiniboines traded beaver pelts to the English in Canada in return for manufactured goods, and then brought the English wares to the Mandans and Hidatsas on the Missouri where they exchanged them for horses, corn, and tobacco.[77]

The nomads who came to the Missouri River villages to deal in horses and corn carried on a more or less continuous trade with Euroamericans beginning in 1738, when la Vérendrye first visited the Mandans on the upper Missouri.[78] Ten years later, French traders were dealing firearms to the Comanches as far south as New Mexico.[79] In 1752, Spanish authorities from New Mexico detained two French traders and confiscated their merchandise. Thomas Vélez Cachupín, the governor of New Mexico, recommended to the Spanish crown that the Frenchmen be executed for their "illicit commerce" with the Indians. Vélez was particularly concerned that the French might trade firearms to the Comanches, "to our great detriment."[80] Despite Vélez's attempt to arrest the commerce, the diffusion of European goods into the plains was rapid and extensive. When the Comanches attacked the Spanish mission at San Sabá in March, 1758, they were well armed with muskets.[81] A few dozen rifles and kettles introduced each year into an average Missouri River village were enough to ensure that every adult villager could have acquired one of those items within fifteen to twenty years of the commencement of trade.[82] Indeed, a Northwest Company clerk, Charles McKenzie, remarked in 1809, "It is incredible the great quantity of merchandize which the Missouri Indians have accumulated."[83]

The transition to equestrian bison hunting had already revolutionized the

[76] Bourgmont, "Exact Description of Louisiana," in Norwall, *Bourgmont*, 110.
[77] "Truteau's Description of the Upper Missouri," in *Before Lewis and Clark*, vol. 2, 379–382.
[78] Wood and Thiessen, eds., *Early Fur Trade*, 22.
[79] Hyde, *Indians of the High Plains*, 105–106.
[80] Thomas, *The Plains Indians and New Mexico*, 82–110.
[81] Gerald Betty, "Comanche Warfare, Pastoralism, and Enforced Cooperation," *Panhandle-Plains Historical Review*, 68 (1995), 1.
[82] Charles E. Orser, Jr., and Larry J. Zimmerman, "A Computer Simulation of Euro-American Trade Good Flow to the Arikara," *Plains Anthropologist*, 29 (August 1984), 204.
[83] "Charles McKenzie's Narratives," 246.

nomads' material culture: the western plains hunters all adopted the tepee, travois, and, to hunt bison from horseback, the short bow. Commerce in European goods furthered that revolution. The nomads abandoned some traditional crafts in favor of trade goods. Although only few groups had direct contact with European traders in the first half of the eighteenth century, all acquired some European goods through intertribal exchange. Indeed, McKenzie marveled that the Missouri Indians acquired their wares "by intercourse with Indians that visit them from the vicinity of the Commercial Establishments."[84] The Blackfeet received several guns, ammunition, iron arrowheads, knives, and an ax in trade with the Crees of the Eastern woodlands as early as 1728. By the time la Vérendrye visited the Mandans in 1738, the Assiniboines were engaged in the business of carrying French trade goods to the Missouri River.[85] As their commercial ties to Euroamericans became more extensive in the second half of the eighteenth century, the nomads gave up pottery and tobacco planting in preference for kettles and tobacco acquired through trade. David Thompson wrote that in the eighteenth century the Blackfeet had raised tobacco for their own use. "When they became acquainted with the tobacco of the U States brought by the traders," he wrote, "they gradually left off cultivating it," until they ceased entirely by 1800.[86] By the 1830s, when a German traveler, Prince Maximilian of Wied-Neuwied, encountered the Crows, he found that they "cultivate no kind of useful plants: even tobacco is now seldom planted, because they prefer that which they obtain from the traders."[87] In 1811, the naturalist Bradbury noted, "Before the Indians had any intercourse with the whites, they made the heads of their arrows of flint or horn stone. They now purchase them from the traders, who cut them from rolled iron or from hoops."[88]

Although they abandoned some traditional crafts, the nomads integrated European products into their material culture. They became adept at the repair of flintlock rifles, cannibalizing inoperative rifles and systematically recycling parts. When a part was beyond repair it was often converted to another use; blown-out barrels, for instance, became hide scrapers.[89] The development of the parfleche, a rawhide pouch common to many plains nomadic societies in the nineteenth century, likely occurred only after the nomads had acquired metal knives and needles capable of cutting and piercing tough bison leather.[90] Altogether, the fur trade of

[84] Ibid.
[85] *Journals and Letters of la Vérendrye*, 323.
[86] *Thompson's Narrative*, 365.
[87] Maximilian, *Travels in the Interior of North America* (London: Ackermann, 1843), in *Early Western Travels*, vol. 23, 368.
[88] Bradbury, in *Early Western Travels*, vol. 5, 174n.
[89] Peter Bleed and Daniel Watson, "Frontier Flintlocks: A Fault Tree Analysis of Firearm Use at Contact Period Sites of the Great Plains," *Great Plains Research*, 1 (August 1991), 233–248.
[90] John C. Ewers, "Influence of the Fur Trade upon Indians of the Northern Plains," in *People and Pelts: Selected Papers of the Second North American Fur Trade Conference*, ed. Malvina Bolus (Winnipeg: Pegius, 1972), 11.

the eighteenth century transformed the plains nomads' economy. No longer merely subsistence hunters and gatherers, the nomads had become providers of pelts to the European market and consumers of European manufactured goods.

In order to control the flow of European manufactured goods into the grasslands – especially to prevent competing groups from acquiring trade goods – the nomads sought to acquire prime hunting territories and to control trade routes. Of particular concern to the Indians was control over the trade in firearms, the primary article the Indians sought in return for pelts. Between 1710 and 1790, the Indians of the plains engaged in an aboriginal arms race as flintlock rifles spread from the Great Lakes to Texas.[91] Along the Missouri River below the Arikara villages, the Sioux stopped fur traders from St. Louis to prevent them from reaching the upper Missouri villagers. When the Sioux stopped Pierre-Antoine Tabeau's boats in 1803, Tabeau viewed the Indians as commercial competitors: "they hoped themselves to trade the peltries ... by an intermediary commerce."[92] In 1804, the Oglala Sioux threatened to prevent Lewis and Clark from proceeding up the Missouri unless the captains presented them with gifts.[93] The fur trader Henry Brackenridge wrote in 1811 that the Sioux imposed a tax – a kind of import duty – on his expedition and threatened to loot his boats if he did not comply.[94] Other groups also attempted to control trade; in 1806, the Hidatsas tried to prevent Charles McKenzie from trading directly with the Cheyennes.[95] In the late 1820s, the Blackfeet harassed Robert Campbell to prevent him from trading with the Crows.[96]

Despite these obstacles, the beaver trade eventually reached every group in the northern plains. The commerce was brief but intense. In his memoirs, David Thompson recalled that the beaver trade brought great wealth to the Indians between the Great Lakes and the northeastern plains as well as to the Euroamerican traders. He wrote, "For several years all these Indians were rich, the Women and Children, as well as the Men, were covered with silver brooches, Ear Rings, Wampum, Beads and other trinkets. Their mantles were of fine scarlet cloth, and all was finery and dress." At the same time, "The Canoes of the Furr Traders were loaded with packs of Beaver." Yet in 1796, an old Cree man who lived with the Blackfeet told Thompson, "we are now killing the Beaver without any labor, we are now rich, but [shall] soon be poor, for when the Beaver are destroyed we have nothing to depend on to purchase what we want for our families."[97] Indeed,

---

[91] Secoy, *Changing Military Patterns in the Great Plains*, 39–95.

[92] Tabeau, *Narrative of Loisel's Expedition*, 107.

[93] Lewis and Clark, *History of the Lewis and Clark Expedition*, ed. Elliott Coues, vol. 1, 133.

[94] Henry Brackenridge, *Journal of a Voyage Up the River Missouri Performed in 1811* (Baltimore: Coale and Maxwell, 1816), in *Early Western Travels*, vol. 6, 65.

[95] "McKenzie's Narratives," 274.

[96] "Narrative of Robert Campbell's Experiences in the Rocky Mountain Fur Trade, 1825–1835, Dictated to William Fayel in 1870," Robert Campbell Papers, Missouri Historical Society.

[97] *Thompson's Narrative*, 204–205.

by the beginning of the nineteenth century, the nomads of the northeastern plains had all but exterminated the beaver between the Mississippi and Missouri rivers.[98] In 1804, Lewis and Clark remarked that on the Niobrara River, "Beaver-houses have been observed in great numbers on the river, but none of the animals themselves."[99] Thompson wrote that after 1797, "almost the whole of these extensive countries were denuded of Beaver, the Nations became poor, and with difficulty procured the first necessaries of life." He concluded, "A worn out field may be manured, and again made fertile; but the Beaver, once destroyed cannot be replaced."[100]

The diffusion of European goods throughout the plains and the integration of the nomads into the Euroamerican market was nothing less than an economic revolution. When they embraced equestrianism, the nomads had abandoned their reliance on a variety of resources. They compensated for those losses by increased trade with the Missouri River villagers. When Euroamerican fur traders came to the plains, the nomads forsook some traditional crafts – the planting of tobacco, the manufacture of stone arrowheads – and instead acquired goods from Euroamericans in exchange for beaver pelts. The extensive inter-tribal trade in the plains meant that even those societies not directly engaged in the production of pelts or the interaction with Euroamerican traders felt the effects of trade; this trade, the exchange of horses and foodstuffs, eventually came to include manufactured goods as well. The horse – the vanguard of the European ecological invasion of the plains – initiated the specialization of the nomads as hunters and traders. The fur trade – the European economic invasion of the plains – furthered the transformation of the nomads' resource use. The near-extermination of the beaver in the late eighteenth century demonstrated to some Indians and Euroamericans the inherent dangers of such specialization.

III

In addition to the horse and the fur trade, European diseases helped create the plains nomadic societies in the eighteenth century. Familiar European diseases such as smallpox and measles were particularly devastating to American Indians, who had no acquired immunities to Old World contagion.[101] Native Americans lacked those immunities because, in all probability, their ancestors had migrated to America from Asia through the Arctic environment of the Bering Strait land

[98] White, "The Winning of the West," 324.
[99] Lewis and Clark, *History of the Expedition*, vol. 1, 107.
[100] *Thompson's Narrative*, 206.
[101] For Native American depopulation, see Alfred W. Crosby, Jr., "Virgin Soil Epidemics as a Factor in the Aboriginal Depopulation in America," *William and Mary Quarterly*, 3d ser., 33 (April 1976), 287–299.

bridge. Because the microbes that cause smallpox, measles, and other diseases cannot survive long among sparse populations, the Arctic migration acted as a disease filter. Therefore, although pre-Columbian North Americans may have suffered from pinta, yaws, venereal diseases, hepatitis, encephalitis, polio, and some varieties of tuberculosis and intestinal parasites, they were free of smallpox, measles, whooping cough, bubonic plague, typhus, yellow fever, scarlet fever, amoebic dysentery, influenza, and several other deadly Eurasian illnesses.[102]

In the Old World, deadly communicable diseases were an often unavoidable facet of everyday life. Eurasian pastoralists shared dozens of diseases with their livestock. Measles, for instance, is probably a strain of rinderpest and smallpox is related to cowpox. In 1347, rats and fleas carried another zoonotic disease, bubonic plague, from the central Asian steppes to Europe with disastrous results. By 1350, the plague had killed one-third of the European population. Moreover, the inadequate sanitation of Old World cities repeatedly produced outbreaks of typhoid. Such epidemics were not the norm, however. For the most part, dense populations in the Old World existed in an uneasy equilibrium with "crowd diseases" – so-called because they persisted in thickly populated areas where new hosts were always available – such as smallpox and measles. The victims of such diseases were usually children. In Europe between the sixteenth and eighteenth centuries, 80 percent of the victims of smallpox were children under ten years of age, and 70 percent were under two years of age. Over time, a kind of balance developed between crowd diseases and host populations. The diseases became endemic childhood killers, accounting for 3 to 10 percent of all deaths.[103]

When hosts carried endemic crowd diseases to remote, previously unexposed populations, however, the result was a devastating epidemic. Beginning in the sixteenth century, when Old World contagion reached the populations of the New World, millions of Native Americans perished. Such a figure is necessarily an inexact estimate. Much of the difficulty of calculating Indian populations stems from Euroamerican observers' habit of counting the number of lodges and then multiplying by the number of people they believed inhabited an average lodge. In the plains, this factor could vary from five to fifteen. Historians cannot know how many Native Americans died as a result of Old World diseases, but based on the virulence of the diseases and an understanding of how epidemics behave, it appears likely that mortality was extremely high.[104] The fur trader

---

[102] Cronon, *Changes in the Land*, 85; Crosby, *Ecological Imperialism*, 197–198; see also Crosby, *Columbian Exchange*, 122–164.

[103] William H. McNeill, *Plagues and Peoples* (Garden City: Anchor, 1976), 45–46, 197–198; Crosby, *Columbian Exchange*, 44; Crosby, *Ecological Imperialism*, 30–32.

[104] For the transmission of diseases, see McNeill, *Plagues and Peoples*, 69–71, 176–207. For Indian demography, see Gregory R. Campbell, ed., "Plains Indian Historical Demography and Health," *Plains Anthropologist*, 34 (May 1989). Also see Douglas H. Ubelaker, "North American Indian Population Size, A.D. 1500 to 1985," *American Journal of Physical Anthropology*, 77 (1988), 289–294. For a criticism of the assumptions and methodology of some historical demographers,

James Mackay wrote of the plains in 1797, "These Countries are in general very healthy, in Consequence of which the Indians are not subject to but very few Diseases, and those generally the fruits of their intemperance, amongst those they reckon dysenteries and the Venereal." Mackay warned, however, that "of all those Scourges and Plagues, the most Terrible is the Small Pox, truly they are attacked of it but very rarely, but when it does visit them, it Strikes them with a Mortality as Frightful as Universal."[105]

The first appearance of Old World contagion in the plains is open to debate. Perhaps smallpox, which the Spanish had unwittingly transmitted with deadly effect to Mexico in 1520, also spread to the grasslands. An unknown disease reached eastern Texas and the southern plains in 1691.[106] Battiste Good's winter count calls 1734–35 the "used-them-up-with-bellyache winter"; oral tradition maintains that fifty Sioux died.[107] In general, affliction followed the paths of commercial interaction between Indians and Euroamericans. In the eighteenth century, contagion devastated the Pueblos of New Mexico and the horticultural villagers of the Missouri River rather than the plains nomads because European fur traders centered their commercial enterprises among the villagers. The densely settled, relatively sedentary villagers were thus more likely to contract diseases than the nomads, who spent much of the year isolated in small, outlying bands.

Smallpox was the deadliest scourge of the Indians of the plains in the eighteenth century. *Variola*, the technical name for the disease, is caused by an airborne virus that enters the body through the respiratory tract. One might also contract the disease if one comes in contact with a fresh pox scab or pustule. Once lodged in a new host, the smallpox virus incubates for about two weeks. According to Joel N. Shurkin, the disease begins relatively mildly with chills, fever, headache, and back pain. These symptoms are followed by a fever, which may reach as high as 40° Celsuis (104° Fahrenheit). During this phase the victim may become delirious or lapse into a coma. As the fever subsides, the victim develops a facial rash and sore throat. Soon the rash becomes painful pox sores, which eventually overtake the entire body. Shurkin described the lesions as "red splotches which swell, spread, and erupt into hideous wounds that eventually scab over." When the sores swell and erupt, the victim's fever rises again to about 39° Celcius. The lesions leave the survivor with permanent scars.

That is, of course, if one survived. Mortality depended largely on the particular strain of the disease one happened to contract. Ninety percent of the victims

---

see David Henige, "Their Numbers Become Thick: Native American Historical Demography as Expiation," in James Clifton, ed., *The Invented Indian: Cultural Fictions and Government Policies* (New Brunswick: Transaction Publishers, 1990), 169–191.

[105] "Captain Mackay's Journal," in *Before Lewis and Clark*, vol. 2, 494.

[106] John C. Ewers, "The Influence of Epidemics on the Indian Populations and Cultures of Texas," *Plains Anthropologist*, 18 (May 1973), 104–115.

[107] Mallery, "Picture-Writing," 300.

of discrete smallpox, in which the pox sores did not touch each other, survived. Half died when afflicted with confluent smallpox, in which the sores were close enough to touch. In the case of hemorrhagic smallpox, in which the victim suffered subcutaneous bleeding, death was inevitable. A survivor of one of the less virulent strains of the disease maintained antibodies which guarded against later affliction, even of the most deadly strain.[108]

A devastating epidemic of smallpox, perhaps in combination with other, unknown diseases, struck the plains between 1780 and 1782. The pestilence began in Mexico in August, 1779. The viceroy of New Spain reported that by December there had been 44,286 cases of smallpox and 8,821 deaths in Mexico City. Hospitals were overwhelmed and corpses filled the streets.[109] Baron Alexander von Humboldt, who surveyed Mexico in 1803 and 1804, reported that nine thousand people had died in Mexico in 1779.[110] The epidemic similarly devastated the Indian villagers north of Mexico. The first villagers to fall victim to the epidemic were the Pueblos of New Mexico. Arriving on the heels of three years of drought, the first wave of the disease killed thirty-one people in Albuquerque in the spring of 1780. The second wave began in January, 1781. Before the end of February the parish priest of Albuquerque had given up recording the names of the dead. Altogether, the disease killed half of the Pueblos, perhaps as many as five thousand people. The epidemic transformed the ethnic composition of New Mexico: by 1793, there were two-thirds as many mestizo settlers as Indians in the Rio Grande valley.[111]

Within months of its first appearance in New Mexico, the epidemic reached the Missouri River villagers to the northeast. Before 1780, a typical Missouri River village consisted of twenty to forty lodges each containing about fifteen people. The relatively densely settled villages were thus acutely liable to Old World contagion. According to Jean Baptiste Truteau, smallpox reduced the number of Arikara villages from thirty-two to two. He wrote in 1795, "A few families only, from each of the villages, escaped; these united and formed the two villages now here, which are situated about a half mile apart upon the same land occupied by their ancestors."[112] Pierre-Antoine Tabeau reported that the number of Arikara warriors was reduced from four thousand to five hundred.[113]

[108] Joel N. Shurkin, *The Invisible Fire: The Story of Mankind's Victory Over the Ancient Scourge of Smallpox* (New York: Putnam, 1979), 25–27; Crosby, *Columbian Exchange*, 44.

[109] Sherburne F. Cook, "The Smallpox Epidemic of 1779 in Mexico," *Bulletin of the History of Medicine*, 7 (July 1939), 940n.

[110] Alexander von Humboldt, *Political Essay on the Kingdom of New Spain*, trans. John Black (New York: Knopf, 1972), 39. Humboldt's essay was originally published in French in 1811.

[111] Spicer, *Cycles of Conquest*, 166, 195; Marc Simmons, "New Mexico's Smallpox Epidemic of 1780–81," *New Mexico Historical Review*, 41 (October 1966), 319–326.

[112] "Journal of Truteau on the Missouri River, 1794–1796," in *Before Lewis and Clark*, vol. 1, 299.

[113] Tabeau, *Narrative of Loisel's Expedition*, 123–124; Brackenridge, in *Early Western Travels*, vol. 6, 122.

Altogether, the reports indicate that the Arikara population fell from fifteen thousand to about fifteen hundred as a result of the epidemic.[114]

At the same time, losses to smallpox forced the Mandans to forsake their nine villages on the Heart and Missouri rivers and to congregate in two sites.[115] For decades, their abandoned villages remained as ghastly reminders of the scourge.[116] The Hidatsas also suffered; when the Assiniboines raided the Hidatsas in 1781, they found the village filled with dead and dying. In sum, the 1780–82 smallpox epidemic killed no fewer than one-third to one-half of the sedentary horticulturists living along the Missouri.[117] The mortality among the upper Missouri villagers may have been still higher. According to one estimate that assumed thirty-five lodges in each village and ten people in each lodge, the pre-epidemic population of the Arikaras, Mandans, and Hidatsas may have been nineteen thousand. When Lewis and Clark visited the upper Missouri in 1804, they reported that the population of the three societies was just under six thousand.[118]

Some nomads suffered, but far less so than the villagers. The Assiniboines who stumbled into the disease at the Hidatsa village carried the scourge back to their kinspeople. After visiting the Assiniboines in 1796, David Thompson wrote, "the Natives allowed that far more than one half had died, and from the number of tents which remained, it appeared that about three fifths had perished." Similarly, the Piegans contracted the disease from the Snakes of the northern Rocky Mountains. According to Saukamapee, a Cree who had lived with the Piegans since his youth, scouts discovered a Snake camp with "something very suspicious about it; from a high knowl they had a good view of the camp, but saw none of the men hunting, or going about; there were a few Horses, but no one came to them." After a council, the Piegans decided to attack. Upon entering the Snake lodges, "our war whoop instantly stopt, our eyes were appalled with terror; there was no one to fight with but the dead and the dying, each a mass of corruption." Shortly thereafter, the disease erupted in the Piegan camp. The Indians were surprised: "We had no belief that one Man could give it to another, any more than a wounded Man could give his wound to another." The pestilence, the Piegans told Thompson in 1787, "came over us all, and swept

[114] Holder, *Hoe and the Horse on the Plains*, 85.
[115] Maximilian, in *Early Western Travels*, vol. 23, 254, 317–318.
[116] Gough, ed., *Henry's Journal*, vol. 1, 217.
[117] E. Wagner Stearn and Allan E. Stearn, *The Effect of Smallpox on the Destiny of the Amerindian* (Boston: Bruce Humphries, 1945), 147–149. For the 1780 smallpox epidemic in the plains, see Ewers, "The Influence of Epidemics," 104–115; Campbell, "Plains Indian Historical Demography," v–xiii; Michael K. Trimble, "Infectious Disease and the Northern Plains Horticulturalists: A Human Behavior Model," *Plains Anthropologist*, 34 (May 1989), 41–59; Holder, *Hoe and the Horse on the Plains*, 84–86.
[118] Donald J. Lehmer, "Epidemics Among the Indians of the Upper Missouri," *Selected Writings of Donald J. Lehmer*, Reprints in *Anthropology*, vol. 8 (Lincoln: J & L Reprint Co., 1977), 107.

away more than half of us by the Small pox, of which we knew nothing until it brought death among us."[119] The Crows contracted the disease from the Hidatsas. They told the fur trader François-Antoine Larocque that before the epidemic, they had numbered two thousand lodges; in 1805 he counted only three hundred.[120] The Brulés called the winters of 1779–80 and 1780–81 "used-them-up-with-smallpox winters."[121] The Oglalas recorded in their winter count that the disease struck them in 1782.[122]

Equestrian bison hunting saved the nomads from greater mortality. The nomads were isolated in small populations for much of the year as they pursued bison. Whereas the estimated population density of the Mandans and Hidatsas was over twenty-seven people per square kilometer, the population per square kilometer of the Comanches, Cheyennes, Arapahos, and Kiowas ranged between five and fewer than two.[123] These differences in population density and therefore in the incidence of epidemics are reflected in Kiowa folklore. In one story, the Kiowa trickster-hero, Saynday, met Smallpox on the plains. Smallpox told Saynday that he was a confederate of the Euroamericans, sometimes traveling before them and sometimes just behind. When he learned that Saynday represented a society that he had yet to visit, Smallpox attempted to learn from the trickster where the Kiowas could be found. Protesting that the Kiowas were few and poor, Saynday suggested that Smallpox might rather visit the Kiowas' enemies, the Pawnees, who lived in large villages by the river. The prospect of large numbers of people crowded together in villages tempted Smallpox to spare the few, dispersed Kiowas.[124] Eurasian disease did not indiscriminately destroy all Indians. In the eighteenth century, epidemics flowed through the Great Plains like the waters of the Missouri River during a spring flood, inundating the valleys but leaving the high ground unaffected.

Altogether, between 1780 and 1870, the population of plains sedentary horticulturists probably declined by 79 percent. During the same period, the population of the nomads likely declined by 45 percent, with most of that loss occurring at the end of the nineteenth century.[125] (See Table 2.1.) These figures are only

---

[119] *Thompson's Narrative*, 323, 336. The elder, Saukamappee (Young Man), said that two days elapsed between the raid on the Snake camp and the outbreak of the disease among the Piegan – certainly too brief a time for the virus to incubate. For smallpox among the nomads, see also Hyde, *Indians of the High Plains*, 165, 174.

[120] "François-Antoine Larocque's 'Yellowstone Journal,'" in Wood and Thiessen, eds., *Early Fur Trade*, 206.

[121] Mallery, "Picture-Writing," 308.

[122] Beckwith, "Mythology of the Oglala Sioux,", 353.

[123] Katherine A. Spielmann, *Interdependence in the Prehistoric Southwest: An Ecological Analysis of Plains-Pueblo Interaction* (New York: Garland, 1991), 61.

[124] Marriott and Rachlin, *American Indian Mythology* (New York: Crowell, 1968), 143–146. For a different interpretation of the same folktale, see Crosby, *Ecological Imperialism*, 207–208.

[125] James Mooney, *The Aboriginal Population of America North of Mexico*, Smithsonian Miscellaneous Collections, vol. 80 (Washington: Smithsonian Institution, 1928), 12–13.

Table 2.1 *Mortality in the Great Plains, 1780–1877*

Villagers	1780	1877	Percent Reduction
Mandan	3,600	257	93 %
Caddo	8,500	643	92
Wichita	3,200	409	87
Pawnee	10,000	1,521	85
Kansa	3,000	500	83
Hidatsa	2,500	466	81
Arikara	3,000	670	78
Omaha	2,800	1,061	62
Osage	6,200	3,000	52
Oto-Missouri	900	452	50
Ponca	800	753	6
Total	**44,500**	**9,732**	**79 %**

Nomads	1780	1877	Percent Reduction
Assiniboine	10,000	1,719	83 %
Atsina	3,000	600	80
Comanche	7,000	1,695	76
Blackfeet	15,000	4,560	69
Kiowa and Kiowa-Apache	2,300	1,433	38
Crow	4,000	3,300	18
Sioux (Teton)	20,000	18,106	9
Cheyenne	3,500	3,236	8
Arapaho	3,000	2,964	1
Total	**67,800**	**37,613**	**45 %**

Source: James Mooney, *The Aboriginal Population of America North of Mexico* (Washington, D.C.: Government Printing Office, 1928), 13.

rough estimates, but they indicate that whatever the exact mortality rates – figures that will probably never be known for sure – the mortality among the villagers greatly exceeded that of the nomads.

The devastation of the villages reinforced nomadism in the plains. During the 1770s, the Cheyennes still lived in earth-lodge villages, and two bands of the Sioux – the Oglalas and the Minneconjous (which means, "those who plant by the stream") – had settled near the Arikaras to plant corn. After the outbreak of the smallpox epidemic in 1780, the Cheyennes and the Sioux abandoned agriculture for good, except for a brief return to the earth lodges by a Sioux band, the Sans Arcs, in the mid-1810s. The Sans Arcs' experiment with farming came to an end after an outbreak of either smallpox or measles at the end of the decade.[126] In 1786, despite the efforts of the New Mexican governor, Juan Bautiste de Anza, to persuade them, the Comanches refused to settle in agricultural villages.[127]

The 1780–82 epidemic shifted the balance of power in the plains from the villagers to the nomads. For most of the eighteenth century, the villagers – by virtue of their palisades and their greater numbers – had little to fear from other groups. The villagers' dominance had begun to wane when the Sioux, Comanches, and others acquired horses; the horse gave the nomads the ability to mount quick raids on the villages. The epidemic of 1780–82 left the nomads virtually unchallenged for authority in the plains. Prince Maximilian wrote that in the wake of the 1780–82 epidemic, the Sioux sacked the largest remaining Mandan village.[128] Tabeau, who lived among the Arikaras from 1803 to 1805, regarded the villagers as little more than peons of the Sioux, "a certain kind of serf who cultivates for them."[129]

After 1782, episodes of smallpox continued to induce Missouri River villagers to abandon planting for equestrian nomadism. One such group was the Omahas, whom the naturalist John Bradbury had mentioned in his discourse on the honeybee in 1811. The Omahas had remained agriculturists along the Missouri despite the epidemic of 1780–82, only to be nearly destroyed when the pestilence swept the Missouri again in 1801–02. The second outbreak of the disease reduced the number of Omahas from an estimated thiry-five hundred to three hundred. Before the epidemic, the Omahas had been one of the most powerful groups on the Missouri. They were the "terror of their neighbors," according to one traveler.[130] Truteau wrote in 1794 that the Omaha chief Blackbird "is feared and respected and is in great renown among all strange nations, none of whom dare to contradict him openly or to move against his wishes."[131] After the epidemic, however, the Omahas were left, according to William Clark, "to the insults of their neighbors, who had previously been glad to be on friendly terms with them."[132] Thomas Farnham, who toured the plains in 1839, wrote that the 1801–02 smallpox epidemic "so disheartened those who survived that they burnt

[126] Tabeau, *Narrative of Loisel's Expedition*, 151–152; Hoebel, *Cheyenne*, 6–9; White, "The Winning of the West," 324. For the brief return of the Sans Arcs to farming, see James R. Walker, "The No Ears, Short Man, and Iron Crow Winter Counts," in *Lakota Society*, ed. Raymond J. DeMallie (Lincoln: University of Nebraska Press, 1982), 133–134.
[127] Flores, "Bison Ecology and Bison Diplomacy," 465.
[128] Maximilian, in *Early Western Travels*, vol. 23, 317–338.
[129] Tabeau, *Narrative of Loisel's Expedition*, 130–131.
[130] Thomas Farnham, *Travels in the Great Western Prairies* (London: Bentley, 1843), in *Early Western Travels*, vol. 28, 146
[131] "Journal of Truteau on the Missouri River, 1794–1795," in *Before Lewis and Clark*, vol. 1, 282.
[132] Reuben Gold Thwaites, ed., *Original Journals of the Lewis and Clark Expedition* (New York: Harper, 1904), 109–110.

their village and became a wandering people."[133] The Omahas thus belatedly opted for the alternative that the nomadic societies had chosen in the mid-eighteenth century.

In the late eighteenth and early nineteenth centuries, the Sioux, Cheyennes, Omahas, and others faced a social and ecological dilemma. As villagers they risked European contagion. As equestrian nomads their land-use strategy lacked the added security of planting and demanded social fragmentation. Those groups that had chosen to abandon their diverse resource base and become nomads better survived the smallpox epidemic of 1780–82. Yet by the middle of the nineteenth century, the nomads' singular reliance on the bison had become a grave ecological liability.

The eighteenth-century Great Plains was a maelstrom of cultural, economic, and ecological change. Transforming social and biological forces stormed into the grasslands from all directions. Indians migrated to the plains from the Western mountains and the Eastern woodlands, drawn there or forced there by hunger or war. Horses entered the plains from the Rio Grande and the northern Rocky Mountains; manufactured goods flowed into the plains from the British and French traders around Hudson Bay and the Great Lakes; smallpox invaded the grasslands from Mexico in 1780. The nomadic societies emerged from this tumult of cultural, economic, and environmental change. In response to the European ecological and economic invasion of North America, the Sioux, Cheyennes, and others created a new social organization and resource strategy based on the exploitation of the bison. The horse, the fur trade, and epidemic disease together created the nomadic hunters. The emergence of the plains nomads in the eighteenth century was thus largely a reaction to the European conquest of North America.

That conquest was a cooperative enterprise. Horses and smallpox – an Old World animal and an Old World disease – destroyed the dominance of the Missouri River villagers and levered the nomads to power in the grasslands. The ecological and economic forces brought by the Europeans were intertwined. Trade brought the horse to the plains. Smallpox largely affected the villages where Euroamerican fur traders concentrated their activities. Trade in horses, furs, and foodstuffs furthered the specialization of the nomads as bison hunters. The arrival of the fur traders led to the destruction of the beaver. In the eighteenth-century plains, ecological and economic changes were inseparable.

The genesis of the nomads was as much ecological as social and economic. Environmental change was endemic to the semi-arid, drought-prone grassland. The introduction of exotic biota to the region created still more change. The

---

[133] Farnham, in *Early Western Travels*, vol. 28, 146.

ecologist Charles S. Elton argued that the usual result of such an invasion is an "ecological explosion." He meant that the population of invading plants, animals, or microbes erupted in a virgin soil environment.[134] In the eighteenth-century plains, however, although horses and smallpox thrived it was not a dramatic upsurge in a plant or animal population that followed the arrival of European biota, but the creation of nomadic, equestrian societies.

Although nomadic bison hunting ultimately proved to be less sustainable than the reliance on planting, gathering, and hunting in a variety of environments, the transformation of many groups from woodland planter-hunters to grassland bison hunters was not a step backward in human evolution. The semi-arid western plains environment, rich in wildlife but too dry for agriculture, dictated the potentials and limitations of resource use. Indeed, rather than exhibiting backwardness, the nomads – characterized by mobility, social anomie, and economic specialization – anticipated later social and economic developments in the plains.

The bison was at the center of the vortex of economic and ecological change in the Great Plains. Indians drew horses into the plains as a means to pursue the herds. The bison's flesh and skins fed, clothed, and housed both the nomads and the fur traders. The bison sustained the nomads during the smallpox epidemic of 1780–82. Yet by positioning themselves to survive the European invasion in the eighteenth century – by becoming specialized bison hunters – the plains nomads made themselves doubly vulnerable. First, dependence on the bison left the equestrian nomads subject to unpredictable changes in the semi-arid grassland. Second, by abandoning their ecological safety nets and embracing the emerging Euroamerican market, the plains nomads bound their fate to the Euroamerican economic and ecological complex. In the nineteenth century, the dynamic grassland environment, commercial exploitation of the bison, and epidemic disease would bring an end to the nomads' dominance of the western plains.

[134] Charles Elton, *The Ecology of Invasions by Plants and Animals* (London: Chapman and Hall, 1958), 15.

3

The Nomadic Experiment

When the equestrian nomads rose to dominance in the Great Plains at the end of the eighteenth century, the bison was the largest mammal in North America, but it was not the largest animal ever to have inhabited the continent. Between twelve thousand and fourteen thousand years ago, during the last Ice Age, glaciers edged into the plains to the north and forests covered much of the plains to the south. In this period – the Pleistocene epoch – large herbivores now extinct such as the mammoth (*mammuthus primigenius*) and the giant bison (*bison latifrons*) foraged in mid-continental North America. As the Ice Age ended, global warming and human predation conspired to kill off the giant mammals (a lethal combination of anthropogenic and environmental pressures that foreshadowed the near-extinction of the bison thousands of years later). The extinction of the large herbivores coincided with the appearance of Paleoindian hunting societies in North America. The enormous glaciers of the Pleistocene epoch had lowered the sea level sufficiently to create a land bridge between Siberia and Alaska in what is now the Bering Strait. Paleoindians probably came from Asia to America between twenty-five thousand and twenty thousand years ago, and again between fourteen thousand and ten thousand years ago, while the Bering land bridge existed but glaciers did not block the migration. The large North American herbivores disappeared about eleven thousand years ago. In addition to the probable pressure of human hunters, climatic change contributed to the Pleistocene extinctions. With the end of the last Ice Age came a global desiccation that killed much of the flora that had supported the large herbivores.[1]

The modern bison survived the Pleistocene epoch because they were swifter ahoof, reproduced faster, and required less forage than their giant competitors. Thus, the bison could both outrun pedestrian hunters and bear enough calves to replace those of their number lost to human predation. As grasses came to replace trees in the Great Plains in the warmer and drier period following the Pleistocene epoch, the bison's ability to survive on the thinner forage helped it to dominate the region. The Pleistocene extinctions left the bison – sometimes

[1] Paul S. Martin and H. E. Wright, Jr., eds., *Pleistocene Extinctions: The Search for a Cause* (New Haven: Yale University Press, 1967), 75–200; Grover S. Krantz, "Human Activities and Megafaunal Extinctions," *American Scientist*, 58 (March–April 1970), 165.

called the "dwarf" bison to distinguish it from its giant Ice Age cousin – without a large competitor for the mid-continental pasturage. The herds shared parts of the region with smaller animals such as wapiti (*Cervus elaphus*), pronghorn (*Antilocapra americana*), and mule deer (*Odocoileus hemonius*), but these browsers primarily subsisted not on shortgrasses but on shrubs and forbs.[2] Accordingly, the bison proliferated, in essence a "weed species" that flooded the shortgrass eco-niche after the giant herbivores were gone.[3] The bison's success was a consequence of the inability of larger plant and animal species to survive in the plains. The eventual dominance of the bison was indicative of the ecological order of the grasslands. Survival owed itself not to magnificence but to retrenchment.

To subsist in the domain of shortgrasses and the dwarf bison, the nomadic societies also had to adapt themselves to the constraints of the semi-arid climate. The nomads therefore led an oftentimes hardscrabble existence. As the explorer Stephen H. Long wrote in 1821, "The condition of the savages is a state of constant alarm and apprehension," because "their means of subsistence are precarious and uncertain."[4] Long anticipated the anthropologist Richard B. Lee's analysis of hunter-gatherer societies a century later. Lee argued that although foraging societies such as the !Kung of southern Africa, who relied primarily on food sources other than meat, subsisted securely, mammal hunting is the least reliable of subsistence sources. Hunting societies tend to inhabit harsh, marginal, unproductive regions such as semi-arid plains or Arctic coastlines. Their food procurement is heavily dependent on the often unpredictable migrations and reproduction of their primary prey. Societies such as the plains nomads that relied on mammal hunting were both unlike and considerably less secure and comfortable in their resource use than other subsistence societies.[5]

For the plains nomads, social and economic pressures that attended the pursuit of the bison – scarcity, nearly constant movement, and the division into small hunting and gathering groups – were constant. Faced with these challenges, social degeneration was an ever-present threat. In the eighteenth and nineteenth centuries, there were violent conflicts within as well as among the nomadic societies. Yet the influence of the grassland–bison biome on the nomads was

---

[2] Perhaps thirty-five million pronghorn inhabited pre-Columbian North America, many of them in the Great Plains. See Bart W. O'Gara, "Antilocapra americana," *Mammalian Species*, 90 (American Society of Mammalogists, 6 January 1978), 4. There were, additionally, as many as five million mule deer in the semi-arid West. See Richard J. Mackie, Kenneth L. Hamlin, and David F. Pac, "Mule Deer," and William T. Hesselton and RuthAnn Monson Hesselton, "White-tailed Deer," in Joseph A. Chapman and George A., Feldhammer, eds., *Wild Mammals of North America: Biology, Management, and Economics* (Baltimore: Johns Hopkins University Press, 1982), 871, 894.

[3] Jerry N. McDonald, *North American Bison: Their Classification and Evolution* (Berkeley: University of California Press, 1981), 250–263.

[4] Stephen H. Long, "A General Description of the Country Traversed by the Exploring Expedition," in *Early Western Travels, 1748–1846*, ed. Reuben Gold Thwaites (Cleveland: Clark, 1904), vol. 17, 166.

[5] Richard B. Lee, "What Hunters Do for a Living, or, How to Make Out on Scarce Resources," in Lee and Irven DeVore, eds., *Man the Hunter* (Chicago: Aldine, 1968), 30–43.

not to reduce them to a state of Hobbesian primitivism. Rather, a communal economic ethic united the Indians during times of hardship. Sarah Ann Horn, a prisoner of the Comanches in the 1830s, observed that ethic in practice: "The strength of their attachment to each other, and the demonstration they give of the same, even to the dividing of the last morsel with each other upon the point of starvation, might put many professed christians to the blush!"[6] The nomads' cooperative ethic both helped them to endure the vicissitudes of the semi-arid plains and united them against the ecological and economic forces that threatened to drive their societies apart.

To understand the communal ethic of the nomads properly, it must be placed in its proper historical and environmental context. Three considerations are important. First, the ethic was neither timeless nor universal. The existence of an ethic and its consistent practice are two very different things, as Horn's observation on Christian charity implied. The social injunction to share made it incumbent on the fortunate or industrious to be generous with their horses and bison meat. Yet such communalism did not eliminate disparities in wealth in the nomadic societies. Some families enjoyed larger herds of horses or readier supplies of game. The ethic did not prevent division or conflict. Rather, the nomadic societies are best understood as alternately cooperative and divisive. Second, the ethic discouraged waste of resources but did not prevent it. In some cases, it mandated such waste, when the community shared a feast to reaffirm social solidarity. The nomads were not paragons of conservation. Social taboos against waste were most compelling during lean times. In the summer, when the bison assembled in huge herds for the rutting season, the nomads often splurged on feasts of fresh meat. The feasts compensated for both the social segmentation and the privation of the colder months of the year. Third, the volatile semi-arid climate periodically reduced the bison population, rendering even frugal use of the bison depletive. Thus, bison hunting exacted steep social and environmental costs: social fragmentation, seasonal privation, and episodic waste and depletion of the herds.

I

The bison liberated and empowered the plains nomads. Unlike the villagers of the Missouri River valley, the nomads did not cultivate crops. The bison provided for nearly all their needs. In 1804, the explorer Zebulon Pike called the Sioux "the most independent Indians in the world" because "they follow the buffalo as chance directs." He marveled at their ingenuity; they clothed, lodged,

---

[6] Sarah Ann Horn, *Narrative of the Captivity of Mrs. Horn* (St. Louis: Kremle, 1839), in *Comanche Bondage: Beale's Settlement and Sarah Ann Horn's Narrative*, ed. Carl Coke Rister (Lincoln: University of Nebraska Press, 1989), 190.

and fed themselves from the skin and flesh of the bison. He admired their mobility: "Possessing innumerable herds of horses, they are here at this day, five hundred miles off ten days hence, and find themselves equally at home in either place, moving with a rapidity scarcely to be imagined by the inhabitants of the civilized world."[7] The plains nomads, according to Pike, were independent to the point of indomitability. Yet precisely because the bison provided for them so completely, the plains nomads were in truth extraordinarily dependent on the herds. The traveler John McDougall wrote of the Blackfeet in 1865, "Without the buffalo they would be helpless, and yet the whole nation did not own one. To look at them and to hear them, one would feel as if they were the most independent of all men; yet the fact was they were the most dependent among men." The bison's flesh served as food, its skin as clothing and lodging, its sinew as thread, its horns and bones as tools, even dried bison manure served as fuel. "In short," wrote McDougall, "they lived and had their physical being in the buffalo."[8] Their near-total reliance on the herds forced the plains nomads to adapt their societies to the constraints of the grassland–bison biome.

For most of the year, the bison wandered throughout the grasslands in groups as small as five or as large as one hundred. These groups were of two types. A "cow group" consisted of adult cows, calves, and a few young bulls. From early fall to early summer the number of bison in a cow group averaged about twenty, occasionally reaching seventy or one hundred. A "bull group" consisted of bulls four years or older. Bull groups were small, numbering about five and rarely more than fifteen.[9] The segregation between cows and bulls puzzled early Euroamerican explorers. Traveling between Indian villages in the fall of 1806, Pike remarked, "the male buffaloes were in great abundance yet in all our route from the Osage to the Pawnees we never saw one female."[10] Pike attributed the absence of female bison to the Indians' preference for the meat of cows. James O. Pattie similarly observed in the late 1820s, "It is a singular fact, in the habits of these animals, that during one part of the year, the bulls all range in immense blocks without a cow among them, and all the cows equally without the bulls."[11]

Pike and Pattie were among the few nineteenth-century Euroamerican observers to realize that the organization of bison herds was complex. In the summer, when the shortgrasses were at their thickest and most nutritious, the cow and bull groups joined together into large herds for the rutting season.

---

[7] Zebulon Montgomery Pike, *The Expeditions of Zebulon Montgomery Pike*, vol. 1, ed. Elliott Coues (New York: Harper, 1895), 344, cited in Frank Gilbert Roe, *The North American Buffalo: A Critical Study of the Species in Its Wild State* (Toronto: University of Toronto Press, 1951), 609.

[8] John McDougall, *Saddle, Sled, and Snowshoe* (Toronto, 1896), 261, cited in Roe, *North American Buffalo*, 610.

[9] Tom McHugh, *The Time of the Buffalo* (Lincoln: University of Nebraska Press, 1972), 157.

[10] *Expeditions of Pike*, vol. 2, 516.

[11] James O. Pattie, *Personal Narrative During an Expedition from St. Louis Through the Vast Regions Between that Place and the Pacific Ocean* (Cincinnati: Wood, 1831), in *Early Western Travels*, vol. 18, 50.

Northern herds assembled for the rut later than those to the south, perhaps to ensure that calves would not arrive until late in the succeeding spring, when forage would be easier to find. During the rutting season, a series of contests among the bulls established a rank order. The encounters could be violent, but most often subordinate bulls simply retreated before pawing, snorting, older males, and most battles consisted merely of a brief butting of heads and locking of horns. The dominant bulls' purpose was to drive younger and weaker males away from cows in heat. The reproductive system thus favored stronger individuals. Moreover, once each animal recognized its place in the rank, conflict within the herd was minimal and grazing proceeded without distraction. When forage was scarce, dominant adult bulls and cows appropriated the available supply. The establishment of rank order thus allowed the herd to weed out low-ranking animals.[12]

In the fall, the large herds dispersed again into cow and bull groups. The constituency of the groups was changeable; the animals split up and intermingled randomly. The fluidity of bison aggregations was likely an adaptation to the patchy and unpredictable quality of plains forage, which varied owing to regional fire, drought, and overgrazing.[13] As they searched for forage during the fall and winter, the herds shifted between the western high plains, central mixed-grass plains, river bottoms, and hilly or wooded regions. Charles McKenzie wrote in 1804, "In stormy weather whole droves [of bison] run from the Mountains and plains to seek shelter in the woods" along the Missouri.[14] The German aristocrat Prince Maximilian likewise observed in the 1830s, that in the summer the bison were widely dispersed in the western grasslands but in the winter migrated east to the Missouri to seek shelter in the woods.[15] Despite this general pattern, migrations, like the constituencies of bull and cow groups, were unpredictable. Generally, herds were large and migrations were minimal when bison could obtain forage easily. When forage was scarce, herds were smaller and migrations wider. The bison's search for water as well as grasses complicated this pattern.

[12] McHugh, *Time of the Buffalo*, 160–168, 191–205. Competing theories of herd organization – that bison migrated south in the winter and north in the summer like birds, or that winter herds were larger than summer herds, or that herds of all sizes were found throughout the year and that bison migrated not at all – are either speculative or grounded on observations of bison in relatively small modern preserves that bear little resemblance to the historic grasslands. See J. Dewey Soper, "History, Range, and Home Life of the Northern Bison," *Ecological Monographs*, 11 (October 1941), 348–412; Jeffrey R. Hanson, "Bison Ecology in the Northern Plains and a Reconstruction of Bison Patterns for the North Dakota Region," *Plains Anthropologist*, 29 (May 1984), 93–113.

[13] Douglas Bamforth, *Ecology and Human Organization on the Great Plains* (New York: Plenum, 1988), passim.

[14] Charles McKenzie's Narratives," in W. Raymond Wood and Thomas D. Thiessen, eds., *Early Fur Trade on the Northern Plains: Canadian Traders Among the Mandan and Hidatsa Indians, 1738–1818* (Norman: University of Oklahoma Press, 1985), 239.

[15] Prince Maximilian of Wied-Neuwied, *Travels in the Interior of North America* (London: Ackermann, 1843), in *Early Western Travels*, vol. 23, 245.

Large numbers periodically gathered near watering places, where they grazed heavily.[16]

In order to exploit the bison, the nomads adapted their movements and their social organization to the habits of the herds. Nomadic bison hunting was, in short, a *solar economy*. In the summer, the shortgrasses of the western plains transformed solar energy into carbohydrates, the bison transformed the grasses into protein, and the nomads assembled in large groups for their summer communal hunts. During the course of the summer hunts the nomads accumulated large amounts of meat, some of which they dried for future use. Because the nomads' economy ultimately relied on solar energy, it was renewable. Theoretically, if the nomads confined their harvest of the bison to the natural increase of the species, their economy was sustainable. But the nomadic economy was limited by the ability of shortgrasses to produce carbohydrates. Drought, for instance, interfered with the predictable operation of the nomads' solar economy. The Kiowa pictographic calendar, which begins in 1832, records six summers when the Kiowas held no Sun Dance, a ceremony that usually occurred during the summer when the Kiowa bands assembled for a communal bison hunt. Dendrochronological records indicate that in five of those six summers, rainfall was scarce. Drought probably prevented the Kiowas from performing the Sun Dance and, presumably, the communal hunt.[17]

One consequence of the nomads' dependence on the bison was their continual movement during the warm months of the year. Communal hunting dispersed the bison, while the nomads' horses consumed grasses near campsites, forcing the groups to move camp periodically. Their marches could reach as far as twenty miles a day, but generally were only ten to fifteen miles.[18] The search for forage, however, sometimes forced them to make wider and more frequent migrations.[19] Shortages of water and wood also contributed to the nomads' migrations. Henry Brackenridge noted in 1811 that the "Indians in their journeys generally so shape their course as to pass where ponds of water are known to be."[20] The nomads also

---

[16] Bamforth, *Ecology and Human Organization*, 48–52

[17] Mooney, *Calendar History of the Kiowa Indians*. For the concept of the "solar economy," see Christian Pfister, "The Early Loss of Ecological Stability in an Agrarian System," in Pfister and Peter Brimblecombe, eds., *The Silent Countdown: Essays in European Environmental History* (Berlin: Springer-Verlag, 1990), 37–55.

[18] Edwin Thompson Denig, *Five Indian Tribes of the Upper Missouri: Sioux, Arikaras, Assiniboines, Crees, Crows*, ed. John C. Ewers (Norman: University of Oklahoma Press, 1961), 159; Francis Parkman, *The Oregon Trail*, ed. E. N. Feltskog (Madison: University of Wisconsin Press, 1969), 154; John Palliser, et al., *Journals, Detailed Reports, and Observations, Relative to Palliser's Exploration of British North America, 1857, 1858, 1859, 1860* (London: Eyre & Spottiswoode, 1863), 204; *A Narrative of the Captivity of Mrs. Horn*, 161.

[19] James E. Sherow, "Workings of the Geodialectic: High Plains Indians and Their Horses in the Region of the Arkansas River Valley, 1800–1870," *Environmental History Review*, 16 (Summer 1992), 64–65, 79.

[20] Henry Brackenridge, *Journal of a Voyage Up the River Missouri Performed in 1811* (Baltimore: Coale and Maxwell, 1816), in *Early Western Travels*, vol. 6, 159–160.

traveled seasonally to forest lands in search of lodge and travois poles. The Sioux went to the Black Hills, the Crows to the Crazy Mountains, and the Blackfeet to the Rocky Mountains or their eastern outcroppings, to harvest lodgepole pine (*Pinus contorta*); the Comanches sought Rocky Mountain juniper (*Juniperus scopulorum*). The bison, the horse, water, and wood shaped the nomads' travels.

When the cold weather came, the nomads divided into bands and dispersed to their favorite winter campsites in the wooded river valleys. There, they awaited the bison, who also sought shelter in the valleys during the winter. Winter was potentially a time of hunger. In its winter count, a Blackfoot band recounted that in 1856, their hunting territory was covered with ice, making it difficult both to hunt and to care for their horses.[21] Cold, snowy winters might wreak havoc on the nomads' horses, but hunting was easy as many bison became mired in snowdrifts. If the cold was severe and the snow deep, bison were abundant in the valleys, hunting was easy, and the Indians were not obliged to go far from camp to look for game. Such winters received special mention in the various Sioux pictographic calendars.[22]

The division into bands lasted for most of the year. The bands varied in size depending on the productivity of the land. The Crows, who numbered altogether about three thousand, inhabited the bountiful Powder River valley between the Black Hills and the Bighorn Mountains. Accordingly, they often camped in two large divisions – the River Crows and Mountain Crows. The thirty-five hundred or so Cheyennes of the less productive Laramie Basin, by contrast, divided into ten bands.[23] The two thousand Kiowas of the least productive southern plains scattered into ten to twenty bands, each comprising twelve to fifty lodges.[24]

Like the constituencies of bull and cow groups, membership in the bands was fluid. Generally, any person or family was free to move from one band to another, or to camp alone.[25] The bands operated more or less independently. They combined and dispersed irregularly, depending on the available supply of bison. Even the Crows, who preferred to camp in large groups, were forced to disperse periodically. "We Crows could not all live together," explained a Crow woman, Pretty Shield, to an interviewer. Small groups "were scattered over the Crow country, so that all might find plenty of meat. The great herds of buffalo were constantly moving, and of course we moved when they did."[26] As Pretty Shield

[21] Hugh A. Dempsey, *A Blackfoot Winter Count* (Calgary: Glenbow-Alberta Institute, 1965), 12.

[22] See Garrick Mallery, "Pictographs of the North American Indians," *Fourth Annual Report of the Bureau of Ethnology, 1882–83* (Washington, D.C.: Government Printing Office, 1886); Mallery, "Picture-Writing of the American Indians," *Tenth Annual Report of the Bureau of American Ethnology* (Washington , D.C.: Government Printing Office, 1889), 297, 302.

[23] E. Adamson Hoebel, *The Cheyennes: Indians of the Great Plains* (New York: Holt, Rinehart & Winston, 1978), 37–38.

[24] Robert H. Lowie, *Indians of the Plains* (Lincoln: University of Nebraska Press, 1982), 87.

[25] Ibid., 88–89.

[26] Frank B. Linderman, *Pretty-Shield: Medicine Woman of the Crows* (Lincoln: University of Nebraska Press, 1972), 27.

explained, the decentralized social structure of the plains nomads was contingent on land use.

The migrations and divisions of the nomads militated against stable or authoritative social organizations. According to the fur trader Edwin Thompson Denig, when two bands of the Sioux came together, "their opinions and interests clash, quarrel follows, and separation follows with bad feelings." Indeed, in 1768, according to an Oglala pictographic calendar kept by Ben Kindle, the Oglala and Brulé divisions of the Sioux fought a civil war against the Saone division, which included the Minneconjous, Hunkpapas, Two Kettles, Sans Arcs, and Blackfeet. Another Oglala calendar, kept by No Ears, also records the civil war and traces its beginnings back to the previous winter.[27] The Hunkpapa band to which Sitting Bull belonged was called *Icira-hingla wicotipi*, or "everyone is always disputing one another." The seven bands of the Oglala Sioux, who were known by such unlovely names as the Shove-asides, Disregards-owns, and Bad-faces, were sometimes bitter rivals. In 1841, Red Cloud, who aspired to leadership of the Bad-faces, murdered a rival band chief, Bull Bear.[28] The mid-nineteenth-century Cheyenne were no less fratricidal. In 1837, Porcupine Bear, a leader of a Cheyenne warrior society, stabbed to death a fellow Cheyenne. Exiled from the Cheyenne, Porcupine Bear, six members of his warrior society who had joined in the murder, and their families formed their own band.[29] In 1854, the government agent for the Arapahos concluded that they "can never, in my opinion, be induced to live together as one nation; they are as hostile to each other as almost any other tribe on the plains."[30] Bands could avoid disputes, however, when they did not hunt in the same territory. According to Denig, "each band confining its hunting operations as nearly as practicable to a certain tract of country accustomed to the rule of its own chief, and domestic association with their friends and acquaintances, prevents differences that arise when several bands comparatively strangers are thrown together." The distribution of bands throughout the country, Denig also noted, made more efficient use of the available supply of game.[31]

That supply was unreliable, however. Grass fires were one of the important factors that influenced the movements of the herds. The effect of fire in the plains varied with its intensity, the weather, and the time of year. In a dry year or during the fall, a fire could be disastrous, destroying the litter layer and leading

[27] Martha Warren Beckwith, "Mythology of the Oglala Sioux," *Journal of American Folklore*, 43 (October–December, 1930), 351; James R. Walker, "The No Ears, Short Man, and Iron Crow Winter Counts," in *Lakota Society*, ed. Raymond J. DeMallie (Lincoln: University of Nebraska Press, 1982), 125.

[28] R. Eli Paul, ed., *Autobiography of Red Cloud: War Leader of the Oglalas* (Helena: Montana Historical Society Press, 1997), 64–70; Walker, *Lakota Society*, 20–21.

[29] Hoebel, *The Cheyennes*, 38, 113–114.

[30] Jno. Whitfield, *Commissioner of Indian Affairs Annual Report, 1854*. S.exdoc 1, 33rd Cong., 1st Sess. (Serial 746), 304.

[31] Denig, *Five Indian Tribes*, 15–16.

to a loss of soil moisture.[32] Denig wrote that the Indians feared autumn grass fires: "Nothing they desire less and their laws to prevent it are severe in the extreme. It effectively destroys their hunting by driving away all game and renders the country unfit for pasturage during the winter." Autumn fires were usually the result of lightning, carelessness, or passing war parties. According to Denig, the Indians' greatest fear was of a fire storm. "Sometimes the flames are very destructive and sweep over districts several hundred miles in all directions until extinguished by rain, snow, or contrary winds."[33] According to Battiste Good's winter count, 1762–63 was "the-people-were-burnt-winter," when a grassfire destroyed the encampment and killed many of the members of one of the Sioux divisions. So many survivors were burned on the legs that the division was thereafter called Siçangu or, by the French, Brulé, for "burnt thigh."[34] Fanny Kelly, a captive of the Oglala Sioux in 1864, wrote in her memoir of her captivity that when a fire threatened the Indians during October of that year, the Oglalas, "terrified in the extreme," pulled up the grass by its roots all around their camp and lit a backfire in order to save themselves.[35]

Autumn fires could be extraordinarily destructive to the bison. Alexander Henry the Younger noted in November, 1804, that in the wake of a fall fire storm, "The poor beasts have all the hair singed off, even the skin in many places is shriveled up and terribly burned, and their eyes are swollen and closed fast. It was really pitiful to see them staggering about, sometimes running afoul of a large stone, at other times tumbling down hill and falling into creeks not yet frozen over. In one spot we found a whole herd lying dead."[36] Charles McKenzie, also traveling in the northern plains in the fall of 1804, wrote, "In the course of a few days we observed whole herds of Buffaloes with their hair singed – some were blind; and half roasted carcasses strewed our way."[37] In the semi-arid grasslands, autumn fire was a potential environmental disaster.

In the spring or during a wet year, however, burning increased the productivity of an area. As Denig observed, "Being covered with grass deeply rooted, only the stalk burns, the heat is swept away by the wind, the roots retain the living principle and soon after another crop springs up, more lively and thick

---

[32] Lauren Brown, *Grasslands*, *(New York: Knopf, 1985)*, 49.

[33] Denig, *Five Indian Tribes*, 107–108. G. W. Arthur maintained that northern plains Indians burned the shortgrass plains every autumn and the tall grass plains every spring, to force the bison to congregate in one area or the other. It is unlikely, however, that plains nomads routinely risked a conflagration in the shortgrass plains during the dry season. See Arthur, "An Introduction to the Ecology of Early Historic Communal Bison Hunting Among the Northern Plains Indians," *Archaeological Survey of Canada*, Mercury Series, no. 37 (Ottawa: National Museum of Man, 1975).

[34] Mallery, "Picture-Writing," 304–305.

[35] Fanny Kelly, *My Captivity Among the Sioux* (New York: Citadel, 1933), 159–163.

[36] Elliott Coues, ed., *New Light on the Early History of the Greater Northwest: The Henry-Thompson Journals (1799–1814)* vol. 1 (New York: Harper, 1897), 253–254.

[37] "Charles McKenzie's Narratives," 230.

than the former owing to its having been freed by the fire from all briars and decayed vegetation."[38] The nutritious spring growth in a burned-over area arrived two or three weeks earlier than in unburned patches. Annual burnings kept forbs and grasses unpalatable to the bison from the area. Moreover, burning rapidly returned the nutrients of dead litter to the soil and destroyed plant diseases and pests.[39] Buffalo grass, because it spreads by above-ground stolons, thrived in burned-over patches. The stolons took root as they spread, and new tufts grew as much as an inch or two a day.[40]

The nomads sought to make the migrations and aggregations of the herds more predictable by setting fire to certain patches of grassland. The nomads set their fires in the spring, at a time when the soil and subsurface plant materials were wet or frozen. The cold and damp prevented a general conflagration. Spring burning accelerated the arrival of forage that was especially attractive to grazing animals that had spent the winter searching for food. As the explorer Edwin James wrote in 1820, the plains nomads "like the Mongalls in the grassy deserts of Asia, set fire to the plains in order to attract herbivorous animals by the growth of tender and nutritious herbage which springs up soon after the burning."[41] In the weeks after the appearance of the spring grasses, the nomads hunted burned-over areas attentively.[42]

Despite strategic burning, however, the nomads were largely unable to control the migrations of the herds and, even divided into bands, their subsistence was uncertain. The French fur trader Pierre-Antoine Tabeau wrote in 1805, "If the hunt is a resource so general for the wandering nations, it is no less precarious and there are frequent instances of families and of entire tribes, which notwithstanding their precaution of drying their meat against a shortage, have experienced horrible famine." Indeed, in the last two months of 1804, Tabeau recorded that the Teton Sioux were reduced to starvation.[43] In 1832–33, the Brulé Sioux set up residence in their accustomed winter camps in the wooded Missouri River valley. Ordinarily, cold weather drove the bison into the riverine forests as well, but during the unseasonably warm winter the bison remained in the high plains

[38] Denig, *Five Indian Tribes*, 107.
[39] William Cronon, *Changes in the Land: Indians, Colonists, and the Ecology of New England* (New York, Hill & Wang, 1983), 50–51.
[40] Brown, *Grasslands*, 57.
[41] Edwin James, *Account of an Expedition from Pittsburgh to the Rocky Mountains, Performed in the Years 1819, 1820* (London: Longman, Hurst, Rees, Orme and Brown, 1823), in *Early Western Travels*, vol. 15, 167.
[42] Henry T. Lewis, "Fire Technology and Resource Management in Aboriginal North America and Australia," in *Resource Managers: North American and Australian Hunter-Gatherers*. A.A.A.S. Selected Symposium no. 67, ed. Nancy M. Williams and Eugene S. Hunn (Boulder: Westview, 1982), 49–50. Also see James H. Shaw and Tracy S. Carter, "Bison Movements in Response to Fire and Seasonality," *Wildlife Society Bulletin*, 18 (1990), 426–430.
[43] Pierre-Antoine Tabeau, *Narrative of Loisel's Expedition to the Upper Missouri*, ed. Annie Heloise Abel (Norman: University of Oklahoma Press, 1939), 72–73.

and many Brulés went hungry. Eventually, the starving Brulés dispersed north-ward up the Missouri, west to the headwaters of the White River, and south to the Platte in search of bison.[44]

Even in the absence of famine, the nomads' diet was oftentimes meager. Fanny Kelly, the captive of the Oglalas, wrote that in 1864 the Indians supplemented their diet of bison by consuming what she called grasshoppers – probably Rocky Mountain locusts (*Caloptenus spretus*). Kelly marveled that "the Indians seemed refreshed by feasting on such small game."[45] Sarah Ann Horn, the captive of the Comanches, complained that her captors expected her to subsist as they did for days at a time on nothing but horse meat and berries.[46]

The nomads relied principally on roots and berries to supplement the bison. According to Denig, although the wild fruits and vegetables of the plains were "only suited to the uncultivated taste of the Indians," they nonetheless "form a considerable item in their bill of fare in times of great scarcity."[47] Tabeau agreed: "Necessity has disclosed to the wandering Savages many nourishing roots, which often preserve them from death during the frequent famines to which they are exposed."[48] The most common vegetable resource was the prairie turnip (*Psoralea esculenta*), which the nomads gathered even in times of plenty for its nutritional value and to vary their diet. The nomads ate the less succulent *Psoralea argophylla* only during times of famine.[49]

The importance of gathering to the nomads' survival cannot be underesti-mated. The Brulé starving winter of 1832–33 came to an end only with the spring harvest of prairie turnips.[50] Denig claimed the turnip was "found everywhere on the high prairies. It is either eaten raw or boiled and is collected and dried in large quantities by the Indians for winter use." In addition to the prairie turnip, the nomads gathered a wide variety of plants. The Cheyennes gathered goose-berries, elkberries, red, yellow, and black currants, black and red raspberries, wild plums, and chokecherries.[51] When hunger pressed, the Cheyennes, Arapa-hos, and Kiowas gathered bigroot, a large but unpalatable tuber. The Blackfeet gathered wild rhubarb, wild potatoes, sarvisberries, chokecherries, tender-root, and bitterroot.[52] The Crows and Sioux in the northern plains gathered sarvis-berries, cushion cactus, wild plums, chokecherries, buffalo berries, wild grapes,

[44] Richmond Clow, "Bison Ecology, Brulé and Yancton Winter Hunting, and the Starving Winter of 1832–33," *Great Plains Quarterly*, 15 (Fall 1995), 259–270.

[45] Kelly, *My Captivity*, 123–124.

[46] *Narrative of the Captivity of Mrs. Horn*, 136.

[47] Denig, *Five Indian Tribes*, 10–11.

[48] Tabeau, *Narrative of Loisel's Expedition*, 97–98.

[49] Barry Kaye and D. W. Moodie, "The *Psoralea* Food Resource of the Northern Plains," *Plains Anthropologist*, 23 (November 1978), 329–336.

[50] Clow, "Starving Winter," 266.

[51] George B. Grinnell, *The Cheyenne Indians: Their History and Ways of Life*, vol. 2 (New Haven: Yale University Press, 1923), 166–191.

[52] Walter McClintock, *Old Indian Trails* (London: Constable, 1923), 323–324.

and the seeds or flowers of milkweed, buffalo rye, wild sunflower, and bulrush.[53] So important were fruit and vegetable resources that the Sioux called the summer months the Moon of Red Cherries (July), the Moon When the Cherries Turn Black (August), and the Moon When the Plums are Red (September).[54] "These fruits and roots," Denig wrote, "are a great resource to a people who depend entirely upon the chase for subsistence."[55]

Although roots and berries supplemented the bison, the nomads relied on their horses and dogs as insurance in the case of famine. Before they had acquired horses, the Indians of the plains used dogs as beasts of burden. After they had acquired horses, the nomads expended little effort to maintain their dogs. Like wolves, the Indians' dogs ate whatever portions of the bison the hunters discarded. In instances of famine, however, the nomads looked on their camp dogs as emergency rations. "To prevent a famine," wrote John Wyeth in 1833, "it is their custom to keep a large number of dogs; and they eat them as we do mutton and lamb."[56] Similarly, the horse was not merely a means of hunting and travel but a potential meal. George Catlin claimed that horses were "killed for food by the Indians at seasons when buffaloes and other game are scarce."[57] Fanny Kelly wrote that during a famine in 1864 the Oglalas consumed both their horses and dogs.[58]

Kelly interpreted the Oglalas' sacrifice of their horses and dogs as a testimony to their savagery. Their lack of thrift and foresight, she believed, had led them to hunger. "They use no economy in food," she wrote. "It is always a feast or a famine."[59] Not that Kelly needed further demonstration of what she regarded as Indian primitivism. The Sioux attack on her wagon train and her subsequent captivity were for her evidence enough. What Kelly and other nineteenth-century Euroamericans viewed as savagery, however, was an adaptation to the volatile and desiccated plains environment. The ecological order of the plains

[53] J. W. Blankinship, *Native Economic Plants of Montana*. Montana Agricultural College Experiment Station Bulletin 56, 1905, in Richard I. Ford, ed., *An Ethnobiology Source Book* (New York: Garland, 1988).

[54] John G. Neihardt, *Black Elk Speaks: Being the Life Story of a Holy Man of the Oglala Sioux* (Lincoln: University of Nebraska Press, 1979).

[55] Denig, *Five Indian Tribes*, 10–12.

[56] John B. Wyeth, *Oregon; Or a Short History of the Long Journey from the Atlantic Ocean to the Region of the Pacific by Land* (Cambridge, 1833), in *Early Western Travels*, vol. 21, 49. See also Melburn D. Thurman, "On the Identity of the Chariticas: Dog Eating and Pre-Horse Adaptation on the High Plains," *Plains Anthropologist*, 33 (May 1988), 159–170. The Comanches, however, maintained a taboo against eating dogs. See Hoebel, *The Political Organization and Law-Ways of the Comanche Indians*. Memoirs of the American Anthropological Association (Menosha: American Anthropological Association, 1940), 17.

[57] George Catlin, *North American Indians: Being Letters and Notes on Their Manners, Customs, and Conditions, Written During Eight Years Travel Amongst the Wildest Tribes of Indians in North America, 1832–1839* (Philadelphia: Leary, Stuart, 1913), vol. 2, 66.

[58] Kelly, *My Captivity*, 110.

[59] Ibid., 76.

enforced retrenchment. In a region given to drought and grassfire, and characterized by the unpredictable wanderings and divisions of the bison, the equestrian nomads necessarily endured periods of want.

II

The unpredictable alternation of abundance and scarcity that typified the nomads' reliance on the bison found cultural expression in their folktales. The tales present the bison as both a mythic source of social and environmental stability and a wily, elusive antagonist. These folktales abound with references to social instability during the transition to nomadism. According to these legends, the social fragmentation and privation of equestrian bison hunting forced the nomads to struggle to maintain a cooperative social ethic. The Cheyennes, for example, explain that their traditions of consensus building and group solidarity emerged from the challenges of nomadic bison hunting. In the early days when "people used to wander about the country," the Cheyennes were uncooperative and selfish. In one tale, a man abandons his family in the plains. Faced with starvation, the man's wife and children are spared when the animals of the plains come to their rescue. A bison approaches and falls dead before them, offering itself for their sustenance. When the family returns to the Cheyennes, they testify to the cooperative spirit of the animals and insist that every Cheyenne "will have to take an oath that you will be honest and care for all the tribe."[60] The Cheyenne myth located the origins of their communalism in their encounter with the bison.

Another Cheyenne tale, however, reflects an antagonistic relationship with the bison. In this tale, a young woman takes her son and leaves her husband, determined to return to her relatives. Her husband follows her, not knowing that she is a bison who has assumed human form. On the journey, he repeatedly overtakes the woman and boy at night, only to find them vanished in the morning, with only the tracks of a cow and calf to follow. Eventually, the trio reaches the buffalo people. According to the tale, the buffalo people at that time hunted and butchered humans. They are determined to kill the man. They subject him to a series of tests, asking him, for instance, to identify his wife – now in the form of a bison – as she mingles in the herd. If he fails, they will kill him. With the help of his son, who signals to his father the identity of his mother, the man succeeds. Impressed, the bison people sacrifice one of their number for the man to eat. When the man returns to the Cheyenne, he encourages them to hunt and eat the bison, and indeed brings them the technology – the bow and arrow – to do so.

[60] Karl N. Llewellyn and E. Adamson Hoebel, *The Cheyenne Way: Conflict and Case Law in Primitive Jurisprudence* (Norman: University of Oklahoma Press, 1941), 69–73.

Like the first tale, this story locates the origin of important Cheyenne social norms in an interaction with bison. Unlike the first tale, however, the interaction is not entirely beatific. The tale presents an intimate relationship between human beings and the bison that is alternately competitive and cooperative. The Cheyenne rely on the bison but must resort to trickery to overcome them.[61]

The Atsinas – linguistic and cultural relatives of the Cheyennes – also tell contradictory tales of the bison. The abundant bison served as the basis of their cooperative economy, and indeed, according to the tales they modeled their cooperative social ethic on the behavior of the herds. Yet, trickery first brought the bison into the world. In one Atsina folktale, an unmarried woman gives birth to a son. She and the boy's father determine to abandon the child. They bury the boy in a bison wallow, where seven bulls discover and rescue him. The bulls raise the boy to adulthood, first sacrificing numbers of their herd for him to eat and later teaching him the use of the bow and arrow so that he can hunt cows himself. Though the man is loath to leave the herd, the bulls finally return him to the Atsinas, to whom he brings the herds' spirit of cooperation. The first act of his mission to teach selflessness to the Atsinas is to seek reconciliation with his parents.[62] As in the Cheyenne myth, in the Atsina tale the nomads model their ethic of cooperation on the animals of the plains – and the bison in particular.

In another Atsina legend, an old woman keeps the bison and the summer in a bag in her lodge. She keeps the bag tied tightly shut and allows one calf out at a time, which she promptly kills for herself. Meanwhile, everyone else is famished and miserable in land covered with snow and without game. To redress this unhappy situation, the Atsina culture hero and trickster Nix'ant transforms himself into a dog and wins the old woman's confidence. The Nix'ant-dog distracts the woman, leaps into the bag, and drives summer and the bison into the world.[63] The story warns against selfishness, equates the appearance of the bison with the well-being of the Atsinas, and clearly approves of Nix'ant's cunning.

The Arapahos, Blackfeet, Cheyennes, and Kiowas tell a similar story. In the Kiowa version, the suspicions of the Kiowa trickster-hero, Saynday, are aroused by a secretive family whose lodge is pitched on the outskirts of camp. While the rest of the Kiowas suffer hunger in the absence of bison, the stand-offish family is mysteriously well fed. Saynday transforms himself into a small dog and wins the affections of the youngest member of the family, a little girl. Although her father forbids her to take the dog into the lodge, Saynday eventually gains access and discovers that a slab in the center of the lodge covers an entrance to a tunnel. Saynday enters the tunnel and drives the underground bison to the surface. The

[61] Grinnell, *By Cheyenne Campfires* (Lincoln: University of Nebraska Press, 1971), 87–104.

[62] Ibid., 94–97. The Blackfeet tell a similar story. See Wissler and D. C. Duvall, *Mythology of the Blackfeet*. Anthropological Papers of the American Museum of Natural History, vol. 2, pt. 1 (New York: American Museum of Natural History, 1908), 121–125.

[63] A. L. Kroeber, *Gros Ventre Myths and Tales*. Anthropological Papers of the American Museum of Natural History, vol. 1, pt. 3 (New York: American Museum of Natural History, 1907), 65–67.

father, discovering Saynday's trick, waits for him at the entrance to the tunnel with his bow drawn, but Saynday changes himself into a cocklebur and hides in the matted hair of the last bison to emerge from underground. In the Cheyenne version of the story, Wihio, the Cheyenne trickster, deceives the owner of a sack containing the bison, takes possession of it, and returns with it to his family. He does not heed the warnings of the sack's former owner, however, who had counseled him not to open it more than four times. When Wihio opens the sack a fifth time, all the bison rush out and crush him.[64] Like the Kiowa and Atsina tales, the Cheyenne tale reiterates the importance of cleverness, and the centrality of subsistence on the bison.

The tales of Nix'ant, Saynday, Wihio, and the other trickster-heroes of the western plains – Napi (Blackfoot), Iktoemi (Sioux), Isaka-wuate (Crow), and Sitconski (Assiniboine), for example – reflected the uncertainties of nomadic bison hunting. The historian Robert Darnton, in his study of trickster tales of early modern France, has argued that such stories are common in societies in which life is hard and hunger is familiar. Tricksters inhabit an arbitrary and amoral universe in which the greatest failings are stupidity and naiveté. Wit and clear-headedness are the necessary tools of survival in an unpredictable environment. The nomads of the western plains, subsisting precariously in a changeable environment, taught and reaffirmed the value of cunning through trickster tales. Indeed, Darnton argues that the Indians of the plains, African-American slaves, and the early modern French represent the three great traditions of trickster folktales.[65] If the folktales of the nomads tell of the importance of sharing within the group, they also tell of the arbitrariness of existence in the plains, and the importance to survival of alertness and cleverness.

In practice, the nomads insisted on cooperation within the group while remaining wary of those without. To mitigate the impermanence, social fragmentation, and privation of nomadic life, the nomads developed an ethic of communal cooperation. The ethic was as much a response to the precariousness of subsistence as were spring burnings and the division into hunting and gathering groups. The influence of the environment on the nomads' communalism was particularly evident in their veneration of the bison, but it was also evident in other aspects of their culture: the social injunctions to share, to maintain social harmony, and to sacrifice individual interests to the good of the community. If the culture of the nomads regarded those without the group as potential enemies, they regarded those within as kin.

The ethic of cooperation and fictive kinship prevailed in the legal cultures of the nomadic societies. In most of the nomadic groups, the redistribution of

[64] Alice Marriott, *Saynday's People: The Kiowa Indians and the Stories They Told* (Lincoln: University of Nebraska Press, 1963), 12–23; Grinnell, *By Cheyenne Campfires*, 302–305.
[65] Robert Darnton, *The Great Cat Massacre and Other Episodes in French Cultural History* (New York: Basic Books, 1984), 55–61.

property served to placate disputing or aggrieved parties and they struggled to
prevent the possession of property from undermining the solidarity of the
group. In 1850, a Cheyenne hunter borrowed a horse from a fellow Cheyenne,
Wolf-Lies-Down. The borrower left a bow and an arrow as symbolic collateral,
but after a year the borrower had yet to return the horse. Wolf-Lies-Down petitioned for his horse, and the borrower returned to him not only the original horse
but a second horse as well. After the matter was concluded, the warrior society
to which Wolf-Lies-Down belonged pledged comradeship to the warrior society
of the borrower.[66]

The legal traditions of the Comanches also sought not to determine culpabil-
ity or to apportion punishment, but to placate aggrieved parties. The Comanches
adjudicated cases with formal politeness; disputing parties addressed one
another as "brother" or "sister." Judges, however, were unknown; it fell to the
persons involved to strike a deal. In most cases, the exchange of goods satisfied
grievances. In cases of adulterous or absconded spouses, for instance, a gift of
horses or goods usually settled the matter. Parties settled disputed inheritances
or broken contracts – for instance, a failure to compensate a healer for services
rendered – through a similar process of bargaining. Although unstructured,
Comanche transactional legal traditions enjoined disputants to settle their affairs
cooperatively.[67]

The Crows, too, settled their disputes amicably. Denig found it strange "that
such a savage nation, living without any law and but little domestic regulation of
any kind, should be able to settle all their individual quarrels with each other
without bloodshed." The Crows settled most disputes through the exchange of
horses. "Thus, if an Indian elopes with another's wife, the unfortunate husband
will seize upon the whole of the offender's horses." If the offender had none, the
cuckold took them from the man's relatives. In time, with his relatives' help, the
paramour could buy back his horses. "Any large thefts, and all disputes concerning women, are arranged on this system," wrote Denig. Indeed, he wrote, "Any
crime or misdemeanor can be paid for among the Crows except murder."[68] The
Crows, like the Cheyennes, Comanches, and other nomads, thus relied on transactions – a formal sharing of resources – to settle disputes and prevent the frac-
turing of the community.

The nomadic societies also strove to harness individualistic, competitive
impulses to the welfare of the group. Groups rewarded young men for their
initiative and competence in what might be loosely termed economic behavior:
hunting, raiding, and the stealing of horses from other groups. Leaders of warrior
societies kept a close watch on young men, restraining them from endangering
themselves or the group, while praising those who excelled as warriors or horse
thieves. By attaching prestige to these pursuits – and to the sharing of the

[66] Llewellyn and Hoebel, *The Cheyenne Way*, 127–128; Hoebel, *The Cheyennes*, 59–60.
[67] Hoebel, *Law-Ways of the Comanche Indians*, 52–53, 125–127.
[68] Denig, *Five Indian Tribes*, 150–151.

resources they produced – the nomads sought to channel the individual quest for prestige toward the group's well-being.[69] There is no reason to believe, however, that the awarding or withdrawal of esteem functioned perfectly to slacken social tensions. In many cases, social approbation failed to contain ambition and the nomads resorted to their fluid social structures to resolve conflict; disgruntled young men switched bands or struck out on their own. The nomadic societies thus resolved conflict through both fusion and fission.[70] Leaving the group was a last resort, however. In general, the nomads strove to resolve ongoing social tensions through reconciliation.

Those tensions were most evident in disputes over private property. The nomads' communal economic ethic disdained the accumulation of wealth. Like the nomads' decentralized social structure, their anti-accumulationist ethic was a product of their nearly constant migrations. As Denig wrote of the nomads, "Their moving habits also prevent the accumulation of much baggage. All useless articles must be thrown away to make room for the more necessary implements. Thus personal property cannot be acquired to any amount." To Denig, the nomads' disinterest in accumulation was one of the deficiencies of their savage temperament. It prevented them from storing provisions, it produced "a carelessness of character and an apathy of disposition," and worst of all, made them indifferent consumers of some European trade goods.[71]

Disputes over horses were the most common conflicts over property within the nomadic societies.[72] The nomads' folktales warned against the accumulation of too many horses in the hands of a few. In a Blackfoot tale, a man who amasses a large herd of horses for himself never shares his wealth with his less fortunate kinspeople. Ordinarily, a person with many horses was expected to loan them to poorer hunters in return for a portion of their kills.[73] One night, in a dream, a ghost stallion drives off the man's herd. He awakes to find his horses indeed missing, and he spends eternity wandering the plains dreaming of and searching for his horses.[74] The tale was a pointed warning against individual engrossment of valuable community assets.

As the Blackfoot tale suggests, the nomads not only discouraged the accumulation of individual wealth but valued the sharing of property. As Denig wrote of the Crows, "There are no poor people among this nation." Denig derided the Crows' "system of begging" in which borrowers "invariably forget to return" articles. Yet he grudgingly acknowledged that the Crows' "liberality" was

---

[69] See Bernard Mishkin, *Rank and Warfare Among the Plains Indians* (Seattle: University of Washington Press, 1940).

[70] See Lee and DeVore, "Problems in the Study of Hunters and Gatherers," in *Man the Hunter*, 12.

[71] Denig, *Five Indian Tribes*, 97.

[72] See, for example, Jane Richardson, *Law and Status Among the Kiowa Indians* (Seattle: University of Washington Press, 1940), 125.

[73] John C. Ewers, *The Blackfeet: Raiders on the Northwestern Plains* (Norman: University of Oklahoma Press, 1958), 81.

[74] Francis Fraser, *The Bear Who Stole the Chinook: Tales from the Blackfoot* (Vancouver: Douglas & MacIntyre, 1990), 38–40.

"absolutely necessary to their national existence." He wrote, "Situated as they are in the constant fear of enemies, and liable at any time to lose their whole stock of animals," the Crows shared their horses in order to survive. "However much they may like their horses, or dislike to part with them, yet each man feels he depends on his neighbor for support when they are taken off."[75] The readiness to pool their resources helped the Indians to weather the insecurities of the nomadic horse culture. The expectation of such generosity was a characteristic of all the nomadic societies.[76]

The nomads' ethic of social cooperation extended particularly to those who were unable to provide for themselves. Denig wrote of the Crows, "Another remarkably good trait in their character is that they do not suffer the aged and infirm to be left behind and perish."[77] The Blackfeet, too, prohibited the abandonment of the elderly or the injured. In a Blackfoot tale, one winter a band leaves behind to die a hunter who, depending on the version of the story, is either old or injured and unable to hunt. The man and his family would have starved were it not for a group of mysterious hunters dressed in wolfskins who supply them with meat. Eventually, the family discovers that the hunters are wolves who are repaying the infirm hunter for his custom of never harvesting more game than necessary to feed his family. The family not only survives the winter but discovers that the band that had left them to die had themselves nearly starved – a pack of wolves, it seemed, had driven away all the game.[78] Apart from the tale's injunction against wasting game, the story enjoined the nomads to provide for the destitute.

The nomads' communal mores emerged in response to the privations of equestrian bison hunting. Their folktales and legal concepts encouraged them to band together to survive in the precarious plains environment. Toward the environment and competing groups, the nomads maintained a posture of alert suspicion. Within a group, however, cooperation was the rule – even if the rule was not always obeyed. Scarcity sometimes rent the nomadic societies with violent divisions, but privation did not reduce the nomads to Ishmaelites. In the grim struggle for survival, they looked for security in social cooperation.

III

The nomads' communal economy and laws and customs enforced the interests of the group and the subordination of individual concerns. Some of the most

[75] Denig, *Five Indian Tribes*, 153–154, 160–161.
[76] Lowie, *Indians of the Plains*, 115.
[77] Denig, *Five Indian Tribes*, 161. Denig implied that some plains groups were not so charitable toward the old and infirm, but he did not specify the group or groups to which he referred.
[78] Fraser, *The Bear Who Stole the Chinook*, 109–111, 125–129. In another version of the story, the hunters were not wolves but deer.

important of those laws prohibited overhunting of game. Like wolves, the nomads were predators in the grasslands. In order to survive, they needed to adjust their resource use to the ecological order of the Great Plains. Like wolves and other predators, however, they were not always frugal in their use of the bison. Wolf packs sometimes kill more prey than they need to survive.[79] Likewise, the nomads, according to the naturalist John Bradbury, "often kill many more than they can possibly dispose of. . . . [H]unting parties are frequently followed by wolves, which profit by this wanton destruction."[80] Despite their injunctions against waste, the nomads' use of the bison was thus sometimes wasteful. This paradox was a consequence not only of the tenuousness of the nomads' reliance on the bison, but of the social pattern of dispersal and congregation essential to the pursuit of the bison.

Despite the influx of European manufactured goods into the plains during the late eighteenth-century trade in beaver pelts, the nomads relied on the bison to provide for them. In 1767, they were so unfamiliar with trade goods that Antonio Ulloa, an agent of the Spanish crown, observed that the "nations in the interior of Missouri" had not yet become accustomed to handling rifles.[81] Alexander Henry the Elder noted in 1776 that the Assiniboines eschewed European manufactured goods: "The wild ox alone supplies them with everything which they are accustomed to want."[82] Tabeau wrote of the Cheyennes in 1804, "The nation has only a half-knowledge of the value of merchandise and prides itself none the less, on being ignorant in this respect." Like Henry, Tabeau attributed the nomads' disregard for European wares to the utility of the bison. "None of these nations values our merchandise highly, and, if we except some iron implements, they have more liking for their skins," he wrote. "They find in the buffalo cow . . . everything that is necessary to them and much that is superfluous."[83]

The retrenchment that Tabeau viewed as savagery was in fact an adaptation to the plains environment. The nomads' frugality was a product of the land use strategy that they had created around the horse and the bison. Except for horses, the nomads' possessions were few. Apart from European goods such as rifles, ammunition, and metal tools, the nomads could manufacture most of the things they needed – food, clothing, lodging, and implements – from the roving herds of bison. Indeed, it was often more effort for the nomads to store provisions than to migrate in search of the herds. As Denig noted, "they seldom have a large supply of meat in their homes, living for the most part on rather short allowance."[84]

[79] Barry Lopez, *Of Wolves and Men* (New York: Charles Scribner's Sons, 1978), 54–55.
[80] John Bradbury, *Travels in the Interior of America in the Years 1809, 1810, and 1811* (London: Sherwood, Neely, and Jones, 1819), in *Early Western Travels*, vol. 5, 174–175.
[81] Antonio Ulloa, 7 January 1767, Louisiana Territory Papers, Missouri Historical Society, St. Louis, Missouri.
[82] Alexander Henry, *Travels and Adventures in Canada and the Indian Territories Between the Years 1760 and 1776*, ed. James Bain (Rutland, Vt.: Charles E. Tuttle, 1969), 317.
[83] Tabeau, *Narrative of Loisel's Expedition*, 153, 162–163.
[84] Denig, *Five Indian Tribes*, 95–97.

Such a strategy could lead to waste. The explorer Matthew Cocking observed that on an expedition to the Blackfoot country his Assiniboine guides "killed a great many Buffalo, only taking what they Choosed to Carry."[85]

The nomads certainly preached against waste. Eagle Plume, a Kiowa, recalled that on his first bison hunt in 1861, an older hunter, Lone Bear, told him, "there are rules about hunting just as about fighting. When you see the herd, you don't want to rush at them. Wait until somebody older than you are gives the signal. Don't kill more meat than you think you can skin and your horse can pack home. That way it won't be wasted and lie around rotting."[86] The injunction to wait for an older man's signal enforced the primacy of the community over the individual hunter, and not incidentally the control of older men over younger hunters. The mandate to kill only as much game as was needed discouraged overhunting that might have led to famine.

Many of the nomadic societies conceived of the mandate against overhunting in religious terms. As General Randolph B. Marcy wrote during his exploration of the southern plains in 1852, the bison's "only enemy then was the Indian, who supplied himself with food and clothing from the immense herds around his door; but would have looked upon it as a sacrilege to destroy more than barely sufficient to supply the wants of his family."[87] In return for the bison allowing themselves to be killed, the nomads offered a portion of the hunt in sacrifice. The explorer Stephen Long wrote in 1821 that the nomads "are generally in the habit of offering in sacrifice a portion of the game first taken on a hunting expedition."[88] The Cheyennes turned the head of the first bison killed to the four directions and then to the sun; they shared its meat as sacred food at a ceremonial feast that concluded the hunt.[89] Many of the plains groups that practiced the summer religious ceremony collectively referred to as the Sun Dance made veneration of the bison an important part of their rituals. Whether religious or secular, the injunction against overhunting prevented exhaustion of the game on which the nomads relied.

The rules against overhunting were also entirely consistent with the nomads' communalism. The Indians extended their ethic of cooperation to include the bison, believing that the animals, like individuals within the group, sacrificed themselves for the good of the human community. The fur trader Tabeau wrote in 1804, "In general, the bear, the deer, and the cow are the kinds of genii that

[85] Lawrence J. Burpee, ed., "Journal of Matthew Cocking, from York Factory to the Blackfeet Country, 1772–73," *Proceedings and Transactions of the Royal Society of Canada* (Ottawa: Hope and Sons, 1908), 333.

[86] Marriott, *The Ten Grandmothers* (Norman: University of Oklahoma Press, 1945), 26–30.

[87] Randolph B. Marcy, *Exploration of the Red River of Louisiana, in the Year 1852* (Washington: Tucker, 1852), 104.

[88] Long, in *Early Western Travels*, vol. 17, 162.

[89] Grinnell, "Some Early Cheyenne Tales," *Journal of American Folklore*, 78 (July–September, 1907), 182–183.

take pleasure in this form and lead this wandering life through kindness for the Savages, in order to furnish subsistence for them. Accordingly, the Savages hunt only with consideration and with a sort of religious respect."[90] The nomads followed the example of the animals and offered their help to their fellows. During Eagle Plume's first hunt, a wounded calf charged his mentor, Lone Bear. Eagle Plume killed the calf and saved the older hunter. "That's the way," congratulated Lone Bear. "That's what you've always got to do. Always remember if you help people in time of danger, they'll help you out when you need it. It's that way in life, not only in hunting."[91] The nomads' customs indicate that they understood that just as their survival depended on the cooperation of the community, their continued subsistence depended on cooperation with their game.

In a year of average precipitation, consistently prudent hunting such as that advocated by Lone Bear might have comfortably sustained the nomads. In 1821, the trader Jacob Fowler estimated that a large camp of Kiowas, Comanches, Cheyennes, and Arapahos used 100 bison per day. If this camp's consumption of bison was typical, the nomads needed annually to harvest about six or seven bison per person to obtain sufficient food, lodging, and clothing.[92] Thus, to subsist, the estimated sixty thousand nomads in the plains in the nineteenth century would need to kill between three hundred sixty thousand and four hundred twenty thousand bison every year. To procure meat and hides to trade for corn with the villagers of the Rio Grande and Missouri rivers and their tributaries, however, they must have killed many more.[93] The estimate of Pierre Chouteau, a prominent St. Louis fur trader, was probably close to the truth. In 1859, Chouteau calculated that the nomads harvested four hundred fifty thousand bison every year for their own consumption and for intertribal trade.[94]

Was an annual destruction of nearly half a million bison – most of them two- to five-year-old cows selected for their tasty meat and pliable hides – sustainable? Seemingly so: the nomads' harvest for subsistence and intertribal trade was less than two percent of the estimated bison population of twenty-seven to thirty million. On modern game preserves, the bison reproduces at an annual rate of 20 percent or higher.[95] If those figures are applicable to the historic grasslands, the plains nomads harvested no more than nine percent of the 4.9 to 7.1 million

[90] Tabeau, *Narrative of Loisel's Expedition*, 195–196.
[91] Marriott, *Ten Grandmothers*, 26–30.
[92] Dan Flores, "Bison Ecology and Bison Diplomacy: The Southern Plains from 1800 to 1850," *Journal of American History*, 78 (September 1991), 479; Elliott Coues, ed., *The Journal of Jacob Fowler: Narrating an Adventure from Arkansas through the Indian Territory, Oklahoma, Kansas, Colorado, and New Mexico, to the Sources of the Rio Grande del Norte* (New York: Harper, 1898), 61, 63.
[93] Katherine A. Spielmann, *Interdependence in the Prehistoric Southwest: An Ecological Analysis of Plains-Pueblo Interaction* (New York: Garland, 1991), 150.
[94] Journal of Elias Marsh, M.D., St. Louis to Fort Benton, May–August, 1859 (31 May 1859). Journals and Diaries Collection, Missouri Historical Society.
[95] Joel Berger and Carol Cunningham, *Bison: Mating and Conservation in Small Populations* (New York: Columbia University Press, 1994), 99–101, 132–135, 145–148; Flores, "Bison Ecology," 476.

calves born every year. Thus, the pressure of the nomads was conceivably well within the capacity of the prolific herds to sustain.

Ecological factors, however – wolf predation, fire, habitat degradation, and, above all, drought – depressed the bison's actual annual increase. Some of these factors were present in the historic plains to a greater extent than on modern, managed, enclosed preserves. Annually, natural mortality and competition from other grazers might have combined to eliminate as many bison as were born each year. Wolf predation (which probably killed between one and two million bison every year), competition from other grazers, particularly the Indians' own horses (two million), accidents (between one and three million), and drought (as many as four million) could have combined to exceed the natural increase of the bison.[96] Given the fluctuating poles of the bison's reproduction and mortality, a yearly Indian harvest of between three hundred sixty thousand and four hundred fifty thousand bison was less than the bison's natural increase only when wolves, fire, competition from other grazers, and accidents claimed a moderate number. During the periods of severe drought which visited the plains every decade or so, the destruction of wildlife was probably so extensive that it rendered depletive any harvest of the bison, even if only for bare subsistence – although many of the bison harvested during dry years might have died anyway as a consequence of drought.

A sustainable harvest of the bison was not a static formula but fluctuated in response to environmental change. Could the nomads have recognized and responded to such changes or to a decline in the bison population? Any decline would have been difficult to discern; divided into small bands for most of the year, the various nomadic societies had little opportunity to assemble to discuss their hunting experiences. A decline in the numbers of bison might well have appeared to be the consequence of its typically unpredictable migrations. Moreover, owing to regional fluctuations in the bison's productivity and density, seasons of scarcity were likely interspersed with seasons of plenty, and whereas some nomads may have found the bison scarce, others may have enjoyed a productive year.

Even had they recognized a decline, the inherent instability of the nomadic societies made it difficult always to enforce the mandates against waste. While traveling in raiding parties, the nomads were likely to consume only some of the bison they killed. The French fur trader and explorer la Vérendrye described an Assiniboine migration in 1738: "If the scouts perceive any herds of buffalo on the way, as often happens, a cry is raised which is quickly heard by the reatguard, and all the most active men in the columns join the vanguard so as to surround the beasts, numbers of which they kill, whereupon each man takes all the meat he

---

[96] Andrew Isenberg, "Social and Environmental Causes and Consequences of the Destruction of the Bison," *Revue Française d'Études Américaines*, 70 (Octobre 1996), 15–27.

wants."[97] Skins may have occasionally proved unsuitable for tanning and meat unfit for consumption, causing the nomads to kill a greater number of bison. War or disease might well have forced the Indians to abandon caches of meat.

Like other groups that depended primarily on hunting for subsistence, such as the caribou hunters of northern Canada or the reindeer hunters of the Eurasian Arctic, the nomads sometimes squandered their primary resource, taking only the best parts of the fattest cows.[98] "They are most improvident with regard of Provision. It is amazing what numbers of Buffaloes or other Quadrupeds the[y] destroy," wrote François-Antoine Larocque of the Crows in 1804. "When hunting they take but the fattest and cut part of an animal and carve [leave] the remainder."[99] Charles McKenzie described the wastefulness of a Cheyenne hunting party in 1806:

> I here witnessed greater slaughter upon Buffalo than I hade been accustom to see at the Missurie – I have been with the Shawyens a hunting, or surround the cattle, with[in] 20 acres of their Camp, when they killed (without saying so much) 250 fat Cows which they left on the field as they fell; excepting the Tongues which they dried for a general feast.[100]

During her captivity among the Oglalas, Fanny Kelly similarly observed her captors' occasional waste of the bison. "The Indians often, for the mere sport, make an onslaught, killing great numbers of them, and having a plentiful feast of 'ta-tonka,' as they call buffalo meat," she wrote. "Each man selects the part of the animal he has killed that best suits his own taste, and leaves the rest to decay or be eaten by wolves, thus wasting their own game."[101]

How could the nomads, who so depended on the herds, be so wasteful? This paradox reveals the tension between the nomads' social organization and the sustainability of equestrian bison hunting. The hunts that Larocque, McKenzie, and Kelly described were special events. They occurred during the summer, the most productive season in the plains, when the nomads indulged in the luxury of the fat, large herds. Both McKenzie and Kelly described the consumption of the bison following these wasteful summer hunts as feasts. The feasts served an important social purpose. Only in the summer, when large herds of bison assembled, could the various nomadic societies find enough meat in one place to allow them to congregate together. These hunts presented an opportunity for the

---

[97] *Journals and Letters of Pierre Gaultier de Varennes de la Vérendrye and His Sons*, ed. Lawrence J. Burpee (Toronto: The Champlain Society, 1927), 317.

[98] See Tim Ingold, *Hunters, Pastoralists, and Ranchers: Reindeer Economies and their Transformations* (Cambridge: Cambridge University Press, 1980), 69–75.

[99] "François-Antoine Larocque's 'Yellowstone Journal,'" in Wood and Thiessen, eds., *Early Fur Trade on the Northern Plains*, 209.

[100] "Charles McKenzie's Narratives," 282.

[101] Kelly, *My Captivity*, 76.

nomads to reaffirm their social solidarity against the privation and social fragmentation that threatened it.

The bison's habits forced the nomads to cooperate during the summer hunts.
Bison are among the most social of North American animals. They communicate
with each other to warn of danger and cooperate to protect themselves against
predators. Much of the communication within a herd consists of grunts and bel-
lows. These noises, varied in pitch, tone, and rhythm, serve as social signals. A
cow and her calf, for instance, locate each other by means of particular calls. In
times of danger, the cow and calf can summon each other by means of a "dis-
tress" noise. The bison's body movements also serve as a means of communication. If a cow senses a lurking predator, she may retreat in a bounding gait that
signals danger to others in the herd. Similarly, a bull may signal potential danger
by staring motionless with his ears swung forward and head raised. The most
common reaction to danger, however, is flight. When alarmed, the herds dis-
pense with rank order; the lowest-ranking animal may initiate the flight, and
even the highest-ranking members follow automatically.[102] In sum, whether
standing or fleeing, the bison relies on its gregariousness to protect it from
predators in the plains. Other open-space grazers – the caribou and the reindeer
of the tundra – also employ this "clumping" tactic to guard against predators.[103]
In some cases, pronghorn antelopes and white-tailed deer sought refuge from
wolves by mingling with a bison herd.

Like pedestrian hunting in the pre-horse plains, equestrian bison hunting
during the summer demanded social cooperation and organization if the
endeavor was to be successful. One hunter on horseback could kill several bison
before the herd scattered, but it would take days for the nomads to locate the fleeing herd again, and the distances between large summer herds were great. The
nomads therefore submitted to greater social authority during the summer.
They borrowed from their pedestrian hunting traditions and appointed a committee to police the hunt. Usually called "soldiers" by Euroamerican observers
and anthropologists, the Indian terms are better translated as "marshals." "The
most effective executive functionaries of the Indians are the 'soldiers'" wrote
Francis Parkman in his journal in 1846. "They are very necessary – they direct
the place to encamp – they direct the movements of a 'surround' and prevent the
buffalo from being frightened by vagrant hunters."[104] Thus the nomads, who at
all other times of the year disdained central authority, obeyed the marshals for
the duration of the summer hunting season.

The organization of nomadic societies during the summer differed markedly
from the bands that divided, intermingled, moved about, and hunted according
to their own initiatives during the fall, winter, and spring. The marshals dictated

[102] McHugh, *Time of the Buffalo*, 151–153, 187.
[103] Ingold, *Hunters, Pastoralists, and Ranchers*, 43.
[104] *The Journals of Francis Parkman*, vol. 2, ed. Mason Wade (New York: Harper, 1947), 445.

when the group should break camp, at what pace they should move, where they should encamp, and when they might hunt.[105] Except for the scouts who rode ahead of the moving camps searching for signs of a large herd, the marshals forbade members of the group to stray. The fur trader Tabeau wrote in 1804, "the soldiers are strict and severe in the execution of their duties. In reality, these laws are an absolute necessity, especially among nomadic peoples who would not be able to subsist if an individual had the right to kill a cow, to put to flight an entire herd, and to destroy the source of their common food. Thus all possible pains and precautions are taken to prevent these things."[106] The marshals, in effect, enforced the social interests of the group over the interests of individuals.

The marshals represented the social consensus. Among the Oglala Sioux, the summer hunts began with a council of adult men. The council deliberated on every matter of the hunt: the hunting territory, the route to follow, and the duration of the hunt. Only when they had produced a consensus did they adjourn. As Denig wrote in 1856, "All questions agitated in Indian councils must have unanimous approval to expect a successful result."[107] After reaching a consensus, the council chose the *akicitas*, or marshals, who would direct the hunt. To be appointed to the *akicitas* one had to be an experienced hunter of good repute. Only rarely did nominees refuse an appointment to the office. After the council had selected them, the *akicitas* usually deputized members of their warrior societies to help them direct the hunt, thus rotating responsibility among the various societies.[108] Once they had been invested with the insignia of their office – a streak of black paint across the right cheek – the *akicitas* commanded absolute obedience. They were excused from ordinary camp duties during their tenure as marshals. In keeping with the spirit of the *akicita*, which sought to build consensus and strengthen the community, a marshal was liable to severe sanctions if he abused his authority.[109]

Most important, the marshals prohibited anyone from hunting bison without their permission. If a hunter transgressed this law – and such offenses were rare – the marshals destroyed the offender's lodge and weapons and confiscated his horses. Yet the object of the penalty – apart from discouraging violations – was not to punish but to correct the offender's behavior. If the offender showed remorse, his belongings would be replaced or returned and his station in the

[105] Raymond J. DeMallie, ed., *The Sixth Grandfather: Black Elk's Teachings Given to John G. Neihardt* (Lincoln: University of Nebraska Press, 1984), 144.

[106] Tabeau, *Narrative of Loisel's Expedition*, 195–196. For the exercise of the police societies, see also James, in *Early Western Travels*, vol. 14, 297; Maximilian, ibid., vol. 23, 293.

[107] Denig, *Five Indian Tribes*, 172.

[108] Clark Wissler, *Societies and Ceremonial Associations of the Oglala Division of the Teton-Dakota.* Anthropological Papers of the American Museum of Natural History, vol. 11, pt. 1 (New York: American Museum of Natural History, 1912), 13. The same rotation existed among Kiowa societies. See Lowie, *Societies of the Kiowas.* Anthropological Papers of the American Museum of Natural History, vol. 11, pt. 11 (New York: American Museum of Natural History, 1916), 849.

[109] Walker, *Lakota Society*, 74–80.

group restored. The spirit of consensus prevailed; the marshals endeavored not to drive away those who violated the hunting laws, but to rehabilitate them and thus strengthen the community.

That spirit of community was nowhere more evident than in the case of the Cheyenne hunter Sticks-Everything-Under-His-Belt. According to Cheyenne informants, before the beginning of a summer communal hunt Sticks-Everything-Under-His-Belt announced his intention to defy the marshals and hunt alone. As punishment, the Cheyennes subjected Sticks-Everything-Under-His-Belt to a kind of internal exile: no one offered to help him in any way and he was excluded from all community activities. He was denied the cooperation of the community essential to everyday survival. After some time, Sticks-Everything-Under-His-Belt petitioned to return to the good graces of the community. "From now on, I am going to run with the tribe," he said. "Everything the people say, I shall stay right by it."[110] Thus not only the communal hunt but the sanctions to enforce its edicts reaffirmed social solidarity.

Like pedestrian hunters, the equestrian nomads attempted to take advantage of the bison's gregariousness and surround the herd, preventing the herd from scattering and allowing the hunters to kill many animals at one time. The hunters surrounded the herd on horseback, waiting for the signal of the marshals. On cue, the hunters attacked. According to Tabeau, "As soon as the scent comes to them, the herd take to flight, and, seeing themselves surrounded, do no more than turn and get in one another's way." The hunters kept the confused herd encircled, singling out young cows to kill. (See Figure 3.1.) Before the late 1860s, when repeating, breech-loading rifles arrived in the plains, the hunters disdained the use of firearms; muzzle-loaders were too unwieldy to reload during the chase. Rather, the hunters rode alongside the cows and fired arrows into the animals' flanks. With a bow and arrows, an average mounted hunter could kill as many as two or three bison in one run; communal hunts generated two or three hundred bison carcasses in one day.[111] During the next few days, the camp was given over to preserving the meat. In 1806, Alexander Henry the Younger described a Cheyenne camp following a communal hunt: "The space between each Tent was filled up and occupied by stages or Grilles for drying meat, and were all covered with Buffalo Flesh, those people having killed upwards of Two hundred of those animals only Two days ago."[112] The hunting of bison and the curing of meat during the summer thus demanded the labors of the entire community.

---

[110] Llewellyn and Hoebel, *The Cheyenne Way*, 124–127; Hoebel, *The Cheyennes*, 58–59.

[111] Tabeau, *Narrative of Loisel's Expedition*, 198. Pierre-Jean De Smet described a Flathead communal hunt in 1840; four hundred hunters killed over five hundred bison in three hours. See De Smet, *Life, Letters, and Travels of Father Pierre-Jean De Smet, S.J., 1801–1873* (New York: Harper, 1905), vol. 1, 231–232.

[112] Barry M. Gough, ed., *The Journal of Alexander Henry the Younger, 1799–1814, Volume I: Red River and the Journey to the Missouri* (Toronto: The Champlain Society, 1988), 263.

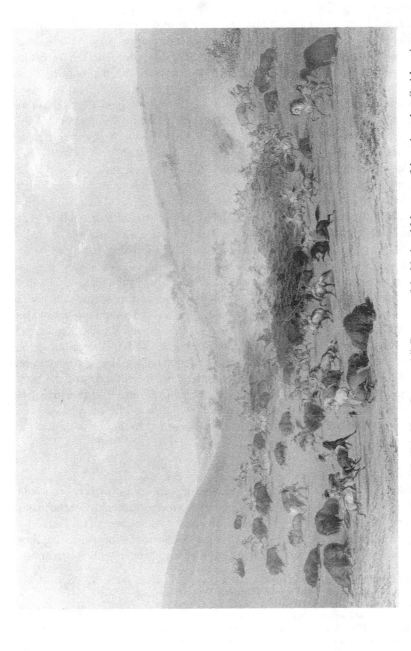

Figure 3.1. George Catlin, "Buffalo Hunt Surround." Courtesy of the National Museum of American Art, Smithsonian Institution.

Social custom enjoined hunters to share the meat they had acquired, thus ensuring that the families of aged, injured, or dead hunters could secure game. The English fur trader David Thompson wrote of the nomadic Indians of the northern plains: "Especially in provision is great attention [paid] to those that are unfortunate in the chace."[113] Every hunter's arrows were marked so that he could identify his kills, but if an arrow had broken off or fallen out, the dead bison became the property of the first person to lay claim to it. Often, according to the American explorers Meriwether Lewis and William Clark, hunters secured only a portion of the game they had killed. When Clark joined with the Sioux for a communal bison hunt in 1804, he returned to his exploring party with the meat of only five of the ten bison he had felled. Because Clark had hunted with firearms, the Indians found no identifying arrows and seized the explorer's other kills.[114] If there were many people to feed, a hunter might be left with only the bison's hide.[115] The hunter thus shared the meat that he had procured but retained the bison's skin, the part of the animal with the highest trade value.[116] This loophole in the nomads' social contract contributed to the explosion of the robe trade with Euroamericans in the mid-nineteenth century.

The summer hunts epitomized the nomads' communal economy. By pooling their resources they stood a better chance of surviving in the plains. Laws that prohibited hunting alone during the bison's summer rutting season established the primacy of community over individual rights. The summer hunts also demonstrated the precariousness of the nomads' singular dependence on the bison. Divided into bands during the lean winter and spring months, the nomads often endured famine. When they congregated together in the summer, they affirmed their social solidarity by squandering the resources of the large summer herds. The inherent fragility of the nomadic societies threatened to undermine the sustainability of equestrian bison hunting. The nomadic societies could endure only if they reconciled their social orders to the constraints of the grasslands.

Zebulon Pike, Fanny Kelly, and other nineteenth-century Euroamericans would have found it hard to imagine that the equestrian nomadic societies of the plains had originated as recently as the eighteenth century in response to the introduction of the horse, the fur trade, and epidemic disease from Europe, or that they continued to change as they adapted to the plains environment. By 1800, the

---

[113] *David Thompson's Narrative of His Explorations in Western America, 1784–1812.* Publications of the Champlain Society XII (Toronto: Champlain Society, 1916), 355.
[114] Meriwether Lewis and William Clark, *The History of the Lewis and Clark Expedition*, vol. 1, ed. Elliott Coues (New York: Harper, 1893), 209–210.
[115] Fraser, *The Bear Who Stole the Chinook*, 13–14; Hoebel, *Law-Ways of the Comanche*, 119–120.
[116] See Stephen Aron, *How the West Was Lost: The Transformation of Kentucky from Daniel Boone to Henry Clay* (Baltimore: Johns Hopkins University Press, 1996).

nomadic societies bore little resemblance to their pre-Columbian precursors. The interaction of indigenous and European ecology, economy, and culture had transformed them. The process of interaction and improvisation continued throughout the nineteenth century. Like the plains themselves – which ten thousand years before the aegis of the nomads had been a humid forest populated by giant herbivores – the nomadic societies were in constant flux.

Given the ecological problems of the late twentieth century – resource exhaustion, pollution, overpopulation – the temptation to romanticize hunter-gatherers such as the equestrian plains nomads is nearly overwhelming. Indeed, in 1968, the economic anthropologist Marshall Sahlins called hunting and gathering communities the "original affluent societies." Hunter-gatherers, he argued, enjoyed not only reliable sources of food obtained at a minimum of effort but also considerable leisure time. His polemical attack on the assumption that hunter-gatherers lived a meager existence on the edge of starvation was a needed corrective to the prevailing notion that agriculture and sedentism were necessarily more enlightened resource strategies than hunting and gathering.[117] His generalizations are accurate for societies that relied primarily on gathering, but he minimized the inherent precariousness of societies that relied primarily on mammal hunting for their subsistence.

Perhaps, had Euroamericans not overrun the American West after the mid-nineteenth century, the western plains nomads might have consciously sought to construct a resource strategy to sustain their nomadic experiment. This conceit ignores, of course, the fact that had Europeans not come to North America, neither would have the horses and the epidemics that drove Indians into the western plains. In the final analysis, this version of the concept of sustainability presumes timelessness; it posits the ability of human societies to arrest economic, cultural, and environmental change. Sustainability is not a chimera, but neither is a sustainable resource strategy an unchanging formula. Rather, it must continually adjust to social and ecological change.

The plains nomadic societies and the western plains environment were in flux from the mid-eighteenth century until the collapse of the bison population in the 1880s. The direction of change in the eighteenth- and nineteenth-century plains, however, was decidedly not toward sustainability. There is much to admire in the nomads' cooperative economy and communal ethos, but to idealize the nomadic societies ignores the historical process – the interaction of ecology, economy, and culture – that produced them. Equestrian bison hunting was not only hastily conceived but short-lived; the nomads' dominance of the plains lasted only about a century and a half. Their resource strategy was thus not a tested, enduring system but rather an innovation, a response to the difficulties of subsistence in the western plains just as equestrian nomadism itself was a

[117] Marshall Sahlins, *Stone Age Economics* (Chicago: Aldine-Atherton, 1972), 1–39.

response to the European ecological and economic invasion. The nomads' social organization and resource strategy were not static but continued to evolve in the nineteenth century as commerce with Euroamericans overswept the plains. The nineteenth-century nomadic societies were precariously suspended between social solidarity and segmentation, centripetal and centrifugal forces, sustainable and unsustainable exploitation of the bison.

Irreconcilable contradictions characterized the nineteenth-century nomadic societies. Created, in part, by trade, the nomads disdained the accumulation of individual wealth. Dependent on horses to pursue the bison, they found that the possession of horses threatened their communalism. Dependent on the bison for their sustenance, the nomads sometimes violated their own injunctions against the waste of this resource in the interests of mobility and community solidarity. These ongoing tensions were not resolved until Euroamericans brought trade in bison robes to the plains. When the robe trade tipped the balance in the nomadic societies toward commerce and individual aggrandizement, their communalism proved to be fleeting. With the onset of the robe trade, the plains nomads, like the Paleoindians who had helped to destroy the large herbivores of the Pleistocene epoch, turned to the destruction of the bison.

4

The Ascendancy of the Market

In the middle decades of the nineteenth century, the nomadic societies of the western plains encountered a new wave of Euroamerican ecological and economic expansion. The eighteenth-century invasion had levered the mounted bison hunters to dominance in the western plains; the renewed incursion of the nineteenth century devastated both the nomads and the bison. In part, the social and environmental catastrophe of the mid-nineteenth century resulted from the scale of the invasion. The bison robe trade of the American Fur Company far exceeded the commerce in beaver pelts of the eighteenth-century *voyageurs*. The smallpox that ravaged the inhabitants of the western plains between 1837 and 1840 was more virulent than the epidemic of 1780 to 1782. Yet the extensive economic and environmental changes in the western plains in the mid-nineteenth century were not simply the product of exogenous forces, however powerful. Social changes that had attended the nomads' transition to mounted bison hunting in the eighteenth century contributed to their receptivity to trade in the mid-nineteenth century and therefore to the depletion of the bison and the spread of disease.

Steamboats began to ascend the Missouri River to tap the labor and resources of the western plains in the early 1820s. In 1832, an American Fur Company steamboat reached the mouth of the Yellowstone River in the northern plains.[1] The steam technology that made possible the ascent of the Missouri by large riverboats was not environmentally benign. Consumption of firewood by steamboats was probably the primary cause of riparian deforestation in the United States in the first half of the nineteenth century.[2] The destruction of forests along the Missouri degraded the bison's winter habitat, contributing to the absence of bison from the Missouri by mid-century. More important, by the 1840s, the western plains nomads were annually bringing to the steamboats over

---

[1] Louis Hunter, *Steamboats on the Western Rivers: An Economic and Technological History* (Cambridge: Harvard University Press, 1949), 47–49.

[2] Michael Williams, *Americans and Their Forests: An Historical Geography* (New York: Cambridge University Press, 1989), 149–157; F. Terry Norris, "Where Did the Villages Go? Steamboats, Deforestation, and Archaeological Loss in the Mississippi Valley," in Andrew Hurley, ed., *Common Fields: An Environmental History of St. Louis* (St. Louis: Missouri Historical Society Press, 1997), 78–81; Ari Kelman, "A River and Its City" (Ph.D. dissertation, Brown University, 1998).

100,000 bison robes. This commercial production was in addition to their annual harvest of roughly half a million bison for subsistence and intertribal trade – an amount that the bison population could withstand only in the absence of drought or other environmental castastrophes. Therefore, even a small increase in hunting pressure would have depleted the bison population – and the impact of Indian commercial hunters on the bison was not light. An annual trade of 100,000 robes raised the nomads' yearly harvest of the bison by no less than 20 percent.

The robe trade was both a continuation and a departure from the nomads' eighteenth- and early nineteenth-century economic practices. It continued and indeed heightened their economic specialization as hunting societies. However, although the nomads had engaged in trade in bison products with Missouri River villagers since the eighteenth century, their energetic exploitation of their primary resource for commerce with Euroamericans was a startling transformation of their use of the resource that sustained their very existence. Eighteenth-century exchanges in beaver pelts and horses certainly anticipated the nomads' eventual integration into the robe trade. Measured by the beaver population's decline, the beaver trade produced significant change in the northern plains. Yet the beaver was not important to the nomads' subsistence, and the commerce in beaver pelts remained peripheral to the nomads' central economic activities of hunting and processing bison. Eighteenth-century exchanges alone do not explain the transformation of Euroamerican commerce from a marginal to a central economic activity within the nomadic societies.[3]

Environmental historians studying regions other than the Great Plains have explained the participation of Indians in the fur trade in ways that provide sophisticated clues to the nomads' adaptation to the commerce in bison robes. William Cronon has argued that in seventeenth-century New England, Indians adopted new economic behaviors in the aftermath of epidemics and resultant demographic collapse. The Indians' participation in the fur trade, he contended, was an improvisation in a period of crisis.[4] Yet, unlike the Indians of New England, the western plains nomads had largely avoided the impact of disease in the eighteenth century. The cultural dislocation caused by the smallpox epidemic of the late 1830s probably enhanced the nomads' participation in the robe trade, but they were fully integrated into it before that outbreak. Their initial participation in the trade demands another explanation.

---

[3] For beaver and bison exchanges in the plains, see Joseph Jablow, *The Cheyenne in Plains Indian Trade Relations, 1795–1840* (Lincoln: University of Nebraska Press, 1994); John Ewers, "The Influence of the Fur Trade upon the Indians of the Northern Plains," in Malvina Bolus, ed., *People and Pelts: Selected Papers of the Second North American Fur Trade Conference* (Winnipeg: Peguis, 1972), 1–26; David J. Wishart, *The Fur Trade of the American West, 1807–1840* (Lincoln: University of Nebraska Press, 1979).

[4] William Cronon, *Changes in the Land: Indians, Colonists, and the Ecology of New England* (New York: Hill and Wang, 1983), 82–92.

Richard White has explained the Choctaws' integration into a trade in deer-skins in the eighteenth century as the result of a combination of environmental and economic factors. Exotic diseases in the lower Mississippi valley forced the Choctaws to abandon their lowland villages in favor of upland forests rich in deer. The Choctaws' concentration on deer hunting paralleled the shift of the plains nomads from reliance on a diversity of resources to mounted bison hunting. Eco-social changes in the lower Mississippi valley were, however, less extensive than those in the plains. Unlike the nomads, the Choctaws remained in the same region; they continued to combine hunting and planting and, when Euroamerican traders arrived, they maintained their economic tradition of enveloping trade in rituals of gift-giving and alliance.[5]

Although the participation of the plains nomads in the robe trade was a direct consequence of neither disease nor migration, it did result from similar eco-social discontinuities and dislocations, particularly their transition to mounted bison hunting in the eighteenth century. The nomads' commerce in horses and beaver pelts, the rising importance of bison hunting, and the division of ethnic groups into largely autonomous bands were all necessary antecedents of the rise of trade. Above all, however, was the emergence, in the eighteenth century, of a gendered division of labor in the nomadic societies. As pedestrian bison hunters, men, women, and children had participated in the surround of the herd or the drive to the pound or the jump. After the advent of the horse, however, hunting became the domain of men and older boys. Women and girls were relegated to the dress-ing of meat and hides, the management of the camp, and the gathering of wild roots and berries. Among the groups that had once raised crops – the Crows, Cheyennes, Sioux, Arapahos, and perhaps the Atsinas and Assiniboines – women had been largely responsible for agriculture. The shift to mounted, nomadic hunting eliminated women's significant contributions to subsistence and their control over their own labor in the garden plots. Women in plains nomadic societies were by no means slaves of their husbands and fathers. The fur trader Pierre-Antoine Larocque noted in the early nineteenth century that these women were well treated by their husbands and fathers and, relative to the Indians of other regions, not overworked.[6] Yet the transition to equestrian bison hunting in the eighteenth century radically reduced the importance of women's separate sphere of production, preparing the way for both the decline of women's status and the ascendancy of the bison robe trade.

Twenty years ago, many anthropologists studying women in past cultures argued that women inherently occupied positions of social inferiority. They

[5] Richard White, *The Roots of Dependency: Subsistence, Environment, and Social Change among the Choctaws, Pawnees, and Navajos* (Lincoln: University of Nebraska Press, 1983), 1–36.
[6] "François-Antoine Larocque's 'Yellowstone Journal,'" in W. Raymond Wood and Thomas D. Thiessen, eds., *Early Fur Trade on the Northern Plains: Canadian Traders Among the Mandan and Hidatsa Indians, 1738–1818* (Norman: University of Oklahoma Press, 1985), 208.

disagreed about the reasons for inferiority; the responsibilities of rearing children and, for Marxist theorists, the socially corrosive effects of capitalism were the two most prominent explanations. Recently, however, anthropologists have looked to the spiritual and social roles of women to challenge the very idea that women have occupied an inferior social position. This school of interpretation has achieved the greatest sway over anthropologists' and historians' understanding of American Indian women. The anthropologist Raymond J. DeMallie, for instance, has argued that women in Sioux society, although limited by cultural notions of appropriate gender roles, nonetheless exerted profound cultural authority as healers, visionaries, and through female sodalities. Women in the nomadic societies certainly exercised significant cultural and moral authority. As the experience of mid-nineteenth-century Euroamerican women demonstrates, however, reverence for the cultural authority of "women's sphere" and the narrowing of women's economic autonomy can occur simultaneously.[7]

The status of women in the nomadic societies was inextricably tied to the environmental and social transformations that had occurred since the mid-eighteenth century. Women's cultural authority notwithstanding, the combined effects of nomadism and trade had left the economic status of women in the nomadic societies markedly unequal to that of men decades before the advent of the robe trade. Inequitable gender relations eventually tipped the tenuous balance – between individual and community, private accumulation and public charity, waste and economy of resources – toward social segmentation and the unsustainable exploitation of the bison. Since the eighteenth century, the ethic of social and economic solidarity had kept the inherent centrifugal forces on the nomadic societies in check. The injunction to share the products of bison hunting had once united nomadic groups, mitigated differences in status, and discouraged, however imperfectly, the over-exploitation of the herds. The weak link in this system was the unequal status of women within the nomadic societies. The arrival of the steamboats and the Euroamerican commerce in bison robes struck at this weakness. Expansion of the trade in bison robes furthered the unequal status of women and magnified economic competition in the nomadic

---

[7] For "women's sphere," see Barbara Welter, "The Cult of True Womanhood: 1820–1860," *American Quarterly*, 18 (Summer 1966), 151–174; Nancy F. Cott, *The Bonds of Womanhood: 'Woman's Sphere' in New England, 1780–1835* (New Haven: Yale University Press, 1977). For the precapitalist inequality interpretation, see Michelle Zimbalist Rosaldo and Louise Lamphere, eds., *Women, Culture, and Society* (Stanford, Ca.: Stanford University Press, 1974). For the capitalist inequality interpretation, see Eleanor Burke Leacock, *Myths of Male Dominance: Collected Articles on Women Cross-Culturally* (New York: Monthly Review Press, 1981). For arguments in favor of cultural equality, see Patricia Albers and Beatrice Medicine, eds., *The Hidden Half: Studies of Plains Indian Women* (New York: University Press of America, 1983), particularly Raymond J. DeMallie's essay, "Male and Female in Traditional Lakota Culture," 237–266; see also Daniel Maltz and JoAllyn Archambault, "Gender and Power in Native North America," in Laura F. Klein and Lillian Ackerman, eds., *Women and Power in Native North America* (Norman: University of Oklahoma Press, 1995), 230–249.

societies, as men sought to advance their own status by relying on the labor of socially subordinate women who dressed robes for trade. Social inequality and competition for status lifted the restraints on resource exploitation, eventually devastating not only the bison but the nomads themselves.

I

At the beginning of the nineteenth century, the nomads' consumption of Euroamerican trade goods was minimal. At that time, according to the fur trader Edwin Denig, the Assiniboines "were the poorest of all Indians, and used knives made of the hump rib of a Buffalo, hatchets of flint stone, cooking utensils of clay or skin, awls and other tools made of bone, and arrow points or spear heads of stone." According to the French fur trader Pierre-Antoine Tabeau, the Teton Sioux in the first years of the nineteenth century had "not yet used intoxicating liquors enough so that they have a passion for them." The fur trader Charles Larpenteur testified that the Crows did not trade for alcohol in the early nineteenth century, and Catlin wrote that as late as the 1830s the Blackfeet "stubbornly resisted the Traders in their country, who have been gradually forming an acquaintance with them, and endeavoring to establish a permanent and profitable system of trade." Until the second third of the nineteenth century, the nomads relegated commerce with Euroamericans to the margins of their economies.[8]

Between the late 1810s and the early 1830s, following the coming of the steamboat to the upper Missouri River, the pressure of the market revolution, and the revocation of federal laws that had strictly limited the operations of fur traders in the trans-Mississippi West, traders poured into the northern plains to induce the nomads to begin hunting bison for commerce. According to the winter count of Lone Dog, a Yancton Sioux, Euroamerican traders established their first posts in Sioux territory in the late 1810s. George Catlin predicted in 1832 that the Blackfeet's resistance to trade would not last long. "Trinkets and whiskey . . . will soon spread their charms amongst these, as it has amongst other tribes." By 1855, Denig testified to the extent of consumerism among the northern plains nomads. He wrote that "the Blackfeet and Crow nations perceive at once the convenience and utility of European articles, especially portions of clothing,

---

[8] Denig, *Five Indian Tribes of the Upper Missouri: Sioux, Arikaras, Assiniboines, Crees, Crows*, ed. John C. Ewers (Norman: University of Oklahoma Press, 1961), 69; Pierre-Antoine Tabeau, *Narrative of Loisel's Expedition to the Upper Missouri*, ed. Annie Heloise Abel (Norman: University of Oklahoma Press, 1939), 171; Charles Larpenteur, *Forty Years a Fur Trader on the Upper Missouri, 1833–1872*, vol. 1 (Chicago: Lakeside, 1933), 45; George Catlin, *North American Indians: Being Letters and Notes on Their Manners, Customs, and Conditions, Written During Eight Years' Travel Amongst the Wildest Tribes of Indians in North America, 1832–1839*, vol. 1 (Philadelphia: Leary, Stuart, 1913), 59.

horse gear, and other things. They readily throw aside the cord and use a bridle for a horse's mouth, [and] will pay well for a saddle. They pride themselves on the cut of their coat." Even the Assiniboines, whom Denig had once described as backcountry rustics, began to trade bison robes for manufactured goods. "What was once filthy skin clothing has given way before good and handsome apparel of American manufacture," Denig wrote. An entry in a Sioux winter count reflects the rise of consumerism: Lone Dog's calendar marks the winter of 1853–54 by the first appearance of Spanish blankets as an article of trade. As traders invaded the northern plains, the nomads' consumption of Euroamerican goods increased exponentially. Consumerism moved from the margins toward the center of the nomadic societies.[9]

The rise of consumption, however, was not the cause of the robe trade but a symptom of it. The trade's origin was in the Indians' transition to nomadism in the eighteenth century. The nomads acutely felt the consequences of that transition in their gender relations and division of labor. The adoption of the horse had obviated both pedestrian bison hunting and, among many of the nomadic groups that had migrated to the western plains from the woodlands to the east, farming. Women's participation in these two subsistence activities had been crucial. Pedestrian bison hunting had required the labor of both men and women. Women's planting and foraging had contributed not only to group subsistence but to their status and autonomy. The rise of mounted bison hunting transformed labor and gender roles, however. The nomads, especially in the northern plains, relied on raiding rather than breeding to replenish their horse herds. Therefore, horse stealing, an exclusively male activity, became centrally important to the nomadic economy. The increased reliance on mounted bison hunting, another exclusively male activity, furthered the differences between the economic importance of male and female labor. Men, in short, became "procurers" of the vital resources of horses and bison, while women, who dressed hides and managed pack horses, became "processors" of those resources.

Significantly, a transformation of notions of property ownership attended changes in labor roles. Whereas the meat and hides produced in the collective pedestrian hunt had been communal property, mid-nineteenth-century commercial hunters owned the game they killed. In processing robes for trade women acquired neither a share in the robe's ownership nor in the goods that it purchased. Hunters were still obliged to share their meat with the poor. The Sioux custom of "tail-tying," for instance, by which a person staked a claim to meat by knotting the tail of a slain bison, insured that no one went hungry. Yet, by the mid-nineteenth century, tail-tying carried a stigma of shiftlessness and

[9] Garrick Mallery, "Picture-Writing of the American Indians," *Tenth Annual Report of the Bureau of American Ethnology* (Washington, D.C.: Government Printing Office, 1889), 277–278, 283; Catlin, *North American Indians*, vol. 1, 59; Denig, *Five Indian Tribes*, 88–95.

dependency. The hunter, in any case, maintained ownership of the tongue and the hide, the parts of the bison with the highest trade values.[10]

The significance of the changes in the gender division of labor and individual property rights among the nomads emerges starkly in comparison with the village-dwelling Pawnees. The Pawnees encountered many of the same forces as the nomads: the arrival of the horse, the devastation of smallpox, and the lure of Euroamerican commerce. The Pawnees, however, elected to remain in their villages and rely on a combination of planting and regular excursions to the high plains to hunt bison. Neither the labor of male hunters nor individual property rights in the products of the hunt overran communal control of the economy. Pawnee leaders continued to oversee the redistribution of the products of the hunt and the cornfields. Most important, the Pawnees resisted the invitation to participate in the robe trade.[11] The Pawnees' ability to resist Euroamerican traders demonstrates that the exogenous pressure of the market was a necessary but not the only factor in the rise of commerce. Trade also depended on the willingness of the Indians. The nomads – decentralized bands of specialized hunters – proved to be far more receptive to trade than the village-dwelling Pawnees.

Patrilocal, largely autonomous bands of nomadic bison hunters were the basic work units of the commercial robe trade. Husbands and fathers in such bands relied on their wives and daughters to dress robes for trade. Rituals surrounding marriage therefore became inextricably bound to the market in bison robes. Since at least the eighteenth century, the ritual exchange of goods accompanied a woman's marriage or separation from her husband; a man might marry only if he paid a token bride price to the parents of his intended. With the acceleration of the trade in bison robes in the middle of the nineteenth century, however, and with the importance of women's labor in the preparation of robes for trade, such exchanges increasingly assumed a new economic significance. Particularly among the Sioux and Cheyenne, as the robe trade assumed a dominant position in the nomads' economy, the exchange of gifts accompanying marriage compensated a father for the loss of his daughter's labor value.[12]

Hunters often needed the labor of more than one woman to dress bison robes for trade with Euroamericans. In the 1830s and early 1840s, there were still enough bison to make commercial hunting relatively facile. The bottleneck in

[10] Alan Klein, "The Political-Economy of Gender: A 19th-Century Plains Indian Case Study," in Albers and Medicine, eds., Hidden Half, 143–173; Klein, "The Plains Truth: The Impact of Colonialism on Indian Women," Dialectical Anthropology, 7 (1983), 299–313; Klein, "The Political Economy of the Buffalo Hide Trade: Race and Class on the Plains," in John Moore, ed., The Political Economy of North American Indians (Norman: University of Oklahoma Press, 1993).

[11] White, Roots of Dependency, 178–191.

[12] See John H. Moore, "Cheyenne Political History, 1820–1894," Ethnohistory, 21 (Fall 1974), 334, 340, for a similar argument. Moore contended that the Cheyennes shifted from matrilocal, matrilineal clans to male-dominated warrior societies in response to the threat of war both with other groups and with Euroamericans.

the production of robes occurred in the preparation of the skins. Dressing a robe was a labor-intensive process that required staking it to the ground for a few days to allow it to dry while rubbing it with the brains of a bison or wapiti to keep it pliant, scraping the fleshy side to soften it, and smoking it in a small lodge for a few days to make it resistant to water.[13] A greater number of laborers in a household increased the efficiency of the process. One woman could prepare ten robes for the market in a year's time, but, according to a Blackfoot hunter, his eight wives could prepare 150 robes each winter.[14] When the number of female laborers proved to be insufficient, the nomads resorted to raiding. The Comanches had trafficked in slaves since the early eighteenth century, but by the 1830s and 1840s slave-catching had become a major economic activity. The Comanches frequently raided south into Chihuahua, Durango, and Coahuila to procure female laborers, as well as horses and mules. The traveler Thomas Farnham described the Comanches in 1839 as "exceedingly fond of stealing the objects of their enemies' affection. Female children are sought with the greatest avidity, and adopted or married."[15] When the Comanches captured the Texas settlers Sarah Ann Horn and Rachel Plummer in 1834 and 1836, the women reported that their captors primarily set them to work dressing bison robes. Plummer's Comanche master, in fact, established a monthly quota. After 1830, the Blackfeet no longer sold or traded their women captives, but kept them to process robes.[16]

To supplement the labor of women captives, Indian men sought multiple wives. Polygyny increased markedly among the nomadic societies in the midnineteenth century. A fur trader who visited the Blackfeet in 1787 observed that no man had more than three or four wives. By 1810, another fur trader reported that some men had six or seven wives. Hunters also pressed women into marriage at ever-younger ages. In 1787, Blackfoot women usually married between the ages of sixteen and eighteen. By 1885, when the trade in bison robes had run its course, a missionary among the Blackfeet reported that the age of first marriage had fallen to twelve. In the late 1850s, some Crow girls married when they were between ten and thirteen years old.[17]

Significantly, polygyny was confined to some of the wealthiest and most prestigious men. In 1833, Prince Maximilian of Wied-Neuwied, a German aristocrat

[13] Catlin, *North American Indians*, vol. 1, 52.

[14] Oscar Lewis, *The Effects of White Contact on Blackfoot Culture with Special Reference to the Role of the Fur Trade*. Monographs of the American Ethnological Society, vol. 6 (New York: Augustin, 1942), 39, 50.

[15] Thomas Farnham, *Travels in the Great Western Prairies* (London: Bentley, 1843), in Reuben Gold Thwaites, ed. *Early Western Travels 1748-1846* (Cleveland: Clark, 1904), vol. 28, 151.

[16] "A Narrative of the Capture and Subsequent Sufferings of Mrs. Rachel Plummer, Written by Herself," in *Held Captive by Indians: Selected Narratives, 1642-1836*, ed. Richard VanDerBeets (Knoxville: University of Tennessee Press, 1973), 340; Sarah Ann Horn, *A Narrative of the Captivity of Mrs. Horn* (St. Louis: Kremle, 1839), in *Comanche Bondage: Beale's Settlement and Sarah Ann Horn's Narrative*, ed. Carl C. Rister (Glendale: Clark, 1955), 156; Lewis, *Blackfoot Culture*, 50.

[17] Denig, *Five Indian Tribes*, 153; Lewis, *Blackfoot Culture*, 38-40, 50.

traveling in the plains, wrote that the wealthiest hunters had eight or nine wives. Catlin wrote that chiefs, doctors, and notable hunters or warriors commonly had six or eight wives. Denig observed of the Crows in 1856, "About one-half the nation have a plurality of wives."[18] Eleven of the twenty-two most prestigious Kiowa men in 1870 had more than one wife. These men not only flouted their wealth by maintaining a large household, but their many wives increased their riches and prestige by generating greater numbers of robes for the market.[19] Multiple wives were, in essence, an investment that only successful commercial hunters could afford. Among the Sioux, the majority of marriages by purchase – as opposed to elopement or other arrangement – were second or third marriages in polygynous unions.[20] The concentration of many wives in the lodges of a few hunters was an engrossment of women's wealth-producing labor by a minority of hunters.

Polygyny itself was older than the trade in bison robes. In 1786, Domingo Cabello, the governor of Texas, wrote that Comanche men married "as many women as they are able to maintain." Larocque observed in the early nineteenth century that many Crow men had more than one wife. Numerous wives, like a large herd of horses, signified a man's wealth and prestige without imperiling the mobility of the community. Moreover, polygyny could function as a kind of social safety net. A man might take as a second or third wife a recent widow or a young woman whose father was deceased or disabled. For hunters whose many wives helped produce wealth through trade, the enduring social ethic of generosity enjoined them to provide for less fortunate families. The expansion of polygyny in the mid-nineteenth century, however, was at its root not in the interests of charity but of private accumulation. "Amongst those tribes who trade with the Fur Companies," wrote Catlin, "the women are kept for the greater part of the year, dressing buffalo robes and other skins for the market; and the brave or chief, who has the greatest number of wives, is considered the most affluent and envied man in the tribe."[21]

The southern plains nomads were on the fringes of the trade in bison robes, but they supplied both horses and captive women to the northern plains commercial hunters. For the southern plains nomads, the accumulation of wealth came in the form of herds of horses. Among the Kiowas, status became closely tied to wealth in the mid-nineteenth century. In particular, a man's upward progress along four social grades was in large part determined by industriousness

---

[18] Catlin, *North American Indians*, vol. 1, 135; Denig, *Five Indian Tribes*, 156.

[19] Bernard Mishkin, *Rank and Warfare Among the Plains Indians* (Lincoln: University of Nebraska Press, 1992), 54–55.

[20] DeMallie, "Male and Female in Traditional Lakota Culture," in Albers and Medicine, eds., *Hidden Half*, 237–266.

[21] Odie B. Faulk, ed., "A Description of the Comanche Indians in 1786 by the Governor of Texas," *West Texas Historical Association Yearbook*, 37 (1961), 178; Catlin, *North American Indians*, vol. 1, 133–134. The anthropologist Oscar Lewis argued that fur trade caused the pursuit of individual wealth to dominate Blackfoot society. See Lewis, *Blackfoot Culture*, 44–46.

in the theft and husbandry of horses. The Kiowas were more successful than the Cheyennes in harnessing the competition over horses and directing it toward participation in relatively stable social institutions. In 1837, in a stunning example of the decline of communal control over economic behavior among the southern plains horse traders, the members of a Cheyenne warrior society beat Gray Thunder, the keeper of a Cheyenne fetish, for his refusal to perform a ritual that would have sanctioned the warriors' planned horse raid. Because the summer horse-trading season was coming to a close, the warriors were unwilling to heed Gray Thunder's call to wait for a more spiritually auspicious moment to perform the ceremony. The warriors embarked on their raid without the blessings of the priest. The rejection of religious form and communal control over warfare became more common among the Cheyennes as the economic motivations for horse stealing rose. Yellow Wolf, one of the most successful Cheyenne war leaders in the mid-nineteenth century, abstained from all ceremonies having to do with war because they encouraged unrewarding wars of revenge rather than the profitable theft of horses.[22]

The trade in bison robes and horses furthered the segmentation of the nomadic societies, as traditional alliances and patterns of authority eroded under the pressures of commerce. In the 1830s, the robe trade divided the Cheyennes, who had been one of the most unified of the nomadic societies in the early nineteenth century. One portion of the Cheyennes migrated south to the Arkansas River valley to trade at Bent's Fort. This faction allied with the Arapahos and engaged the Kiowas and Comanches for control of the commerce in horses from New Mexico. The other faction remained in the northern plains and allied with their former enemies, the Sioux. In succeeding years, this northern alliance fought the Crows for access to the bison herds of the Powder River region. Trade exacerbated the split between the Mountain Crows and the River Crows, as the former sold their robes at the American Fur Company post on the Yellowstone and the latter traded their robes at Fort Laramie on the north branch of the Platte River. Among the Blackfeet and other groups, younger hunters resisted the authority of established leaders as they accumulated individual wealth. Rather than waiting for established leaders to organize large war parties and distribute spoils, younger warriors began to organize their own raids for horses and loot.[23]

In the eighteenth century, the plains nomads had labored to develop and practice a cooperative economy. At the same time, however, the transition to nomadism had privileged the labor of men and eroded women's economic autonomy. In the nineteenth century, the nomads' cooperative spirit ebbed as

---

[22] Mishkin, *Rank and Warfare*, 35–54; Jablow, *Cheyenne in Plains Trade Relations*, 68–69.

[23] Moore, "Cheyenne Political History," 340–341; Donald J. Berthrong, *The Southern Cheyennes* (Norman: University of Oklahoma Press, 1963), 3–99; E. Adamson Hoebel, *The Cheyennes: Indians of the Great Plains*, 2d ed. (New York: Holt, Rinehart & Winston, 1978), 9–10; Denig, *Five Indian Tribes*, 134–135; Frank B. Linderman, *Pretty-shield: Medicine Woman of the Crows* (Lincoln: University of Nebraska Press, 1972), 20–21; Lewis, *Blackfoot Culture*, 52–53.

the robe trade increased in economic importance. Although the accumulation of wealth was at odds with their ethic of solidarity, at the same time it was the predictable result of their adaptation to the horse and the market, and above all, of the rise of gender inequality in the eighteenth century. The nomads' economic behavior in the mid-nineteenth century was embedded in a social context of anomie and inequality that had begun to emerge a century earlier. These social changes – particularly the decline of women's economic autonomy – were the root causes of the nomads' participation in the robe trade.

II

A notorious bison hunt occurred in the early 1830s near Fort Pierre, an American Fur Company trading post at the juncture of the Bad and Missouri rivers. According to the accounts of two Euroamericans, several hundred Sioux hunters slaughtered roughly fifteen hundred bison in one day, cut only the tongues from the animals, and traded them at the fort. However, neither of the two Euroamericans who wrote of the incident, Edwin Thompson Denig and George Catlin, witnessed it, and their accounts are different. Denig, a trader, whose description of the Indians of the northern plains is sober and generally reliable, heard the story from Fort Pierre traders after coming to the post in 1833. He did not write of it, however, until he recorded his memoirs in the early 1850s. According to Denig, the hunt occurred in 1830 on the east side of the Missouri, across from the fort. The hunters, Yanctonnai Sioux, killed fifteen hundred bison – a figure determined by the post trader who collected the tongues the Yanctonnais brought back to Fort Pierre.[24] Unlike Denig's matter-of-fact recital of the story, Catlin's account is disapproving. Like Denig, he learned the story from Fort Pierre traders. In many details, his account is similar to Denig's: the hunt occurred directly across from the post, producing fourteen hundred tongues for trade. According to Catlin, however, the slaughter occurred not in 1830 but only a few days before his arrival at Fort Pierre in May, 1832. Were this true, he might have noticed fourteen hundred fresh bison carcasses across the river from the fort, but he failed to mention it. Aside from disagreeing with Denig on the date of the slaughter, Catlin (or his source) provides (or invents) a lurid denouement: the Sioux hunters traded the tongues for "but a few gallons of whiskey, which was soon demolished, indulging them in a little, and harmless, carouse."[25]

Perhaps Catlin injected into the story this moral disapproval of the commerce in alcohol to accentuate the wastefulness of the Indian hunters. Yet, although Catlin mentioned alcohol and Denig did not, it would have been remarkable if alcohol had not been part of the transaction. By the 1830s, alcohol was a dominant

[24] Denig, *Five Indian Tribes*, 30.
[25] Catlin, *North American Indians*, vol. 1, 289.

commodity in the robe trade. Unlike the more mundane items of the trade, such as metal goods, firearms, ammunition, and woven cloth, whose weight and bulk impeded the hunters' mobility, alcohol, once consumed, did not burden the nomads. Moreover, whereas the nomads needed only so many knives or rifles, their demand for alcohol knew no limit. Watered down, a gallon of alcohol sold for sixteen dollars, or five prime bison robes. Catlin, a newcomer to the western plains in 1832, could still be shocked by the exchange of bison tongues and robes for whiskey. Denig, a seasoned trader and no teetotaler himself, may have been inured to the ubiquitous presence of alcohol in the trade in bison products by the time he wrote his memoirs.[26]

Both the naive Catlin and the hard-boiled Denig, however, were astounded by the scale of the Indians' slaughter at Fort Pierre. Catlin wrote that between five hundred and six hundred Sioux hunters participated in the hunt. A force of that size certainly could have killed between fourteen and fifteen hundred bison in an afternoon. Large numbers of Sioux camped at Fort Pierre from time to time, particularly in the late spring when they came to the post to trade the bison robes they had processed during the preceding winter. The pertinent question is not whether the Sioux could have killed so many bison at once but why they might have done it. If this hunt occurred as the Yanctonnais congregated at Fort Pierre from their separate winter camps, they may have purchased the alcohol for a celebration of solidarity that typically wasted large numbers of bison. According to eighteenth- and early nineteenth-century Euroamericans, communal bison hunts commonly produced between two hundred and three hundred carcasses in a day, but the incentives of trade may have spurred the hunters to greater destruction. The incident – whatever the scale of the slaughter – exemplified the new commercial motivations for the destruction of the bison by the western plains nomads in the middle third of the nineteenth century.

As the plains nomads accumulated robes for commerce with Euroamericans, they steadily increased their harvest of the bison. This depletion of the herds was not unique. By the mid-nineteenth century, the fur trade in eastern North America, the Rocky Mountains, and the Pacific Northwest had nearly extermi-nated many species of fur-bearing game. As Denig wrote, "The tendency of every fur trade is towards extinction of the game and diminishing the value of the country for hunting."[27] For the nomads, this environmental change had sig-nificant social consequences. As the bison herds diminished, the nomads increasingly wrestled over access to remaining hunting territories. Those groups that were unable to prevail sank into poverty.

The commercial harvest of the bison rose sharply in the first third of the nineteenth century. In the eighteenth and early nineteenth centuries, the Plains

---

[26] For alcohol in the North American fur trade, see White, *Roots of Dependency*, 69–96.
[27] Denig, *Five Indian Tribes*, 123.

Indians – villagers and nomads alike – traded only a few thousand bison robes a year to Euroamericans. In the winter of 1800–01, the British fur trader Alexander Henry sent only 31 bison robes to Montreal. Over the next seven years, he sent nearly 4,000 beaver pelts but only 150 bison robes. In 1805, the Northwest Company, based in Montreal, received from all its posts only 1,135 bison robes. In 1812, the American Fur Company purchased 12,000 bison robes from the plains nomads. Yet between 1825 and 1830, fur trading outfits shipped over 785,000 robes through New Orleans, an average of over 130,000 a year. In 1825 alone, traders shipped 184,000 robes through New Orleans. In 1831, an Indian agent, John Dougherty, reported to Lewis Cass, the Secretary of War, that the fur trade "is certainly more profitable now, than at any former period."[28]

The American Fur Company, which dominated the trade in the western plains, determined to control the marketing of bison robes in the East and to avoid the problems that had plagued the beaver pelt market. In the early 1830s, the market in beaver pelts had collapsed as competing fur companies flooded the market with pelts. Dealers in pelts bought up supplies when prices were low and held them until the market rebounded. In order to avoid glutting the emerging market in bison robes, Ramsay Crooks, the American Fur Company agent in New York, resolved to fix a low price for robes. "A higher price might be obtained," he wrote, "but we deem it prudent to make the rate moderate and divide them among so many hands as will create a competition and restrain them from putting too high a value on the article, thereby insuring the consumption of the whole collection annually, and having the market clear for the succeeding crop."[29] Thus, the American Fur Company's profits depended less on the price of the robes than on the volume shipped east. The American Fur Company was able to sell the robes at a moderate price and still reap a profit because the herds were immense and the costs of procuring the robes were low. This marketing strategy, however, meant heavy pressure on the herds.

The bison had always been an integral part of the fur trade as a source of food for Indian and Euroamerican trappers and traders. Beginning in the 1830s, however, and continuing until the 1870s, the bison's skin became the most marketable natural resource in the plains. George Catlin wrote in the 1830s that "the fur trade of these great western realms ... is now limited chiefly to the purchase of buffalo robes." From the early 1830s to the late 1840s, the trade in bison robes increased markedly. The Jesuit missionary Pierre-Jean De Smet estimated that

[28] E. Douglas Branch, *The Hunting of the Buffalo* (Lincoln: University of Nebraska Press, 1997), 72–73; Hiram M. Chittenden, *The American Fur Trade of the Far West*, vol. 2 (New York: Harper, 1902), 555; Merrill G. Burlingame, "The Buffalo in Trade and Commerce," *North Dakota Historical Quarterly*, 3 (1929) 260, 264; John Dougherty to Lewis Cass, November 19, 1831. Fur Trade Collection, Missouri Historical Society, St. Louis.

[29] Ramsay Crooks to Pratte, Chouteau, & Co., March 3, 1835. American Fur Company Letterbooks, Letterbook One, 247. See also letter from Crooks to Pratte, Chouteau, & Co., April 17, 1835. American Fur Company Letterbooks, Letterbook One, 323. New York Public Library.

the American Fur Company purchased 45,000 bison robes in 1839. By 1847, however, according to De Smet, the number of robes shipped to St. Louis had risen to 110,000. William S. Hatton, an Indian agent, conducted a thorough survey of the Missouri River trade between St. Louis and the mouth of the Yellowstone in the summer of 1849, and also concluded that the Indians sold 110,000 robes each year to the Euroamericans.[30] In the 1850s, however, the trade declined. In 1853, the Upper Missouri Outfit of the American Fur Company purchased 88,927 bison robes.[31] In 1857, the upper Missouri posts collected only 75,000 robes.[32] In 1859, Pierre Chouteau of the American Fur Company estimated that the firm bought 50,000 robes a year.[33]

Although the nomads knew how to utilize nearly every part of the bison – flesh for food, horns and bones for tools and implements, hoofs for glue, sinew for thread – when they hunted bison for the fur trade they sought only the animal's marketable parts: its skin and, less often, its tongue. In pursuit of robes and tongues, Indian hunters were exceptionally destructive. Josiah Gregg, who traversed the southern plains in the 1830s, wrote in 1845 that if the bison were hunted only for food, "their natural increase would perhaps replenish the loss; yet the continued and wanton slaughter of them by travellers and hunters and the still greater havoc made among them by the Indians, not only for meat, but often for the skins and tongues alone (for which they find a ready market among their traders) are fast reducing their numbers, and must ultimately effect their total annihilation from the continent."[34] Mid-century Indian commercial hunters were so wasteful that packs of wolves frequently followed hunting parties at a respectful distance to feast on the many flayed bison that Indian hunters left in their wake. Catlin estimated that in the 1830s the nomads left enough dead bison on the plains to support 1.5 million wolves. "The white wolves," Catlin wrote, "follow the herds of buffaloes ... from one season to another, glutting themselves on the carcasses of those that fall by the deadly shafts of their enemies."[35] Wolves, wrote Denig, "follow in the wake of the buffalo in bands of several hundreds.... No diminution is apparent in these animals when compared with former years."[36]

---

[30] *Life, Letters, and Travels of Father Pierre-Jean De Smet, S.J., 1801–1873* (New York: Harper, 1905), vol. 1, 179, vol. 2, 635–636; Hatton, *Annual Report of the Office of Indian Affairs*, 31st Cong., 1st Sess., 1849, S. exdoc. 1 (Serial 550), 1074.

[31] Returns of the Upper Missouri Outfit for 1853 (August 14, 1854), Chouteau Collection, Box 47, Missouri Historical Society.

[32] Joel A. Allen, *The American Bisons, Living and Extinct* (Cambridge, Mass.: Harvard University Press, 1876), 188.

[33] Journal of Elias Marsh, M.D., St. Louis to Ft. Benton, May–August, 1859 (May 31, 1859), Journals and Diaries Collection, Missouri Historical Society.

[34] Josiah Gregg, *Commerce of the Prairies* (New York: Langley, 1845) in *Early Western Travels*, vol. 20, 264–265.

[35] Catlin, *North American Indians*, vol. 1, 289–290, 297. See also John K. Townsend, *Narrative of a Journey Across the Rocky Mountains to the Columbia River* (Boston: Perkins and Marvin, 1839), in *Early Western Travels*, vol. 21, 170.

[36] Denig, *Five Indian Tribes*, 119–120.

The enormous number of bison and the readiness of the nomads to supply fur traders with robes attracted a horde of traders to the northern plains. Seeking to exploit the bison rather than leave them for their rivals, the fur companies supplied alcohol and credit to Indians to induce them to hunt extensively. The Indians in turn put extraordinary pressure on fur-bearing game in order to acquire alcohol and manufactured goods at inflated prices. Joshua Pilcher, an Indian agent for the upper Missouri, wrote in 1838 that "our citizens carry on an extensive trade" with the Assiniboines, Crows, Blackfeet, Sioux, and Cheyennes. Their territory, he wrote, "is traversed with carts, wagons, and pack horses."[37] In the Sioux territory, Catlin found "one of the most extensive assortments of goods, of whiskey, and other saleable commodities, as well as a party of the most indefatigable men, who are constantly calling for every robe that can be stripped from these animals' backs."[38] The traders acquired the Indians' robes at rock-bottom prices. In 1832, the traveler John Wyeth claimed "the white trader barters a tawdry bauble of a few cents' value for a skin worth fifty of it. . . . Coffee was sold at two dollars a pound, and so was tobacco."[39] Francis Parkman, who toured the plains in the 1840s, recorded in his diary that at Fort Laramie, "Prices are most extortionate. . . . a common clay pipe sells for half a dollar – a three-bit calico shirt for four dollars – a pair of the very coarsest pantaloons for ten dollars – a gallon of whiskey for 35 dollars, etc."[40] Fanny Kelly, a captive of the Oglala Sioux in 1864, wrote that the Indians "are most outrageously swindled by the traders whom our Government licenses to trade with them. A buffalo-robe which the trader sells for from ten to fifteen dollars, is bought from the Indians for a pint cup of sugar and a handful of bullets."[41] Traders' account books show that Indians received about three dollars' worth of goods for every robe. This "would be amply sufficient for their support," wrote one agent, "were it not that they have to give such exorbitant prices for what they purchase from the whites."[42]

The trade in bison robes was destructive both to the herds and to the nomadic societies. The nomads conducted their communal hunts to obtain food during the summer when the animals were fat, but the winter, when the bison's coat was thick, was "the season in which the greatest number of these animals are destroyed for their robes," according to Catlin.[43] The nomads sought only cows in the summer for their succulent meat and tender hides; they pursued

[37] Joshua Pilcher, *Annual Report of the Office of Indian Affairs*, 25th Cong., 3rd Sess., 1838, S.doc. 1, (Serial 338), 502.

[38] Catlin, *North American Indians*, vol. 1, 280.

[39] John B. Wyeth, *Oregon; or, A Short History of a Long Journey from the Atlantic to the Region of the Pacific* (Cambridge, 1833), in *Early Western Travels*, vol. 21, 84–85.

[40] Mason Wade, ed., *The Journals of Francis Parkman*, vol. 2 (New York: Harper, 1947), 425, 440.

[41] Fanny Kelly, *My Captivity Among the Sioux Indians* (New York: Citadel Press, 1993), 185.

[42] Alexander Ramsey, *Annual Report of the Commissioner of Indian Affairs, 1849*, 31st Cong., 1st Sess. (Serial 550), 1022.

[43] Catlin, *North American Indians*, vol. 1, 285.

primarily cows and young bulls in the winter for their thick and pliable robes.[44] A bison's coat was at its thickest and most valuable between November and February. Thus, commercial hunting occurred when the nomads were divided into bands and largely outside of social controls and strictures on economic behavior. William Gordon, a fur trader, reported in 1831 that there were six or seven trading posts on the Missouri above Council Bluffs, each supplied with between fifteen and twenty thousand dollars' worth of goods. "These are the 'principal depots' whence a great number of wintering posts are established, and called in again in the Spring, at the termination of the winter's trade."[45] The Indian agent John Dougherty reported in 1831 that traders branched out from the main posts to camp with bands during the winter. The association of hunters and traders was so close that the traders followed the nomads to their winter encampments, kept their goods in the lodges of chiefs, and even accompanied the nomads during their hunting expeditions.[46]

The nomads' commercial slaughter of the bison began along the Missouri River, the region most accessible to the Euroamerican traders, and continued in the more remote regions of the northern and central plains. In the early 1830s, while he was staying at Fort Union, a fur-trading post on the upper Missouri, Prince Maximilian wrote, "wild beasts and other animals, whose skins are valuable in the fur trade, have already diminished greatly in number along this river."[47] In the summer of 1849, when the agent William Hatton inspected the Missouri River from St. Louis to the mouth of the Yellowstone River, he met with Sioux, Arikaras, Hidatsas, and Crows, and concluded that the Indians' resources of game along the river were "daily diminishing, and must, before a great while, be almost entirely exhausted." He noted that the bison, in particular, "whose flesh furnishes their principal food, and the robes of which constitute by far the most important article of traffic, are now not near as numerous as a few years since, and the number is every year rapidly diminishing." Hatton attributed the absence of the bison to the fur trade. "The reason of so great a number of robes being sold during the last few years has not been on account of the great abundance of the buffalo, but the unusual diligence and industry of the Indians in hunting them."[48]

The rise, florescence, and decline of trading posts along the Missouri reflected the rapid acceleration of the robe trade in the 1830s and the similarly rapid disappearance of the bison. In 1832, Catlin called Fort Pierre at the juncture of the

[44] Wishart, Fur Trade, 96.
[45] Gordon to William Clark, Superintendent of Indian Affairs, October 27, 1831, Fur Trade Collection, Missouri Historical Society.
[46] John Dougherty, letter to Secretary of War Lewis Cass, November 19, 1831, Fur Trade Collection, Missouri Historical Society.
[47] Maximilian, Travels in the Interior of North America (London: Ackermann, 1843), in Early Western Travels, vol. 22, 379.
[48] Hatton, Annual Report of the Office of Indian Affairs, 1849, 1074.

Bad and Missouri rivers "undoubtedly one of the most important and productive of the American Fur Company's posts, being in the center of the great Sioux country, drawing from all quarters an immense and almost incredible number of buffalo robes, which are carried to the New York and other Eastern markets, and sold at great profit."[49] In 1834, Prince Maximilian estimated the value of the trading goods at Fort Pierre to be eighty thousand dollars.[50] In 1849, the traders at Ft. Pierre collected seventy-five thousand robes – over two-thirds of the robes produced in the northern plains that year.[51] But by the early 1850s, the nomads had hunted out the region surrounding Fort Pierre. According to Denig, the area "used to be the great range for the buffalo, but of late years they are found in greater numbers west of the Missouri." He correctly predicted that "the great diminution of buffalo in the Sioux country will compell that nation to seek subsistence farther west."[52] In 1857, Fort Pierre collected only nineteen thousand robes.[53] By the 1860s, the fur trader Henry Boller could only eulogize the post: "Fort Pierre was one of the largest posts in the Indian country and some years ago was the center of a flourishing trade with the Sioux, which has since greatly fallen off, many of them trading on the Platte and at the posts on the Upper Missouri."[54] Within thirty years of the beginning of the trade in robes at Fort Pierre, hunters had driven the bison from the central plains.

Beginning in the 1840s, the emigration of California-bound Euroamericans through the plains along the Platte River also contributed to the diminution of the bison herds. The emigrants' livestock trampled or consumed the grasses along the Platte, effectively ruining the bison's forage for miles on either side of the trail. In 1853 alone, emigrants herded over one hundred thousand cattle and forty-eight thousand sheep along the Platte. Before 1860, they probably drove over half a million cattle and an equal number of sheep to the Pacific Coast.[55] Emigrants delighted in shooting any bison that strayed too near the wagons. Similar destruction occurred in the southern plains along the Santa Fe Trail. Although the river valleys constituted only about 7 percent of the shortgrass plains, they were crucial winter refuges for the bison. Emigrants' destruction of forage and timber in the river valleys displaced large numbers of bison from their accustomed winter resorts.[56]

In addition to the nomads' commercial predation and the degradation of the

[49] Catlin, *North American Indians*, vol. 1, 234.

[50] Maximilian, in *Early Western Travels*, vol. 24, 91.

[51] Ramsey, *Annual Report of the Commissioner of Indian Affairs, 1849*, 1022.

[52] Denig, *Five Indian Tribes*, 3, 30, 93.

[53] Allen, *American Bisons*, 188.

[54] Henry A. Boller, *Among the Indians: Eight Years in the Far West, 1858–1866* (Chicago: Lakeside, 1959), 22.

[55] John D. Unruh, *The Plains Across: The Overland Emigrants and the Trans-Mississippi West, 1840–60* (Urbana: University of Illinois Press, 1979), 334.

[56] Elliott West, *The Way to the West: Essays on the Central Plains* (Albuquerque: University of New Mexico Press, 1995), 51–83.

river valleys by passing Euroamerican emigrants, the semi-arid climate of the grasslands – in particular the region's susceptibility to drought – conspired to undermine the bison population. In the first forty years of the nineteenth century, precipitation in the plains was above average.[57] Therefore, despite the mounting pressure of Indian hunters, the herds probably found forage sufficient to maintain their numbers. Beginning in 1846 and continuing for the next decade, however, rainfall was below average. The extended drought reduced the carrying capacity of the grasslands at a time when the bison were under extraordinary pressure from commercial Indian hunters.[58] Ecological and economic pressures thus combined to kill millions of bison in the middle of the nineteenth century.

Exotic disease was probably also a factor, albeit a minor one, in the mid-century decline of the bison population. Like commerce, bovine diseases spread from Euroamerican settlements to destroy the bison. Anthrax was the likely killer of large numbers of bison in the Canadian plains in the 1820s and 1830s. The bacterium *Bacillus anthracis*, which causes the disease, came with French livestock to Louisiana in the eighteenth century. It spreads as a hardy spore that can survive in certain types of soil – dry, warm, and alkaline – for decades. Hudson's Bay Company traders noted the outbreak of unidentified diseases among the bison around Great Slave Lake in the summers of 1821, 1823, and 1831. The symptoms of the 1831 outbreak were a sudden choking, frothing at the mouth, and collapse. These symptoms conform to the peracute form of anthrax, in which an apparently healthy animal may suffer sudden seizure, choking, dypsnoea, and death.[59] In her memoir, the Crow woman Pretty Shield recalled that a bison, frothing at the mouth, attacked her when she was a child.[60] Apart from this single, cryptic reference, no documentary evidence of anthraxlike symptoms among the bison south of the Canadian border exists. Nor does evidence exist that the anthrax bacterium ever established an enduring presence in the soil to become endemic in plains wildlife.[61] Its impact, therefore, although dramatic, was probably localized and ephemeral.

It is tempting to categorize separately anthropogenic and environmental causes of bison mortality. To do so, however, would obscure the inseparability of the human and ecological causes of the destruction of the bison. The arrival in the western plains of livestock and their diseases was a late wave in the tide of

---

[57] Merlin P. Lawson, *The Climate of the Great American Desert: Reconstruction of the Climate of the Western Interior United States, 1800–1850*. University of Nebraska Studies, New Series no. 46 (Lincoln: University of Nebraska Press, 1974).

[58] Dan Flores, "Bison Ecology and Bison Diplomacy: The Southern Plains from 1800 to 1850," *Journal of American History*, 78 (September 1991), 482.

[59] Theresa A. Ferguson and Frank LaViolette, "A Note on Historical Mortality in a Northern Bison Population," *Arctic*, 45 (March 1992), 47–50.

[60] Linderman, *Pretty Shield*, 72.

[61] Glenn B. Van Ness, "Ecology of Anthrax," *Science*, 172 (25 June 1971), 1303–1307.

European ecological expansion in North America. The domesticated livestock that destroyed the bison's forage and introduced exotic disease did not come to the plains of their own accord, however; their masters drove them there. Some Euroamericans came west to take advantage of economic opportunities, some to escape the commercialization of agriculture in the East, but in either case the nineteenth-century market revolution was integral to Euroamerican westward emigration.[62] The social, economic, and environmental transformations that contributed to the demise of the bison were not separate categories of change, but embedded in each other.

The decline of the bison population produced widespread destitution among the nomadic societies. The diminution of the herds forced the nomads to move west in search of the remaining bison. As early as 1837 Joshua Pilcher, a fur trader and Indian agent for the Sioux, Cheyennes, and Poncas on the upper Missouri, wrote that those groups formerly "confined themselves pretty much to the Missouri River, but scarcity of buffalo, their chief source of subsistence, has made it necessary for them to seek the means of living in more remote regions."[63] By the late 1840s, according to Denig, the scarcity of bison on the north bank of the Missouri forced the Minneconjou Sioux to move to the south-western bank of the river.[64] By the 1850s, the Teton Sioux and Cheyennes had largely shifted from the Missouri to the Platte River region.[65] The Assiniboines began to push west in the 1840s, hunting bison in the territory of the Crows, Atsinas, and Blackfeet.[66]

The increased warfare among the plains societies as they jostled for control of the remaining hunting territories did not escape the notice of federal authorities. In 1849, Orlando Brown, the Commissioner of Indian Affairs, wrote that the destruction of the bison "must, at no late day, so far diminish this chief resource of their subsistence and trade, as not only to entail upon them great suffering, but it will bring different tribes into competition in their hunting expeditions, and lead to bloody collisions and exterminating wars between them." Indian hostilities, Brown feared, might "seriously disturb" the "peace and security of our frontier."[67] Brown therefore convened a conference of the nomadic societies at Fort Laramie in 1851, in an attempt to define the boundaries of the nomads'

---

[62] For Euroamerican emigration, see Unruh, *Plains Across*; John Mack Faragher, *Women and Men on the Overland Trail* (New Haven: Yale University Press, 1979); Dean May, *Three Frontiers: Family, Land, and Society in the American West, 1850–1900* (New York: Cambridge University Press, 1994).

[63] Joshua Pilcher, *Annual Report of the Office of Indian Affairs*, 25th Cong., 2nd Sess., 1837, S.doc. 1, (Serial 314), 553.

[64] Denig, *Five Indian Tribes*, 22–25.

[65] Remi Nadeau, *Fort Laramie and the Sioux* (Lincoln: University of Nebraska Press, 1967), 23; White, "Winning of the West," 321; Berthrong, *Southern Cheyennes*, 16–26; Hoebel, *Cheyennes*, 10.

[66] Denig, *Five Indian Tribes*, 89–93.

[67] Orlando Brown, *Annual Report of the Office of Indian Affairs*, 1849, 942.

hunting territories. But the accord ended neither overhunting nor competition for resources. In 1855 the new Commissioner, George W. Maypenny, wrote "The great diminution of the buffalo, and other game, from which the Indians of the plains have heretofore derived their subsistence, has so far reduced them to a state of destitution as to compel them to plunder or steal from our citizens or starve." Maypenny concluded, "Under the existing state of things they must rapidly be exterminated by the whites or become extinct."[68]

By the mid-1850s, even the herds in the far western plains had diminished. The Indian agent at Fort Laramie, the main trading post on the upper Platte, wrote in 1855, "The buffalo is becoming scarce and it is more difficult from year to year for the Indians to kill a sufficient number to supply them with food and clothing."[69] During the same year, the agent at Fort Clark in the northwestern plains reported that little game could be found.[70] By 1858, game was also scarce at Fort Benton, in Blackfoot territory. The agent at Fort Benton wrote that previous to the fur trade, the Indians' demands on the herds had been equal to the bison's natural increase. But "when the cupidity of the whites forged the iron arrow point, and ... the Indian was stimulated to draw the bow, myriads of buffalo were recklessly sacrificed ... until at length the entire race has dwindled into comparative nothingness."[71] By the end of the 1850s, the combination of drought and commerce had driven the bison from everywhere but the far western plains. The Blackfeet pressured the remaining herds along the tributaries of the Missouri in northwestern Montana. The Sioux, Northern Cheyennes, Northern Arapahos, and Crows contested for control of the Powder River valley, and the Southern Cheyennes, Southern Arapahos, Kiowas, and Comanches subsisted on the herds around the upper Arkansas and Red river valleys.[72]

Outside of the regions where the bison remained the nomads found themselves impoverished. In the winter of 1846, an Indian agent on the Missouri reported that the Assiniboines of the northern plains were reduced to starvation. They subsisted for a time on deer, elk, and wolves, but these were either too few or too insubstantial to sustain them. After consuming their reserves of dried meat, berries, and roots, they fell upon their own dogs and horses. When the famine became severe, the Assiniboines scattered from the Missouri to the Saskatchewan River in the north and the Red River in the east, to search for food. They left the old behind to die, and some desperate Assiniboines reportedly resorted to cannibalism. The winter count of the Buffalo Followers, a Blackfoot band, calls 1854 the year "when we ate dogs." By 1853, the Saone and Yancton

---

[68] George W. Maypenny, *Annual Report of the Office of Indian Affairs*, 34th Cong., 1st Sess., 1855, S.exdoc. 1 (Serial 810), 331.

[69] Thomas Twiss, Ibid., 403.

[70] Alfred J. Vaughan, Ibid., 396.

[71] Vaughan, Ibid., 35th Cong., 2nd Sess., 1858, S.exdoc. 1, (Serial 974), 435.

[72] William T. Hornaday, *The Extermination of the American Buffalo, With a Sketch of Its Discovery and Life History* (Washington, D.C.: Government Printing Office, 1887).

Sioux on the eastern bank of the Missouri were destitute. In the spring of 1855 those bands, as well as the Assiniboines and Crees, subsisted solely on wild berries, roots, and the occasional putrefying carcass of a drowned bison that washed downriver. In the late 1850s, Boller found the Atsinas of the northern plains "in a starving condition, their main subsistence being upon roots and berries."[73] The quest for wealth brought the bison hunters not prosperity but poverty.

III

Traders introduced more than manufactured goods to the plains nomads; they also transmitted Eurasian diseases to which Native Americans had no acquired immunities. Familiar European diseases such as smallpox, measles, and influenza had devastated American Indians since the sixteenth century. Cholera, which commercial vessels first carried from southeast Asia to Europe and from there to the United States in 1832, decimated both Indian and Euroamerican populations.[74] The first substantial appearance of Old World contagion in the plains was the smallpox epidemic of 1780, which nearly destroyed the horticultural societies of the Missouri. Outbreaks of smallpox occurred repeatedly in the plains during the next fifty years, but they merely presaged the devastating epidemic of 1837–40. Within a decade of that scourge, cholera swept through the central and southern plains. In all, by the 1890s, the Indian population of the plains had declined no less than 60 percent from its late eighteenth-century level.[75]

Like the commercial destruction of the bison, smallpox and other diseases followed the Euroamerican traders. Contagion spread first along the Missouri River and other streams that the traders plied. The 1801–02 smallpox epidemic spread up the Missouri from the Omahas to the Poncas, Kansas, Arikaras, Mandans, and Hidatsas. Henry Brackenridge, a fur trader, noted the great number of abandoned villages on the middle Missouri when he ascended the river in 1811.[76]

---

[73] Vaughan, *Annual Report of the Office of Indian Affairs*, 33rd Cong., 1st Sess., 1854, S.exdoc. 1, (Serial 690), 290–291; Ibid., 33rd Cong., 2nd Sess., 1853, S.exdoc. 1, (Serial 746), 358; Ibid., 1855, 396–397; Hugh A. Dempsey, *A Blackfoot Winter Count* (Calgary: Glenbow-Alberta Institute, 1965), 12; Boller, *Among the Indians*, 35.

[74] For Native American depopulation, see Alfred W. Crosby, Jr., "Virgin Soil Epidemics as a Factor in the Aboriginal Depopulation in America," *William & Mary Quarterly*, 3d ser., 33 (April 1976), 287–299.

[75] James Mooney, *The Aboriginal Population of America North of Mexico*. Smithsonian Miscellaneous Collections, vol. 80 (Washington, D.C.: Smithsonian Institution, 1928). Also see John C. Ewers, "The Influence of Epidemics on the Indian Populations and Cultures of Texas," *Plains Anthropologist*, 18 (May 1973), 104–115.

[76] Henry M. Brackenridge, *Journal of a Voyage up the River Missouri Performed in 1811* (Baltimore: Coale and Maxwell, 1816), in *Early Western Travels*, vol. 6, 69.

The 1801–02 epidemic also spread along the Platte River. In an 1822 report to the Secretary of War, Jedediah Morse estimated, probably exaggeratedly, that half the Indian population along the Platte died during the outbreak.[77] In 1815–16, smallpox broke out along the Red and Rio Grande rivers in Texas, killing perhaps four thousand Comanches. In 1818–19, the disease claimed a number of Assiniboines and Yancton Sioux along the White River of South Dakota.[78]

In 1833, smallpox devastated the Crows in the northwestern plains. Euroamerican traders or Indians probably carried the pestilence to the Crows from the Pawnees in the central plains, who had suffered from an outbreak of smallpox in 1831. Denig claimed that a party of Crows contracted the disease while traveling, and that "before they reached their homes the disease commenced making its appearance." Denig estimated that only one out of every six or seven of the afflicted recovered. Survivors scattered in the hope of escaping the virus. "All order was lost. No one pretended to lead or advise. The sick and dead were alike left for the wolves and each family tried to save itself." According to Denig, the Crows had numbered eight hundred lodges before the epidemic. He calculated that at eight people per lodge, the Crow population was sixty-four hundred. After the epidemic, they numbered but three hundred sixty lodges.[79]

Prior to 1837, smallpox epidemics in the plains were localized episodes. Some of those episodes, such as the scourge of the Crows in 1833, could be extraordinarily destructive, but other societies nearby managed to avoid the contagion and remained largely unaffected. Between 1837 and 1840, however, a smallpox epidemic broke free of the riverine villages and trading posts and fanned out into the plains. The epidemic caused thousands of deaths in the northern plains where the robe trade was most intense. Catlin, who based his estimates on the reports of Joshua Pilcher, the Superintendent of Indian Affairs, wrote that of the forty-one thousand Hidatsas, Crees, Blackfeet, Cheyennes, and Crows in 1836, twenty-five thousand had died by 1840.[80]

The Indian villages along the upper Missouri served as the main fur trade rendezvous sites for the nomads and Euroamerican traders. The villages therefore also served as important conduits for the transmission of European diseases. By the 1830s, fur traders were permanent residents of the Mandan and Arikara villages and the condition of the villages was decidedly squalid. "The whole of the Arikara village, both within and without their habitations, presents a disgusting appearance," wrote Denig. "The spaces between the huts are seldom if ever cleaned, animal and vegetable substances in every state of putrefaction are scattered about, and the consequence of this is fluxes, dysenteries, scurvy, and

[77] Jedediah Morse, *Report to the Secretary of War on Indian Affairs* (New Haven, 1822), 92.

[78] E. Wagner Stearn and Allan E. Stearn, *The Effect of Smallpox on the Destiny of the Amerindian* (Boston: Bruce Humphries, 1945), 75–78.

[79] Denig, *Five Indian Tribes*, 170.

[80] Catlin, *North American Indians*, vol. 2, Appendix A, "Extinction of the Mandans," 294. See also Stearn and Stearn, *Effect of Smallpox*, 94.

other diseases prevail in the summer months."[81] In 1835, for instance, Francis Chardon, the resident trader at Fort Clark, reported that an epidemic of dysentery had broken out among the Mandans.[82] According to the testimony of fur traders, travelers, and Indian agents, sexually transmitted diseases were endemic among the Arikaras and Mandans.[83] Given the density of the population, the inadequate sanitation of the villages, and the close contact between villagers and fur traders, the villages were ideal places for epidemics to begin.

In 1831, for instance, fur traders brought smallpox to the Pawnee villages along the Platte River. According to Catlin, the disease killed between ten thousand and twelve thousand, about half the population of the villages, in the space of a few months.[84] Catlin was sometimes given to exaggeration, but in this case his estimate was probably not far off. John Dougherty, the Indian agent at Fort Leavenworth, visited the Pawnee villages in the fall of 1831. In his report, he concurred with Catlin that half of the Pawnees had perished. The Pawnees told Dougherty that every person under thirty years of age had died. Those Pawnees older than thirty had acquired immunity to the disease during the smallpox outbreak of 1801–02. Because the disease struck so swiftly, Dougherty found the dead lying where they had fallen: in the river, lodged in sand bars, in the pastures and gardens around the village, or in the corn caches. Village dogs and wolves from the surrounding prairie scavenged the corpses. "Their misery was so great and so general," Dougherty wrote, "that they seemed to be unconscious of it, and to look upon the dead and dying as they would on so many dead horses."[85] The Pawnee debacle of 1831 only served to foreshadow the smallpox epidemic that overswept the plains between 1837 and 1840.

The American Fur Company steamboat *St. Peter* brought smallpox to the Mandan village Mih-tutta-hangkush, near Fort Clark, after a severe winter of near-starvation in 1836–37. Chardon wrote in January, 1837, that the Mandans had gone without meat for several weeks. Other fur traders reported that the Hidatsas farther upstream were also short of food. The Mandans' famine stemmed partly from their concentration on the production of pelts and robes rather than foodstuffs. Despite the scarcity of bison meat, Mandan hunters continued to trap beavers for Chardon in the spring of 1837. In May, 1837, the Arikaras came to Fort Clark loaded with bison robes but short of meat. Both the Mandans and the Arikaras continued to grow corn, but by the 1830s, as much as

---

[81] Denig, *Five Indian Tribes*, 54.

[82] Francis Chardon, *Journal at Fort Clark 1834–1839*, ed., Annie Heloise Abel (Lincoln: University of Nebraska Press, 1997), 45. The disease may have been cholera.

[83] Tabeau, *Narrative of Loisel's Expedition*, 183; Maximilian, in *Early Western Travels*, vol. 23, 359; David D. Mitchell, *Annual Report of the Office of Indian Affairs*, 32nd Cong., 1st Sess., 1851, S.exdoc. 1, (Serial 613), 324.

[84] Catlin, *North American Indians*, vol. 2, 28; also see Stearn and Stearn, *Effect of Smallpox*, 79; and White, *Roots of Dependency*, 155–156.

[85] John Dougherty, *Letter from the Secretary of War*, 22nd Cong., 1st Sess., March 30, 1832, doc. 190.

one-third of their production went to feed the Euroamerican traders and another species of Old World immigrant, the Norway rat (*Rattus norvegicus*). The rats had stowed away on steamboats, infested the Upper Missouri villages, and settled down to consume a not insignificant proportion of the Indians' corn caches. Chardon, who kept meticulous count, trapped over seven hundred rats between November 1836 and May 1837. The consumption of so much of the villagers' corn by Euroamericans – both human and rodent – depleted the Indians' provisions on the eve of the epidemic.[86]

The *St. Peter* arrived at Mih-tutta-hangkush on June 18,1837. How the disease was transmitted to the village is impossible to document. In their reports, fur traders routinely went to great lengths to establish their innocence in the outbreaks of diseases among Native Americans. Most claimed to have been unaware of the presence of disease, or to have warned the Indians of the danger only to have their warnings ignored. There might be some truth to those accounts. Given the dependence of their enterprise on the stability and good will of the Indians, the traders had no interest in facilitating an outbreak of smallpox. Moreover, the lure of commerce might well have been strong enough to induce Indians to risk exposure to the disease. It was in the Indians' interest, after all, to bring their robes directly to the Euroamerican traders and avoid commercial intermediaries. Nevertheless, the traders' account of the transmission of smallpox to the Mandans is suspicious: They allege that a Mandan chief stole a blanket belonging to an afflicted passenger aboard the *St. Peter*.[87]

The transmission of smallpox is difficult to intercept because the *Variola* virus is insidious. The incubation period for the disease is two weeks, which allowed the virus to spread from one victim to another aboard the crowded steamboat before anyone became alarmed. A boathand on board the *St. Peter* fell ill on April 29 with a fever. The precise nature of the illness was not known until the steamboat reached Council Bluffs in the middle of May. By that time, several more people on board the boat had developed the symptoms of smallpox. By June 18, however, when the steamboat reached Fort Clark, the carriers of the virus had either died, recovered, or not yet evidenced any symptoms. Bernard Pratte, Jr., the commander of the steamboat, and Joshua Pilcher, the agent for the Sioux and a passenger on the boat, probably believed that the disease had burned itself out. However, a host who has not yet developed symptoms, a recuperating victim, or a corpse can transmit the disease. Three Arikara women who had boarded the steamboat as passengers near Council Bluffs probably carried the disease from the steamboat to the Indians at Fort Clark. The women had fallen ill and had

[86] Chardon, *Journal at Fort Clark*, 96–107; Denig, *Five Indian Tribes*, 46–47; James J. Berry, "Arikara Middlemen: The Effects of Trade on an Upper Missouri Society" (Ph.D. dissertation, Indiana University, 1978); Wishart, *Fur Trade*, 102.
[87] Chardon, *Journal at Fort Clark*, 121.

recovered but were still carrying the virus when the boat arrived at Mih-tutta-hangkush.[88]

Fort Clark was a center of trade in 1837, and almost immediately after the transmission of the disease Indians embarked from the trading post, carrying the deadly microbes to other parts of the plains. Four days after the arrival of the steamboat, a hunting party of Arikaras arrived in the village with dried bison meat. Shortly after – and long before the appearance of the first symptoms of the disease – parties of Arikaras and Mandans set out from the village. On June 26, a party of Arikaras, perhaps carrying the *Variola* virus, set off for the Platte to obtain horses from the Pawnees. The next day another party of Arikaras and Mandans went north to raid the Yancton Sioux.[89]

Chardon first noted a death due to smallpox on July 14. From that day on, his journal shifts from recording the number of rats he killed each day to documenting the course of the disease among the Mandans. According to Chardon, between eight and ten Indians died every day during July and August, and five or six died every day during September. Survivors left the dead where they had fallen: in their lodges, the streets of the village, or along the river. In mid-September a survivor of the epidemic in the Mandans' other village on the Missouri arrived at Mih-tutta-hangkush and reported that eight hundred had died, leaving only fourteen alive. Altogether, Chardon estimated, seven-eighths of the Mandans had died.[90] Chardon – who prudently refrained from venturing into the village during the scourge – may have underestimated the mortality. Between fifteen and sixteen hundred Mandans had met the *St. Peter* in June, 1837. By the end of the year, according to Catlin, only between thirty and forty were still alive.[91] Many, no doubt, had not died but fled from the village. A significant proportion of those who fled probably carried the virus with them.

Before the appearance of the disease at Fort Clark, the *St. Peter* had steamed upriver to Fort Union, the trading post of the Blackfeet and Assiniboines at the juncture of the Missouri and Yellowstone rivers. The outbreak of the disease among the Assiniboines illustrated the strong connection between the lure of Euroamerican commerce and the spread of contagion. After the *St. Peter* brought smallpox to Fort Union, certain bands of the Assiniboines came to the post to trade the bison robes that they had accumulated during the winter. Traders met the Indians about one mile from the post and warned them of the danger of contagion. Unheeding, the Assiniboines pressed on to Fort Union. By coming to the trading post, the Assiniboines merely did what all plains nomads had learned to

[88] Clyde D. Dollar, "The High Plains Smallpox Epidemic of 1837–38," *Western Historical Quarterly*, 8 (January 1977), 15–38.

[89] Chardon, *Journal at Fort Clark*, 118–119.

[90] Ibid., 123–138.

[91] Catlin, *North American Indians*, vol. 2, Appendix A, "Extinction of the Mandans," 293.

do since the eighteenth century: to acquire the most goods in exchange for their robes, they attempted to avoid commercial intermediaries and trade at the posts.

Smallpox ran its course among the Assiniboines during the summer and fall. According to Denig, the mortality rate among the Assiniboine bands that came to Fort Union was nearly 90 percent. Of the two hundred fifty lodges belonging to those bands before the onset of the disease, only thirty lodges or one hundred fifty people survived. Those who died at the trading post were daily thrown into the river by the cartload. Those who fled the post fared no better. Lodges in which whole families lay dead lined the trails leading from Fort Union.[92] Yet Assiniboine hunters continued to bring robes to Fort Union to trade for alcohol despite the ravages of the epidemic. "On being asked how it happened that there were so many robes brought in," the fur trader Charles Larpenteur wrote, "the Indians would say laughingly that they expected to die soon, and wanted to have a frolic until the end came."[93] Survivors of the epidemic found Assiniboine society nearly broken. Remnants of various bands joined together, but twenty years after the outbreak of the disease, all the bands of the Assiniboine together numbered only one hundred lodges.[94] The nearby Blackfeet also suffered terribly during the scourge. Thomas Farnham estimated that of the twenty-five hundred Blackfoot lodges existing before the outbreak of the disease, one or more members of only eight hundred lodges survived.[95]

The devastation of the Indians at Fort Clark and Fort Union suggests that the 1837–40 contagion began as a combination of different strains of smallpox that probably included hemorrhagic smallpox, the most virulent strain of the disease. Contemporary accounts of the symptoms testified to the virulence of the pestilence. Catlin wrote that the first symptom of the disease which afflicted the Mandans in 1837 was a rapid swelling of the body – perhaps a subcutaneous hemorrhage. In many cases, Catlin wrote, death occurred before the appearance of the disease on the skin, probably as a result of high fever.[96] Denig also recorded that two-thirds of the Assiniboines died before any pox sores appeared. He further noted that a high fever and hemorrhages from the mouth and ears precipitated death.[97] Other groups that suffered from smallpox in succeeding months evidenced neither the acute symptoms nor the high mortality of the Mandans and Assiniboines, among whom the estimated death rate ranged from 90 to 98 percent. The most lethal forms of a disease usually burn out quickly, because their carriers die so suddenly that they cannot transmit the contagion.

[92] Denig, *Five Indian Tribes*, 71.
[93] Larpenteur, *Forty Years a Fur Trader*, 134–135.
[94] Denig, *Five Indian Tribes*, 71–72.
[95] Farnham, in *Early Western Travels*, vol. 28, 265–266. For depopulation among the northern plains nomads, see John F. Taylor, "Counting: The Utility of Historic Population Estimates in the Northwestern Plains, 1800–1880," *Plains Anthropologist*, 34 (May 1989), 17–30.
[96] Catlin, *North American Indians*, vol. 2, 298.
[97] Denig, *Five Indian Tribes*, 71.

Although it began along the Missouri, intertribal raid and trade carried the disease out into the plains. In August, 1837, Chardon reported that the disease had reached the Atsinas camped near Turtle Mountain. "A great many of them have died of the smallpox," he wrote. "They swear vengeance against all the whites, as they say the smallpox was brought here by the Steamboat."[98] The Atsina population fell from about five thousand before the epidemic to just over two thousand in 1842.[99] In early 1838, the disease reached the Pawnees and Sioux on the Platte, who transmitted it to the Kiowas on the Arkansas River. Denig recounted that the Saone division of the Sioux "suffered considerably by the smallpox of 1838."[100] In the Kiowan calendar, the winter of 1839–40 is called *Tä dalkop Sai*, or smallpox winter; the disease is indicated by a pictograph of a man covered with red spots. From the Kiowas, the disease spread to the Comanches and other southern plains societies.

In the decades after 1840, smallpox repeatedly afflicted the plains nomads, but it never again had the same deadly effect, because survivors of the 1837–40 epidemic had acquired immunity to the disease. In 1848, emigrants to Oregon transmitted smallpox to the Northern Shoshones, who in turn gave the disease to the Crows. The generation that had been born after the last epidemic suffered terribly. In 1856, the steamboat *Clara*, belonging to the fur trade company of Joseph Picotte, transmitted the disease to the Arikaras, Hidatsas, and Crows. Perhaps one quarter of the Indians exposed to the disease died. In 1861–62 the Kiowas contracted smallpox on a trade excursion to New Mexico, and transmitted the disease to the Cheyennes, Arapahos, and Sioux.[101] Other diseases also contributed to the devastation of the nomadic populations. In 1843, the Plains Crees contracted measles. In 1849, six hundred Crows died of influenza contracted from emigrants on the Platte Trail.[102]

On the heels of the great smallpox epidemic of 1837–40 came the cholera outbreak of 1849–50. Like smallpox, cholera followed in the wake of commerce between Indians and Euroamericans. In the 1840s, the Southern Cheyennes and Arapahos served as commercial intermediaries between the Euroamerican traders at Bent's Fort on the Santa Fe Trail, and the Comanches and Kiowas south of the Arkansas River, obtaining trade goods from Bent's Fort and exchanging them for horses. The Cheyennes and Arapahos returned with the horses to Bent's Fort, where they traded the animals for more manufactured goods. The traders at Bent's Fort shipped the horses east along the Santa Fe Trail to St. Louis, where they sold them to western emigrants, supplying them

[98] Chardon, *Journal at Fort Clark*, 126.
[99] Taylor, "Historic Population Estimates," 24–25.
[100] Denig, *Five Indian Tribes*, 27–28.
[101] James Mooney, "Calendar History of the Kiowa Indians," *Seventeenth Annual Report of the Bureau of American Ethnology* (Washington, D.C.: Government Printing Office, 1898), 274, 311; Stearn and Stearn, *Effect of Smallpox*, 85–86, 97–99.
[102] Denig, *Five Indian Tribes*, 115, 185–186.

with the means to cross the plains.[103] In 1849, those emigrants transmitted cholera to the nomads.

Vibrio comma, the bacterium that causes cholera, can spread by means of unwashed hands, uncooked fruits and vegetables, or contaminated water. The first symptoms, which can arrive suddenly to an otherwise healthy person, are diarrhea, spasmodic vomiting, and painful cramps. Death may occur within a few hours or a day after the appearance of the first symptoms. It was not until the summer of 1832 that increasing commercial contact between American and European ports brought cholera, originally a Southeast Asian disease, to the western hemisphere. A second outbreak occurred in 1848. The citizens of western towns, whose water supplies were inadequate and whose municipal sanitation was rudimentary, suffered severely during the second epidemic. Ten percent of the population of St. Louis died in 1849. In San Antonio, Texas, the number of dead outstripped the ability of undertakers to process the corpses. The bacterium also flourished among emigrants packed into steamboats on the first leg of their journeys to California or Oregon. Forbidden to disembark the dead properly, travelers jettisoned corpses overboard. The disease continued to afflict travelers in the plains as the bacterium survived in the streams and water holes along the Platte and Arkansas rivers.[104]

The Teton Sioux largely avoided smallpox during the first half of the nineteenth century, only to fall victim to measles and cholera in 1848. The rush of emigrants carrying the diseases along the Platte Trail hastened the atomization of the Sioux. The Brulé division, whose territory lay closest to the Platte Trail, suffered from their proximity to the emigrants. Cholera and measles, wrote Denig, "have year after year thinned their ranks, so that but a remnant of this once numerous band remains." The emigrants' transmission of the contagion to the Indians, as well as their destruction of timber and game along the Platte, spurred the breakdown of the Brulé social order. By the 1850s, the Brulés were depopulated, scattered throughout their territory, badly equipped, and without game. "Their former good order and flourishing condition deranged, they are no more the same people," wrote Denig. "Their tempers are soured and all their fierce passions raised against the authors of these evils."[105] The swarm of emigrants along the Platte was no less destructive to the Oglala Sioux. Oglala government, according to Denig, was once well ordered. "In all things regarding their hunting operations and traveling they preserved order, kept together, and were respected and somewhat feared by neighboring bands." After the introduction of measles and cholera, however, the decimated Oglalas were "split into different factions following different leaders, and through a want of game

---

[103] Jablow, The *Cheyenne in Plains Trade Relations*, 67.
[104] Charles E. Rosenberg, *The Cholera Years: The United States in 1832, 1849, and 1866*, 2d ed. (Chicago: University of Chicago Press, 1987), 2–3, 114–116.
[105] Denig, *Five Indian Tribes*, 19.

and unity of purpose are fast verging toward dissolution." Their ultimate destination, predicted Denig in 1855, "will no doubt be to become a set of outlaws."[106]

Smallpox, cholera, and other diseases devastated the Indian population of the
plains in the nineteenth century. Altogether, the native population of the plains
fell from an estimated one hundred forty-two thousand in 1780 to fifty-three
thousand in 1890.[107] The Sioux, Blackfeet, Cheyennes, and others had become
equestrian nomads in the eighteenth century partly to avoid the diseases that
European fur traders had brought to the horticultural villages along the Missouri River. Yet by the nineteenth century their contacts with fur traders had
become so extensive that they were no longer able to evade Eurasian pestilence.

In the eighteenth century, some of the Indians who eventually became nomads
had faced a social and ecological dilemma: to remain as agrarian villagers and
face the threat of European diseases, or to become nomadic bison hunters and
abandon their reliance on a diverse array of resources. In the eighteenth century,
the Sioux, Cheyennes, and others fled their villages and the specter of disease in
preference for the insecurity of dependence on the bison alone. When they
became mounted bison hunters, the nomads necessarily became avid traders,
with both other Indians and Euroamericans, in order to acquire horses and to
compensate for their narrow resource base. In the middle of the nineteenth century, the nomads felt the consequences of their choice. As the bison population
declined – in large part because of the Indians' commercial carnage in the
drought-prone plains – the nomads' subsistence became increasingly precarious.
Finally, the diseases that the nomads had sought (or been fortunate enough) to
avoid in the eighteenth century reached them in the nineteenth century with
devastating results.

After the arrival of European biota and commerce in the grasslands in the
eighteenth century, the Great Plains had resisted European economic and ecological expansion longer and more successfully than any other region in North
America; the plains nomads and the bison dominated the grasslands until the
1860s.[108] The plains nomads resisted Euroamerican conquest because they had
so ingeniously adapted themselves to the European economic and ecological
invasion. The ecological disasters of the mid-nineteenth century were largely a
consequence of those earlier successes. The dominance of the nomads and the
bison began to erode in the 1830s under the combined pressures of the European
economic and ecological conquests. The expansion of the robe trade led to the
commercialization of the nomads' culture and the furtherance of inequitable
social relations. To fuel the accumulation of wealth and the competition for

---

[106] Ibid., 21–22.
[107] Mooney, *Aboriginal Population of America North of Mexico*, 12–13.
[108] Crosby, *Ecological Imperialism*, 279–280.

prestige, the nomads began to eradicate the bison from the plains. Finally, Eurasian diseases followed the paths of commercial interaction to devastate the nomads. The European economic and ecological invasion – which had created the nomadic societies in the eighteenth century – combined to break the dominance of the nomads and the bison in the Great Plains in the nineteenth century.

Throughout the eighteenth and nineteenth centuries, the fate of the plains nomads was bound to the fate of the bison. Like the bison, they traversed the grasslands, divided into small groups during the cold months of the year, and endured the privations of the volatile, semi-arid plains. The trade in robes that decimated the herds also brought suffering to the nomadic societies. Like all human societies, the plains nomads were dependent on nature for their welfare; in their case, their dependence was uncommonly singular and direct. The poverty and misery that followed in the wake of the nomads' decimation of the herds were unique to the ecological disaster that befell them. Yet the dependence of people on nature for their survival transcends the nineteenth-century plains. The hellish social and ecological predicaments that the nomads suffered – an inequitable and impoverishing economic regime, the exhaustion of natural resources, and the affliction of deadly and mysterious diseases – also transcend the circumstances of the nineteenth-century plains. If the fate of the nomads offers a lesson to other societies that share those predicaments, it is to understand both the futility of riches and the fragility of nature.

5

The Wild and the Tamed

As the Civil War approached its end, the citizens of the United States faced the prospect of an Indian war in the Great Plains. John Evans, the governor of the Colorado Territory, predicted in 1864 that the coming hostilities "will be the largest Indian war this country ever had, extending from Texas to the British line involving nearly all the wild tribes of the plains."[1] Contention over the control of natural resources was the root cause of the brewing conflict. In the southern plains, the nomads struggled to preserve their stewardship of the bison herds, while Euroamericans sought access to ranchlands and the gold mines of Colorado.[2] For the southern plains nomads, the conflict reached its nadir on November 29, 1864, when Colonel John Chivington led two companies of Colorado volunteer cavalry in an attack on noncombatant Southern Cheyennes at Sand Creek. Chivington and his men killed one hundred fifty Cheyennes; two-thirds of the dead were women and children. The Commissioner of Indian Affairs and a Congressional committee rebuked those involved in the massacre, but Chivington won broad support among Euroamericans in Colorado, including Governor Evans.

In the northern plains, the conflict between Indians and Euroamericans over the control of natural resources also raged. The dispute of the northern plains nomads with the United States centered on the Bozeman Trail leading from Fort Laramie to the gold mines of Montana. The trail and the emigrants on it cut directly through the Powder River valley, the nomads' best remaining hunting territory in the northern plains. The scattered attacks of the Indians on miners and soldiers turned to concerted warfare in 1866 after the army constructed three forts along the trail to protect emigrants. The United States fared poorly in the conflict. On December 21, 1866, near Fort Phil Kearney, one of the three new posts, a Sioux force lured eighty cavalrymen into an ambush and obliterated the entire unit. In the aftermath of this defeat, Generals William Sherman and Ulysses Grant urged Congress "to provide means and troops to carry on

---

[1] Quoted in Philip Weeks, *Farewell, My Nation: The American Indian and the United States, 1820–1890* (Arlington Heights, Ill.: Harlan Davidson, 1990), 102.

[2] See James Mooney, *Calendar History of the Kiowa Indians* (Washington, D.C.: Smithsonian Institution Press, 1979), 321–322.

formidable hostilities against the Indians, until all the Indians or all the whites on the great plains, and between the settlements on the Missouri and the Pacific, are exterminated."[3] Congress, weary of the human and fiscal costs of war, rather urged a policy of negotiation and created a Peace Commission composed of military and civilian leaders to conclude treaties with the plains nomads.

The Peace Commissioners first addressed the war in the southern plains. (See Map 5.1.) In October, 1867, the Peace Commission convened a meeting with over five thousand Comanches, Kiowas, Southern Cheyennes, and Southern Arapahos in the valley of the Medicine Lodge Creek. The agreements that the assembly produced – the Treaties of Medicine Lodge – purported to end the three years of hostilities between the southern plains nomads and Euroamericans. The treaties allowed Euroamericans to build roads and lay tracks to the Colorado mines, and indeed to settle north of the Arkansas River. The Indians secured the right to hunt south of the Arkansas "so long as the buffalo may range thereon in such numbers as to justify the chase." The treaties, moreover, forbade Euroamericans to settle south of the Arkansas.[4]

By establishing the Arkansas River as the boundary between Indians and Euroamericans, the Treaties of Medicine Lodge appeared to resolve the problems posed by conflicting land use practices. Although the treaties prohibited Euroamericans from settling in the nomads' hunting territory, they did not expressly forbid Euroamerican hunters from pursuing bison south of the Arkansas, except in the nomads' relatively small reservations between the Arkansas and Red rivers in Indian Territory. Indian signatories maintained, however, that the Peace Commissioners had made oral promises to keep Euroamerican bison hunters north of the Arkansas. Richard Bussell, a bison hunter who attended the negotiations, recalled that he and other bison hunters promised not to hunt south of the Arkansas. As Bussell noted, however, "the hunters paid no attention to the treaty."[5] The Treaties of Medicine Lodge, therefore, while establishing

---

[3] "Letter from the Secretary of the Interior, Communicating ... information in relation to the late massacre of United States troops by Indians at or near Fort Phil. Kearney, in Dakota Territory." S.ex.doc. 16, 39th Cong., 2nd Sess.

[4] See Charles Kappler, ed., *Indian Affairs: Laws and Treaties*, vol. 2 (Washington: Government Printing Office, 1904), 887–895, 977–989. The line of demarcation between Euroamerican settlement and Indian hunting territory did not correspond precisely to the Arkansas River but ran along the southern border of the state of Kansas to the juncture of the Cimarron River and Buffalo Creek, then north to the Arkansas River, then down the Arkansas to the state border.

[5] Richard Bussell, interview with J. Evetts Haley, 19 July 1926, Canadian, Texas; Bussell, "Buffalo Hunting," 27 December 1929, Panhandle-Plains Historical Society, Canyon, Texas. Bussell, recalling the Treaty of Medicine Lodge over fifty years after it had been signed, referred to General William S. Harney as "General Harker." He was perhaps confusing Harney with General Charles Harker. Bussell also thought that the conference had convened "in 1871 or 1872." Despite these lapses, he remembered the presence at the conference of the Cheyenne leader Black Kettle, a treaty signatory. The bison hunter Mark Huselby also recalled that "the whites had made an agreement to stay back, but they had begun to encroach upon the plains, which were the Indians' hunting grounds." Huselby, interview with Haley, 18 June 1925, Mobeetie, Texas, Panhandle-Plains Historical Society.

the Arkansas River as the informal boundary between Indian and Euroamerican territory, did not guarantee to southern nomads the exclusive right to hunt bison south of the Arkansas. After 1870, Euroamerican hide hunters poured into the region and within a decade had nearly exterminated the herds.

After the conclusion of the negotiations at Medicine Lodge, the members of the Peace Commission traveled to Fort Laramie on the north branch of the Platte River, hoping to negotiate an end to the war between the United States and the Sioux, Northern Cheyennes, and Northern Arapahos. In his winter count, the Sioux calendarist Lone Dog memorialized the 1868 negotiations – which he termed "many flags were given" – as the principal event of the year.[6] Indeed, the conferences were critical to the northern plains nomads, who hoped to capitalize on their recent military successes against the United States and secure lasting control over their remaining hunting territory.

Like the agreements at Medicine Lodge, the Treaty of Fort Laramie of April, 1868, appeared to end the dispute over resources. In return for cession of the territory south of the Platte River by the northern plains nomads and the promise not to impede the construction of railroads outside of their hunting area, the Peace Commissioners agreed to abandon the forts in the Powder River valley and to close the Bozeman Trail. Moreover, the treaty explicitly guaranteed to the northern plains nomads their undisturbed use of the hunting territory west of the Missouri, north of the Platte, and east of the Bighorn Mountains. "So long as the buffalo may range thereon in such numbers as to justify the chase," the Treaty forbade Euroamericans to settle or to pass through the nomads' hunting territory.[7]

Yet just as the Treaties of Medicine Lodge had only appeared to protect the Indians' hunting territory, the Treaty of Fort Laramie was an imperfect guarantee of the nomads' undisturbed use of the bison herds. The seemingly straightforward treaty was only one part of the contradictory regulation of resource use in the plains. The agreement banned Euroamerican hunters from the Indians' territory, but the law simultaneously allowed scientific exploration, land grants, and mining claims – the legal framework of Euroamerican settlement – to go forward.[8] In 1864, the federal government had set aside land in the Dakota and Montana territories for the construction of the Northern Pacific Railroad. The Treaty of Fort Laramie did not specify a northern boundary of the Indians' hunting territory, virtually ensuring conflict in 1873 when the Northern Pacific, building westward from Duluth, Minnesota, reached the Missouri River. Moreover, in 1874, Lieutenant-Colonel George Armstrong Custer led a scientific

[6] Garrick Mallery, "Pictographs of the North American Indians," *Fourth Annual Report of the Bureau of Ethnology, 1882–83* (Washington, D.C.: Government Printing Office, 1886), 125.

[7] Kappler, *Indian Affairs*, vol. 2, 998–1005.

[8] Hendrik Hartog pointed out to me the problem of multiple sources of legal authority in the nineteenth-century United States. See his article, "Pigs and Positivism," *Wisconsin Law Review* (1985), 899–935.

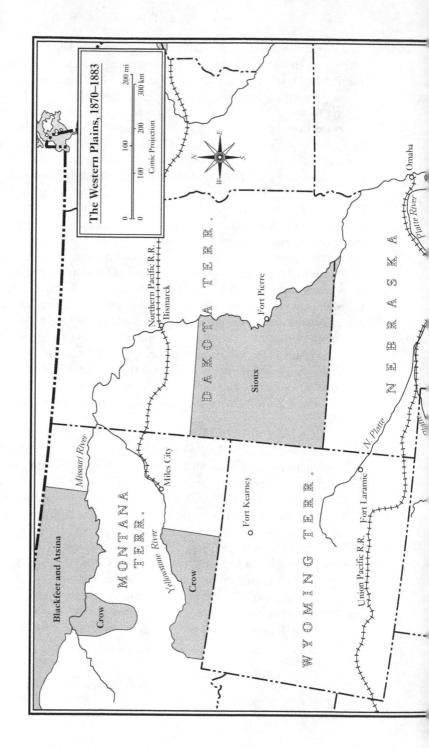

The Western Plains, 1870–1883

0   100   200 mi
0   100   200   300 km
Conic Projection

MONTANA TERR.

Blackfeet and Atsina

Crow

Crow

Missouri River

Yellowstone River

Northern Pacific R.R.

Bismarck

Miles City

DAKOTA TERR.

Fort Pierre

Sioux

WYOMING TERR.

Fort Kearney

Union Pacific R.R.

Fort Laramie

N. Platte

NEBRASKA

N. Platte

Platte River

Omaha

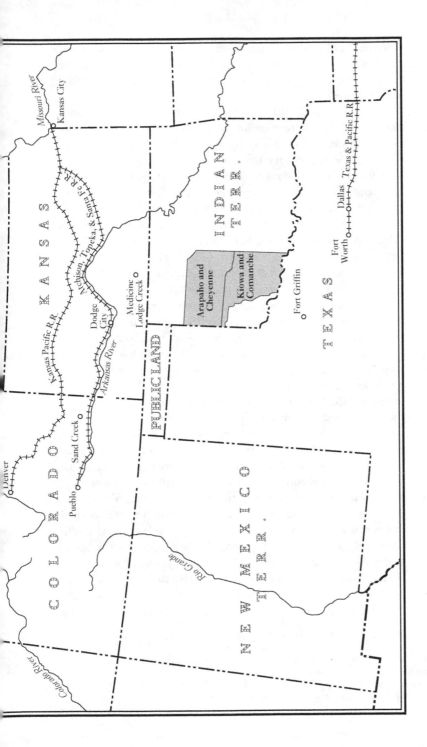

expedition to the Black Hills in the center of the area reserved for the Sioux. Custer's report of an abundance of gold in the Black Hills sparked a rush of Euroamerican miners into the Sioux territory. They were followed in the 1880s by Euroamerican hide hunters.

Above all, the agreements of Medicine Lodge and Fort Laramie were ephemeral because the United States' recognition of autonomous Indian hunting territories was due to expire with the bison. By 1867, both the Indian and Euroamerican signatories to the treaties knew that the bison population was declining rapidly. The diminution of the bison certainly did not escape the notice of General Sherman, a member of the Peace Commission. He wrote to his brother, John Sherman, a United States Senator from Ohio, on June 17, 1868, that "the commission for present peace had to concede a right to hunt buffaloes as long as they last, and this may lead to collisions, but it will not be long before all the buffaloes are extinct near and between the railroads."[9] The language of the treaties Sherman helped to negotiate was temporizing: the Indians "yet reserve the right to hunt ... so long as the buffalo range ... in such numbers to justify the chase." In 1870, Jacob Cox, the Secretary of the Interior, wrote somewhat prematurely that the provisions of the treaties reserving hunting territory to the nomads were moot because the Indians were already unable to subsist on the few remaining bison. "The building of the Union Pacific Railroad has driven the buffalo from their former hunting grounds," he wrote, so "that it was impracticable for the Indians to rely upon this natural supply of food, clothing, and shelter."[10] Sherman and Cox were ultimately proved correct; by 1883, the bison was nearly extinct and the plains nomads submitted to the reservation system.

The historian David D. Smits has argued that the United States Army was primarily responsible for the destruction of the bison. Certainly Sherman, the commander of the Division of the Missouri, suggested more than once that the eradication of the bison would force the plains nomads to reservations. The strategy, if indeed it was Sherman's aim to destroy the bison, was reminiscent of his destruction of Confederate resources during the Civil War. Sherman burned a path through Georgia and South Carolina in 1864–65, while General Philip Sheridan simultaneously conducted a similar campaign in the Shenandoah Valley in Virginia.[11] In the West in the 1860s and 1870s, the Army, when frustrated by its inability to defeat Indians in battle, sometimes resorted to the destruction of their animal resources. In 1864, Kit Carson, a breveted brigadier general in the First New Mexico Volunteer Infantry, ordered the destruction of Navajo sheep

[9] Rachel Thorndike Sherman, ed., *The Sherman Letters: Correspondence Between General and Senator Sherman from 1837 to 1891* (New York: Scribner's, 1894), 320.
[10] Jacob D. Cox, *Annual Report of the Secretary of the Interior*, 41st Cong., 1st Sess., 1870, H.exdoc. 1 (Serial 1449), vi.
[11] James M. McPherson, *Ordeal by Fire: The Civil War and Reconstruction*, 2d ed. (New York: McGraw-Hill, 1992), 443–446, 459–463; McPherson, *Battle Cry of Freedom: The Civil War Era* (New York: Ballantine, 1988), 774–806.

in order to bring the Indians to submission. In 1868, following his attack on a winter camp of Southern Cheyennes on the Washita River, Custer ordered his men to shoot eight hundred horses belonging to the Indians. Colonel Eugene Baker ordered three hundred Blackfeet horses killed following his attack on a Piegan winter camp on the Marias River in 1870.

In the 1870s, Smits argued, soldiers routinely led wasteful bison hunts.[12] Soldiers in the plains, however, were too few and too otherwise occupied to kill enough bison to make a difference to the Indians' subsistence. Their organized hunts killed only a few thousand bison in the 1860s and 1870s. Particularly in the southern plains, the Euroamerican slaughter of the bison in the 1870s was not primarily the work of soldiers, but of civilian hunters. The army declined to enforce treaty provisions banning the hunters from Indian territory and provided the civilian hunters with protection and sometimes ammunition. In other words, Sherman commended the hunters but he did not command them. Although the hunters served Sherman's purposes, they did not come to the plains at his behest but rather to satisfy an industrial economy's appetite for natural resources. The expansive American economy, which brought to the plains not only hide hunters but domestic cattle to replace the slaughtered bison, was primarily responsible for the destruction of the 1870s and early 1880s. Economic forces thus spared the army from fighting the extensive Indian war that Governor Evans had predicted in 1864.

Other historians have attributed the destruction of the bison not to uniformed or civilian hunters but primarily to environmental factors. They have pointed to the impact of drought, the predation of wolves, domestic livestock's pressure on plains forage, and exotic bovine diseases as the likeliest causes of the collapse of the bison population in the 1870s and early 1880s.[13] Environmental factors certainly contributed to the demise of the bison, but the decisive role of the environment is far easier to assert than to prove. Neither the predation of wolves nor the competition of other grazers in the 1870s and 1880s was sufficient to cause the destruction of the bison. Drought had periodically afflicted the plains for centuries, causing the bison population to fluctuate considerably, but the species had always recovered. Environmental factors are important when considered in *combination* with anthropogenic causes of the bison's decline, particularly the unprecedented, large-scale onslaught by Euroamerican commercial hide hunters.

---

[12] David D. Smits, "The Frontier Army and the Destruction of the Buffalo: 1865–1883," *Western Historical Quarterly*, 25 (Autumn 1994), 312–338.

[13] Rudolph W. Koucky, "The Buffalo Disaster of 1882," *North Dakota History*, 50 (Winter 1983), 23–30; Dan Flores, "Bison Ecology and Bison Diplomacy: The Southern Plains from 1800 to 1850," *Journal of American History*, 78 (September 1991), 465–485; Richard White, "Animals and Enterprise," in Clyde Milner, et al., eds., *The Oxford History of the American West* (New York: Oxford, 1994), 247–249; Elliott West, *The Way to the West: Essays on the Central Plains* (Albuquerque: University of New Mexico Press, 1995), 72–83.

If the natural environment contributed to the bison's demise, so too did the cultural environment. The army was the forward arm of federal government policy in the plains, which in turn reflected dominant cultural notions of the rightness of the Euroamerican conquest of the West. Most soldiers, emigrants, hunters, and ranchers in the plains shared a belief in the inevitability of Euroamerican triumph over Indians and the wilderness. They took the droughts, blizzards, and grass fires in the 1870s and 1880s that contributed to the destruction of the bison as evidence of the providential extinction of the herds. The belief that domestic livestock were destined to replace the bison sustained the hide hunters' destructive harvest. Some Euroamericans in the 1870s drew on opposing cultural traditions and argued for a policy of humanity toward both Indians and the bison. They argued that the bison and their primary users, the nomads, were already tame. Yet, the competing notion of the bison and the Indians as wild and therefore inferior to domestic cattle and their Euroamerican masters prevailed. Federal authorities institutionalized these cultural notions and channeled the transforming forces of the American industrial economy into the bison range. Together with inherent environmental pressures, those forces pushed the bison to the brink of extinction.

I

A spasm of industrial expansion was the primary cause of the bison's near-extinction in the 1870s and early 1880s. During this period, Euroamericans hunted bison to satisfy an increasing demand for hides in industrializing America. Leather belts were the sinews of nineteenth-century industrial production: mills relied on heavy leather belting to animate their machinery.[14] In 1850, leather manufacturing, based largely in New York and Pennsylvania, was the fifth-largest industry in the United States, after lumber, flour, boots and shoes, and blacksmithing. The tanning industry grew in value in the second half of the nineteenth century. The value of leather belting produced in the United States rose from over $6,500,000 in 1880 to over $8,600,000 in 1890, an increase of 32 percent.[15]

At the same time, however, the number of tanneries in the United States steadily declined, from over five thousand in 1860 to fewer than two thousand in 1890, as the industry was increasingly concentrated in fewer hands. The consolidation of smaller firms into larger conglomerates, to reduce the costs of

[14] Lucius F. Ellsworth, *Craft to National Industry in the Nineteenth Century: A Case Study of the Transformation of the New York State Tanning Industry* (New York: Arno Press, 1975), 193.
[15] See *Report on the Manufactures of the United States at the Tenth Census* (June 1, 1880). Misc. Doc. 42, 47th Cong., 2nd Sess. (Serial 2130), 9; *Report of the Manufacturing Industries in the United States at the Eleventh Census: 1890*, Misc. Doc. 340, 52nd Cong., 1st Sess., (Serial 3024), 126–127.

production, was typical of late nineteenth-century American business. In the tanning industry, however, consolidation was a symptom of crisis. Other industries lowered their production costs through increased mechanization, but tanning remained a largely labor-intensive process. While labor costs remained relatively high, the price of hides, the raw material of tanning, rose. In 1850, Adirondack tanneries paid an average of $2.20 per hide. By 1870, the average price had nearly doubled. Because the demands of the tanning industry outstripped the domestic supply, 70 percent of the hides tanned in the United States in 1850 were imported from Latin America, primarily from the Argentine pampas.[16] Continuing demand, as well as the high cost of cowhide produced in the United States, prompted the industry's interest in the bison as a relatively low-cost source of hides.

Exploitation of the bison required a heavy investment of industrial capital, energy, and knowledge. Before bison hides could become a viable commodity, tanners had to perfect the chemical process of transforming them into leather. Tanners began experimenting on bison hides in 1870. They eventually perfected a process that relied on soaking the hides in a strong lime solution.[17] The result was a porous but highly elastic leather ideally suited to industrial belting. Other technological innovations facilitated industrial America's absorption of the bison. The early single-shot rifles were too light, inaccurate, and difficult to reload to permit large-scale commercial bison hunting. Toward the end of the Civil War, however, American munitions makers developed accurate, large-bore rifles. In the late 1860s, bison hunters used the Springfield Army rifle, a .50-caliber weapon that fired with the power of seventy grains of powder. In 1872, the Sharp Rifle Manufacturing Company developed a still more powerful weapon that became the most common rifle among the bison hunters. The Sharp "big fifty" fired slugs weighing up to one pound with the power of ninety grains of powder, allowing hunters to fire accurate and deadly shots from several hundred yards away.[18] The extension of railroads to the plains allowed easy shipment to the East. The Union Pacific, which joined the Central Pacific in Utah in 1869, traversed the plains through Nebraska; the Kansas Pacific reached Denver in 1870; and the Atchison, Topeka, and Santa Fe reached Dodge City, in western Kansas, in 1872. The financial panic of 1873 stalled railroad expansion into the northern and extreme southern plains; the Texas and Pacific had reached Dallas and the Northern Pacific had extended to Bismarck, Dakota Territory, when the panic and the ensuing economic depression began. Construction on the Texas and

---

[16] Barbara McMartin, *Hides, Hemlocks, and Adirondack History: How the Tanning Industry Influenced the Region's Growth* (Utica, N.Y.: North Country Books, 1992), 8, 27, 88, 108; Victor S. Clark, *History of Manufactures in the United States, 1860–1914* (Washington, D.C.: Carnegie Institute, 1928), 465–466.

[17] Henry R. Proctor, *A Text-Book of Tanning: A Treatise on the Conversion of Skins into Leather, Both Practical and Theoretical* (New York: E. & F.N. Spon, 1885), 144.

[18] Lewis T. Nordyke, "King of the Buffalo Slayers," *Farm and Ranch* (April 1939), 7.

Pacific resumed in 1878 and had reached nearly to El Paso by 1881. The Northern Pacific resumed construction in 1879 and reached Glendive, Montana Territory, in 1880.[19] In sum, the hunting of the bison in the 1870s and early 1880s
was unquestionably the work of an industrial society. The western plains became
a remote extension of the global industrial economy and an object of its demand
for natural resources.

The destruction of the bison in the plains to fuel the demand for hides was
part of a broad pattern of environmental degradation in industrializing America.
The tanning industry consumed not only animal hides but trees and lime in
enormous quantities; it returned unused portions of those resources to local
environments in the form of pollution. The tanning industry initially concentrated in northeastern Pennsylvania and the Adirondack region of New York,
amidst dense forests of Eastern hemlock (*Tsuga canadensis*), because the bark of
hemlock is rich in tannin, the chemical essential to the production of leather.
Heavy harvesting of Eastern hemlock rapidly depleted the species, whose pace
of reproduction was not suited to industrial consumption. The species grows
slowly, reaching maturity in about three hundred years. Following cutting in the
nineteenth century, the second generation faltered because hemlock seedlings
cannot endure the strong sunlight in cut-over areas. The industry's unsustainable consumption of tanbark had depleted accessible supplies of hemlock in the
Adirondacks by the mid-1880s and a few decades later in Pennsylvania. The
New York Times attributed the 1883 failure of Shaw and Brothers, the largest
tanning company in the United States, to the firm's exhaustion of local tanbark
supplies.[20] Deforestation had widespread environmental as well as economic
consequences, ranging from the destruction of local wildlife habitats to
increased erosion and runoff of soil into streams.[21] Tanneries were also a leading
contributor to the noxious condition of rivers in the industrializing Northeast.
Tanneries discharged large amounts of organic pollution, including particles
of lime and animal hair and flesh, into rivers. Significant quantities of organic
pollution, particularly in combination with inorganic pollutants from textile and
paper mills, overwhelmed the capacity of aerobic bacteria to break down con-
taminants in many rivers in the Northeast.[22] Late nineteenth-century tanneries
were thus an environmental malignancy that destroyed bison, razed forests, and
fouled rivers.

[19] Lloyd J. Mercer, *Railroads and Land Grant Policy: A Study in Government Intervention* (New York:
    Academic Press, 1982), 44–54.
[20] *New York Times* (September 16, 1892), quoted in McMartin, *Hides, Hemlocks*, 119; Gordon G.
    Whitney, *From Coastal Wilderness to Fruited Plain: A History of Environmental Change in Temper-
    ate North America, 1500 to the Present* (New York: Cambridge University Press, 1994), 186–188.
[21] George Perkins Marsh, *Man and Nature, or, Physical Geography as Modified by Human Action*, ed.
    David Lowenthal (Cambridge, Mass.: Harvard University Press, 1965), 186–189.
[22] Theodore Steinberg, *Nature Incorporated: Industrialization and the Waters of New England* (New
    York: Cambridge University Press, 1991), 206–209.

Although the industrial system that brought Euroamerican hide hunters to the plains wrought extensive environmental change, Euroamerican hide hunters were not able to shape the environment to their liking completely; they also adapted themselves to the constraints of the western plains. Because the bison spent most of the year fragmented into small foraging groups, Euroamericans, like bands of nomads, dispersed in search of bison in small hunting outfits often based on kinship ties. A typical hunting outfit consisted of a shooter, a cook, and three or four skinners. John Cook signed on to serve in such an outfit in 1870. Charlie Hart, a survivor of the Confederate prisoner-of-war camp at Andersonville, did the shooting. Cook, Warren Dockum, Cyrus Reed, and Reed's "green, gawky" teen-aged brother-in-law Frank Williamson skinned the animals. A man known to Cook only as Hadley drove the team, cooked the outfit's meals, and managed the camp.[23] Such outfits staked out their camps along the rivers where the bison sought water. In the early 1870s, outfits were camped every few miles along the Smoky Hill, Arkansas, Cimarron, Canadian, Washita, and Red rivers.

Although they seemingly overcrowded the bison's range, dispersal was essential to the hunters' success, just as it was to nomadic Indian hunters. The Euroamericans were generally careful not to encroach on each other's hunting grounds. Colonel Richard Irving Dodge wrote, "there are unwritten regulations, recognized as laws, giving to each hunter certain rights of discovery and occupancy."[24] Like the nomads who battled for the control of hunting territory, hunters did not secure those rights without conflict. The skinner S. P. Merry remembered that "some of the buffalo hunters tried to act hoggish and claimed a certain range for their hunting ground, but they could not do it."[25] Disputes over discoveries of hunting grounds likely represented the exercise rather than the absence of informal regulations. Such arrangements were typical of Euroamerican resource exploitation in the nineteenth-century West. Squatters who moved into public lands and miners who established claims also improvised their regulations.[26]

Although they preferred to be called "buffalo runners," most hide hunters did not pursue bison from horseback like the plains nomads. Instead, they employed a method known as the "still hunt." At dawn, a hunter slipped up to the downwind

[23] John R. Cook, *The Border and the Buffalo: An Untold Story of the Southwestern Plains*, ed., Milo M. Quaife (Chicago: Lakeside, 1938), 159–160.

[24] Richard I. Dodge, *The Plains of North America and Their Inhabitants* (Newark: University of Delaware Press, 1989), 151. See also Frank Mayer and Charles B. Roth, *The Buffalo Harvest*, (Denver: Sage, 1958) 47; H. B. Lovett, interview with L. F. Sheffy, 23 June 1934, Pampa, Texas; and J. W. Woody, interview with Haley, 19 October 1926, Panhandle-Plains Historical Society.

[25] Merry, interview with Haley, Amarillo, Texas, 21 August 1926, Panhandle-Plains Historical Society.

[26] See Malcolm Rohrbough, *Days of Gold: The California Gold Rush and the American Nation* (Berkeley: University of California Press, 1997), 15–16; Arthur F. McEvoy, *The Fisherman's Problem: Ecology and Law in the California Fisheries, 1850–1980* (New York: Cambridge University Press, 1986), 95.

side of a group of bison and concealed himself several hundred yards away in a wallow or behind the rise of a bluff. Using a telescopic sight to scan the herd, he located the lead cow of the group and killed her with his first shot, which he aimed below the animal's shoulder to strike her lungs and the bottom of her heart. The remaining animals could hear the report of the rifle but neither see nor smell their enemy. Nor could they rely on their leader to alert them to the danger. As she collapsed, dropping first to one foreleg, then the other, the hunter picked off several more of the bewildered animals, taking care to kill the wariest bison before they smelled blood and led the herd out of range. Such a "stand" varied in productivity, from as few as ten to as many as fifty hides in one morning's work. The hunter's labors ended before noon, when the skinners took over. Ordinarily, they removed hides until sundown.[27]

Like the Indians who brought their bison robes to trading posts such as Bent's Fort, Fort Union, and Fort Pierre, many Euroamerican hunters hauled their hides to centers of trade. Dodge City, Kansas, was initially the capital of the hide trade. The Santa Fe railroad had hardly reached the city in September, 1872, before "the streets of Dodge were lined with wagons, bringing in hides and meat and getting supplies from early morning to late at night," recalled one of the town's early residents. In the winter of 1872–73, the largest hide dealers in Dodge City, Robert Wright and Charles Rath, shipped over two hundred thousand hides on the Santa Fe; Wright estimated that the other dealers in town shipped another two hundred thousand. The editor of a Dodge City newspaper wrote in 1877 that in Wright and Rath's warehouse, "it is no uncommon thing to find from sixty to eighty thousand buffalo robes and hides."[28] (See Figure 5.1.)

The impact of the hide hunters on the herds in the southern plains was devastating. In 1872, Colonel Dodge wrote that the area near Dodge City was thick with bison. By the fall of 1873, however, "where there were myriads of buffalo the year before, there were now myriads of carcasses. The air was foul with sickening stench, and the vast plain which only a short twelve months before teemed with animal life, was a dead, solitary putrid desert." Even those bison who avoided bullets felt the impact of the hunters. Dodge wrote that "Every drink of water, every mouthful of grass is at the expense of life, and the miserable animals continually harassed, are driven into localities far from their haunts, anywhere to avoid the unceasing pursuit."[29] George Lemmon, a Nebraska rancher, wrote that after 1875, bison rendered no tallow and only stringy meat, "as hide hunters

[27] For descriptions of still hunting, see Homer W. Wheeler, *Buffalo Days: Forty Years in the Old West; the Personal Narrative of a Cattleman, Indian Fighter, and Army Officer* (Indianapolis: Bobbs-Merrill, 1923), 80–81; Cook, *The Border and the Buffalo*, 168–176; Dodge, *Plains of North America*, 151–153. See also T. S. Bugher, interview with Haley, 17–18 July 1925; J. W. Woody, interview with Haley, 19 October 1926, Panhandle-Plains Historical Society.
[28] Robert M. Wright, *Dodge City, The Cowboy Capital* (Wichita, 1913), 75; Ford County *Globe*, quoted in Wright, 158.
[29] Dodge, *Plains of North America*, 150–151.

Figure 5.1. Charles Rath and Robert Wright's Dodge City hide yard, 1874. Courtesy of the Kansas State Historical Society

had the few remaining animals almost run to death."[30] Like those of some other mammals and birds such as the passenger pigeon – millions of which market hunters in eastern North America slaughtered in the 1870s – the bison's communal breeding system relied on the assembly of large groups in the summer. Reproductive success likely declined with group size in the 1870s, as unceasing predation prevented the congregation of the herds in the rutting season, upsetting the bison's patterns of migration and reproduction and thus inhibiting a recovery of the bison population.[31]

How many bison did the hide hunters slaughter in the 1870s? The productivity of the outfits varied. W. S. Glenn, who hunted bison in Texas in 1876–77, recalled that "a remarkably good hunter would kill seventy-five to a hundred in a day, an average hunter about fifty, and a common one twenty-five, some hardly enough to run a camp. It was just like in any other business. A good skinner would skin from sixty to seventy-five, an average man from thirty to forty, and a common one from fifteen to twenty-five."[32] Charlie Hart's outfit stacked up 2,003 hides in six weeks, an average of about 50 hides a day.[33] Bat Masterson's crew, which was camped close to Fort Dodge and, unlike most outfits, took the time to take the meat from the carcasses, averaged only 15 hides a day.[34]

Colonel Dodge conservatively estimated the number of hides shipped on the Santa Fe, Kansas Pacific, and Union Pacific railroads between 1872 and 1874 to be 1,378,359. His figures were largely guesswork because only the Santa Fe provided him with a statement of the number of hides shipped. Dodge assumed that the other two lines shipped a number of hides equal to the Santa Fe's 459,453. Yet the Santa Fe's accounting of the hides it shipped in this period – even if accurate – was no reflection of the actual number of bison killed. Dodge noted that in the early years of the slaughter hunters were especially wasteful. Poor hunters wounded two or three bison for every one they killed; the crippled animals later fell to wolves. Skinners ruined hides as they flayed them, or failed to stretch and stake them to dry properly. When skinners failed to finish their work before sundown, wolves had often torn the unskinned carcasses to pieces by the next morning. Dodge estimated that in 1872 every hide shipped to market represented five dead bison. As they learned their craft, the outfits became

[30] Lemmon Papers, State Historical Society of Nebraska, Lincoln.
[31] Douglas B. Bamforth, "Historical Documents and Bison Ecology on the Great Plains," *Plains Anthropologist*, 32 (February 1987), 1–16. For the passenger pigeon, see Jenny Price, "Flight Maps: Encounters with Nature in Modern America" (Ph.D. dissertation, Yale University, 1998); H. Ronald Pulliam and Thomas Caraco, "Living in Groups: Is There an Optimal Group Size?" in J. R. Krebs and N. B. Davis. eds., *Behavioural Ecology: An Evolutionary Approach*, 2d ed. (Sunderland, Mass.: Sinaver, 1984), 134.
[32] Rex W. Strickland, ed., "The Recollections of W. S. Glenn, Buffalo Hunter," *Panhandle-Plains Historical Review*, 22 (1949), 25–31.
[33] Cook, *The Border and the Buffalo*, 171.
[34] Henry H. Raymond, "Diary of a Dodge City Buffalo Hunter, 1872–73" ed., Joseph W. Snell, *Kansas Historical Quarterly*, 31 (Winter 1965): 350–351.

more efficient. In 1873 every hide represented only two dead bison. Altogether, Dodge estimated that hide hunters slaughtered 3,158,730 bison between 1872 and 1874, an average of just over one million animals each year.[35] The Euroamerican hunters resembled the Indian nomads in many ways; small groups dispersed over a broad range, relying on the bison's gregariousness, and brought their hides to centers of trade. Yet the destructive effect of the hide hunters was significantly greater than that of the more numerous nomads.

If the hide hunters' estimates of their own productivity were correct, the impact of commercial hide hunting was still more devastating than Dodge guessed. Glenn estimated that a "common" hunter killed between fifteen and twenty-five bison a day.[36] The Kansas hunter Frank Mayer set twenty-fives hides as his "regular quota."[37] An outfit that accumulated twenty-five hides a day could amass 2,250 hides in three months. Such a figure was not unreasonable. Charlie Hart and his outfit accumulated 3,361 hides in three months.[38] In one season, a hide hunter known as "Kentuck" brought in 3,700 hides.[39] J. W. Woody claimed to have killed 3,200 in the winter of 1876–77.[40] Thomas Linton of Troy, Kansas, killed 3,000 in 1872. Zack Light killed 2,300 in the winter of 1873–74. Joe McCombs killed 4,900 in Texas in the winter of 1877–78. William "Doc" Carver killed 5,700 in 1875. Orlando Brown killed 5,855 bison during a two-month span in 1876 – indeed, the nearly constant report of his .50-caliber rifle during that time rendered him deaf in one ear.[41] A competent hunter could have a single productive season – or inflate his estimates to appear more successful before his peers – but more common perhaps was Josiah Wright Mooar's tally. He estimated that he killed twenty thousand bison in a career as a hunter between 1870 and 1879 – twenty per day if he hunted three months of every year.[42] The Newton *Kansan* reported in 1872 that at least one thousand hide hunters roamed the southern plains.[43] If that number were in the grasslands for three months of the year, they could easily have supplied tanneries with over two million hides every year. Waste and the disruption of the bison's patterns of subsistence and reproduction could have raised their capacity for destruction higher still.

By what means could so many hides have been transported from the southern plains every year, if not on the Santa Fe, Kansas Pacific, and Union Pacific railroad lines that Dodge surveyed? The central plains railroads were the primary means of shipping bison hides to tanneries, but Dodge's exclusive focus on them

[35] Dodge, *Plains of North America*, 155.
[36] Strickland, "Recollections of W. S. Glenn." 25–31.
[37] Mayer and Roth, *Buffalo Harvest*, 49–52.
[38] Cook, *Border and the Buffalo*, 167.
[39] Wheeler, *Buffalo Days*, 80.
[40] Woody, interview with Haley, 11 February 1928, Panhandle-Plains Historical Society.
[41] Wayne Gard, *The Great Buffalo Hunt* (Lincoln: University of Nebraska Press, 1959), 128–129.
[42] J. Wright Mooar, interview with J. Evetts Haley, 25 November 1927, Panhandle-Plains Historical Society.
[43] Newton *Kansan*, November 28, 1872.

obscured humbler means of transportation. Many hide hunting outfits hauled their hides by the cartload not to railway stations, where dealers paid lower prices, but to markets in Texas, Colorado, and New Mexico. The hunter James Cator, for instance, hauled his hides by wagon to dealers in Las Vegas, New Mexico, and Granada, Colorado.[44] Dodge's estimate of the railroad's hide shipment was but a fraction of the number that were collected at temporary hide markets in the southern plains, such as Buffalo Gap in Taylor County and Hide Town in Scurry County, Texas. Like many mining towns in the Mountain West, these places flourished only briefly before being abandoned when the local resource became scarce.

By the mid-1870s, the army of hunters in the southern plains had pressed the herds south into the Texas Panhandle, far from the Kansas Pacific, Union Pacific, and Santa Fe lines. (See Figure 5.2.) The carnage in Texas in the mid-1870s was at least as extensive as that in Kansas in the early 1870s. Merry recalled that in the Texas Panhandle in 1876, "you could hear guns popping all over the country." To acquire the Panhandle hides, Charlie Rath, who had built a general store in Dodge City in July, 1872, and A. C. Reynolds founded a short-lived hide town alternately known as Rath City and Reynolds City. The town, a makeshift collection of buildings constructed of hides and sod, was briefly a center of the southern plains hide trade. Dealers bought over one hundred thousand hides at Rath/ Reynolds City in the winter of 1876–77. "It was really a hide town," recalled Merry. "There were acres of ground covered with hides."[45] Another center of trade in the Panhandle was Fort Griffin, Texas, established as an Army post in 1867. John Irwin, a freighter for the government, compared the hide yards at Fort Griffin to "a great lumber yard. The hides were stacked tier upon tier in rows."[46] Far from the Kansas railroads, the hides that Euroamericans accumulated in the Texas Panhandle found their way out of the southern plains by the cartload.

The hide hunters' slaughter could not be sustained by a southern plains herd that numbered, at most, 15 million in the late 1860s. A herd of that size probably produced no more than four million calves a year. Wolves, accidents, drought, and competition from other grazers may have killed half that number in their first year. In 1871–72, a severe winter followed by drought destroyed, by one estimate, two hundred thousand head of cattle in western Texas. Although the loss of cattle reduced the competition for the bison's range, the blizzard and drought must have killed large numbers of bison as well. In October, 1873, a grass fire spread for 100 miles along the north side of the Kansas Pacific railroad, destroying millions of acres of forage.[47]

[44] Cator Family Papers, Panhandle-Plains Historical Society.
[45] Merry, interview with Haley, 21 August 1926, Panhandle-Plains Historical Society.
[46] John Chadbourne Irwin Papers, Southwest Collection, Texas Tech University.
[47] "Snow on the Plains," New York Times (13 December 1871), 2; "Great Loss of Cattle in Texas, Ibid. (29 March 1872), 1; "Incidents in Frontier Experiences – How the Monarch of the Plains is Hunted," Ibid. (2 April 1874), 3.

Figure 5.2. Hide hunters' camp in the Texas Panhandle, c. 1874. Courtesy of the Western History Collections, University of Oklahoma Library.

A bovine disease, Texas fever, may also have contributed to the demise of the bison in the southern plains. The disease, which affects grazing animals in warm climates, is caused by parasites transmitted by certain ticks belonging to the *Boophilus* genus. The parasites enter a host animal's bloodstream and attack the red blood cells, causing high fever, anemia, jaundice, and weakness. Texas long-horns were immune to the disease caused by the ticks they carried, but when they were driven to market they spread the affliction to Midwestern livestock. Like anthrax, which may have spread among Canadian bison in the 1820s and 1830s, Texas fever could spread without close contact between domestic and feral animals; the ticks could drop off their old hosts and attach themselves to new ones. Bison were susceptible to the disease. In 1905, when preservation-ists established a bison refuge in Oklahoma where longhorns had formerly grazed, they feared that the bison would be infected. Indeed, two of the first fifteen bison introduced to the refuge died of Texas fever.[48] The illness appeared as far north as Wyoming in 1885, brought by Texas cattle, but because the tick was susceptible to a hard frost, Texas fever was never well established in the northern plains. To the south, however, it may have contributed to the decline of the bison.

By the end of the 1870s, the combination of human and environmental pres-sures had reduced the southern plains bison to a few hundred stragglers. The destruction then moved north. Just as the extension of the Santa Fe Railroad to Dodge City spurred the expansion of commercial hide hunting in the southern plains, the extension of the Northern Pacific Railroad to Miles City, Montana Territory, in 1881, made possible the slaughter in the northern plains. "The prairies ... are covered with the carcasses of bison," wrote a *New York Times* correspondent from Miles City in April, 1880. Yet the hide hunters in the north-ern plains did not equal the destructiveness of their colleagues to the south. The *Times* correspondent estimated that the hunters brought in only ten thousand hides in the winter of 1880.[49] The naturalist William Hornaday thought that the slaughter was greater. He estimated that between 1881 and 1883, hide hunters in the northern plains shipped nearly three hundred thousand hides to the east.[50] The hide hunter Vic Smith wrote in his memoirs that the Montana hunters killed four hundred thousand bison in the winter of 1881–82.[51] Yet in 1884, the Northern Pacific carried only three hundred hides. Although hunters accumu-lated fewer hides than to the south, something certainly destroyed the northern plains bison. A rancher who traveled a thousand miles across the northern plains

[48] T. S. Palmer, "Our National Herds of Buffalo," *Tenth Annual Report of the American Bison Society, 1915–1916* (New York: American Bison Society, 1916), 44–46.
[49] "Montana's Indian Puzzle," *New York Times* (4 April 1880), 2.
[50] William T. Hornaday, *The Extermination of the American Bison, with a Sketch of its Discovery and Life History* (Washington, D.C.: Government Printing Office, 1887).
[51] Victor Grant Smith, *The Champion Buffalo Hunter*, ed. Jeanette Prodgers (Helena, Mt.: Twodot, 1997), 98.

in the early 1880s was, by his own account, "never out of sight of a dead buffalo and never in sight of a live one."[52]

In the northern plains, environmental pressures – both inherent in the grassland and anthropogenic – conspired with hunters to reduce the number of bison to a few stragglers. The decline of the northern plains bison resulted primarily from the combination of drought and ranches. The dominant shortgrasses of the western plains are well adapted to the drought-prone climate. By concentrating roots at the top of the soil, and keeping leafage minimal, shortgrass species conserve their moisture and take advantage of scarce rainfall.[53] Nonetheless, acute drought can devastate the shortgrasses upon which grazing animals such as the bison depend. When drought shrivels shortgrasses in the western plains, it also opens niches for them in the ordinarily more humid grasslands to the east. The mixed-grass plains – so-called because they lie between the semi-arid, shortgrass, western plains and the humid, tall grass, eastern prairies – are far enough from the Rocky Mountains that their dominant species, such as little bluestem, can grow to a height of one to two feet. During severe drought, however, little bluestem is reduced to a tiny proportion of the mixed-grass community, while shortgrass species, which thrive in relatively dry conditions, invade and dominate.[54] Thus in the historic plains drought did not so much destroy the bison's range as it temporarily shifted it to the east.

So long as bison were able to move eastward in search of forage, they could mitigate the impact of drought. By the late 1860s, however, they faced an obstacle. Lone Dog's winter count recorded the arrival of Texas cattle to the region north of the Platte River in 1868–69.[55] In succeeding years, bison increasingly faced competition for rangeland from domestic livestock. Between 1874 and 1880, the number of cattle in Wyoming increased from ninety thousand to over five hundred thousand.[56] By 1883, over five hundred thousand cattle grazed in eastern Montana.[57] Between 1874 and 1890, the cattle population in southern

---

[52] Theodore Roosevelt, *Hunting Trips of a Ranchman* (New York: G. P. Putnam's Sons, 1885).

[53] James K. Detling, "Processes Controlling Blue Grama Production in the Shortgrass Prairie," in *Perspectives in Grassland Ecology*, ed. Norman R. French (New York: Springer-Verlag, 1979), 25–39; Victor Shelford, *Ecology of North America* (Urbana: University of Illinois Press, 1963), 340; Philip L. Sims, J. S. Singh, and W. K. Lauenroth, "The Structure and Function of Ten Western North American Grasslands I: Abiotic and Vegetational Characteristics," *Journal of Ecology*, 66 (March 1978), 270; Sims and Singh, "The Structure and Function of Ten Western North American Grasslands II: Intra-Seasonal Dynamics in Primary Producer Compartments," *Journal of Ecology*, 66 (July 1978), 565; O. E. Sala and W. K. Lauenroth, "Small Rainfall Events: An Ecological Role in Semiarid Regions," *Oecologia*, 53 (June 1982), 301–304.

[54] Robert T. Coupeland, "Effects of Changes in Weather upon Grasslands in the Northern Plains," in Howard B. Sprague, ed., *Grasslands* (Washington, D.C.: American Association for the Advancement of Science, 1959), 293.

[55] Mallery, "Picture-Writing of the American Indians," *Tenth Annual Report of the Bureau of American Ethnology* (Washington, D.C.: Government Printing Office, 1889) 285–286.

[56] Ernest Staples Osgood, *The Day of the Cattleman* (Chicago: University of Chicago Press, 1970), 53.

[57] William Cronon, *Nature's Metropolis: Chicago and the Great West* (New York: Norton, 1991), 220.

Alberta rose to one hundred thousand.[58] Domestic cattle not only encroached on the bison's range but occupied much of the mixed-grass region to which bison migrated during periods of drought. Drought struck the northern plains in the 1870s and early 1880s. Climatologists recorded droughts in eastern Wyoming and northeastern Colorado in 1873, 1879, and 1882. The handful of stations in Montana recorded low summer precipitation in 1877–78 and 1881–83.[59] During his two-year sojourn in the plains beginning in 1882, Theodore Roosevelt killed only a few bison for trophies, but his ranch on the North Dakota-Montana border was one of many that likely prevented northern plains bison from migrating to ranges in the mixed-grass plains to escape drought. Moreover, by occupying the bison's range, cattle made a recovery of the bison population unlikely.

Other inherent environmental causes of bison mortality – blizzard and grass fire – also took their toll on the northern plains bison in the 1870s and early 1880s. When Romanzo Bunn settled in Dakota Territory in 1880, he discovered the bleached skeletons of hundreds of bison in his half-section. The skeletons were largely intact, and Bunn found no broken bones or bullet-marked ribs among the remains. Bunn attributed the deaths to blizzard, such as the one he endured in his first winter in the northern plains in 1880–81. The blizzard that winter covered the plains with a foot of snow; drifts were 20 feet high in some places.[60] Grass fire in Alberta in 1878 destroyed many bison and drove survivors south into the Missouri River valley toward drought, the bullets of hide hunters, and the competition of domestic livestock.

Despite the influx of domestic cattle to the northern plains, exotic bovine diseases probably played less of a role in the decline of the bison there than they did to the south. A retired pathologist, Rudolph Koucky, suggested in 1983 that bovine disease was a factor in the destruction of the bison in the northern plains.[61] However, recent evidence suggests that brucellosis, a disease that causes spontaneous abortion, has only a minor impact on the bison's reproduction. Bison who survived the nineteenth century had high rates of infection of brucellosis, but because of the close contact usually necessary to transmit the disease, transmission more likely occurred not in the 1870s or 1880s but later, when ranchers corralled surviving bison in close proximity to domestic cattle.[62] Similarly, bovine tuberculosis, which was first diagnosed in bison at the Buffalo National Park in Wainwright, Alberta, in 1923, probably did not infect feral

[58] David. H. Breen, *The Canadian Prairie West and the Ranching Frontier, 1874–1924* (Toronto: University of Toronto Press, 1983), 65–66.
[59] Cary J. Mock, "Drought and Precipitation Fluctuations in the Great Plains During the Late Nineteenth Century," *Great Plains Research*, 1 (February 1991), 43–47.
[60] Bunn, "The Tragedy of the Plains," *Forest and Stream*, 63 (29 October 1904), 360–361.
[61] Koucky, "Buffalo Disaster of 1882," 23–30.
[62] Mary Meagher and Margaret E. Meyer, "On the Origin of Brucellosis in Bison of Yellowstone National Park: A Review," *Conservation Biology*, 8 (September 1994), 645–653; Meagher and Meyer, "Brucellosis in Free-Ranging Bison (*Bison bison*) in Yellowstone, Grand Teton, and Wood Buffalo National Parks: A Review," *Journal of Wildlife Diseases*, 31 (1995), 579–598.

bison in the Great Plains in the nineteenth century. Many of the bison at Wainwright descended from several hundred raised in Montana and purchased by the Canadian government in 1906. Most of the Montana herd went to Wainwright, but some went to Elk Island National Park. The Elk Island bison never developed tuberculosis, suggesting that the disease occurred only after the bison arrived in Wainwright. The infection probably came to Wainwright with a shipment of bison from a Canadian rancher who had raised captured bison calves by having his domestic cows nurse them – a common means of transmission of bovine tuberculosis.[63]

In the western plains, anthropogenic and environmental causes of bison mortality worked in concert. When Euroamerican hunters and ranchers added their pressures on the bison to the inherent causes of bison mortality in the dynamic plains, the bison population collapsed almost completely in only a decade and a half. When Hornaday surveyed the bison population in January, 1889, he discovered only twenty-five in the Texas Panhandle, twenty in the foothills of Colorado, ten between the Yellowstone and Missouri rivers, twenty-six near the Bighorn Mountains, and two hundred in Yellowstone National Park.[64] In just a few years, two dynamic forces – the plains environment and the American industrial economy – had combined to nearly obliterate the millions of bison that had inhabited the grasslands.

II

Economic behavior is embedded in culture, an assembly of principles and expectations that, while ever changing and often contested, set standards for conduct in the economic arena. As a consequence of the acceleration of industrialization in the second half of the nineteenth century, economic standards became the subject of political debate. In this period, Euroamericans argued over the legitimacy of labor unions, the promotion of railroad construction, the protection of industries from international competition, and the regulation of the money supply. As the scope of the hide hunters' destruction of the bison became clear, Euroamericans clashed over another issue: the wisdom of permitting the slaughter to continue. Those who opposed the destruction drew on two reform efforts of the post-Civil War United States: animal protection and Indian humanitarianism. The advocates of the slaughter appealed to an emerging belief that the extinction of the bison and the subjugation of Indians, however brutal, was necessary to open the Great Plains to Euroamerican settlement. The triumph of this group's beliefs permitted the rapid destruction of the bison in the 1870s and early 1880s.

[63] Seymour Hadwen, "Tuberculosis in the Buffalo," *Journal of the American Veterinary Medical Association*, 100 (January 1942), 19–22.

[64] Hornaday, *Extermination of the Bison*, 513.

An enthusiasm for animal protection was the most important obstacle to the destruction of the bison. American efforts to prevent cruelty to animals began in the 1820s. Following the example of the Royal Society for the Prevention of Cruelty to Animals, founded in England in 1824, eighteen states enacted laws regulating the treatment of horses, sheep, and cattle between 1828 and 1861. Prominent antebellum reformers endorsed kindness to animals; Charles Lowell preached a sermon on the topic in Boston in 1837. Yet animal protection became a bona fide reform movement in the United States only after the Civil War. Henry Bergh, the son of a wealthy immigrant shipbuilder, founded the American Society for the Prevention of Cruelty to Animals in New York in 1866. Pennsylvania and Massachusetts SPCAs followed in 1867 and 1868, respectively, organized in both cases by wealthy, reform-minded women. By 1874, SPCA chapters were located in more than thirty of the largest cities in the Northeast and Upper Midwest.

The concentration of animal protection societies in the centers of American industry was not coincidental. Nineteenth-century animal protection was largely a reaction to industrialization. Nearly all reformers were middle-class city-dwellers. Critical and fearful of urban mechanization and poverty, they rued the loss of rural innocence, particularly farmers' solicitude for their animals. Preventing cruel treatment of animals in urban America would, they hoped, counteract the aggressive, competitive amorality of the marketplace. According to the historian James Turner, the advocates of animal protection "were conformists, comfortable, at heart happy with their up-to-date industrial world." Sensitive to the ill effects of industrialism, however, they "wanted to protest the sordid acquisitiveness of Victorian capitalism, but not too loudly."[65]

Animal protection was a decidedly feminizing movement, in its sizable female constituency and its invocation of a domestic ethic of anticruelty. Caroline Earle White in Philadelphia and Emily Appleton in Boston were early organizers of SPCAs in their cities, although both were formally excluded from the main sectors of the societies they helped to found. In 1869, White became the president of the Women's Branch of the Pennsylvania SPCA. In a short time, the Women's Branch surpassed the effectiveness, energy, and fund-raising ability of the original Pennsylvania SPCA.[66] Anticruelty was, above all, an explicit effort to extend the nineteenth-century ideology of feminine compassion to men and boys who were presumed to be responsible for most of the cruelties practiced upon animals. Pet-keeping and stories of the cruel treatment of innocent animals were intended to instill in boys an aversion to mistreating animals. Reformers were particularly concerned about boyhood hunting, which, they feared, established a taste for killing. Reformers thus portrayed hunting as a violent intrusion

---

[65] James Turner, *Reckoning with the Beast: Animals, Pain, and Humanity in the Victorian Mind* (Baltimore: Johns Hopkins University Press, 1980), 31–57.
[66] Ibid.

into the animal family. Harriet Beecher Stowe published a story in an American Sunday School Union tract that told of birds rendered motherless by the casual thoughtlessness of young hunters. The analogy to the human domestic sphere was obvious: to visit suffering on a family of animals was akin to violating the sanctity of the human family.[67]

Although anticruelty tracts criticized hunting, they focused their attentions largely on urban and suburban animals: pets, carriage horses, and stray dogs. To prevent the hunting of wild animals was, at first, not a significant part of their mission. But the destruction of the bison excited Bergh to action. In the early 1870s, he received a number of letters decrying the slaughter. "We speak on behalf of the buffalo, antelope, and various wild game of the western prairies," a group of women from Freeport, Illinois, recently returned from a trip through the plains, wrote to Bergh in December, 1872. "Visiting these sickening scenes of slaughter, we find the Plains thickly strewn with carcasses of buffalo, deer, and antelope."[68] High-ranking army officers stationed in the plains also wrote to Bergh objecting to the slaughter. When General William Hazen and Lieutenant-Colonel A. G. Brackett protested to Bergh, he forwarded copies of the letters to ASPCA members, newspapers, and Congressional supporters, hoping to spur the creation of legislation to regulate the hide hunters.

The officers' letters in particular revealed how the effort on behalf of the bison struggled to extend the rhetoric of anticruelty – previously applied only to farm animals, pets, songbirds, and some urban draft animals – to a wild animal. Hazen described the bison as "a noble and harmless animal, timid, and as easily taken as a cow." He called the hunt a "wicked and wanton waste." Brackett also took care to present the bison as both "harmless and defenseless": a gentle, nearly domesticated animal. (See Figure 5.3) "[T]here is as much honor and danger in killing a Texas steer as there is in killing a buffalo," wrote Brackett. "It would be equally as good sport," he argued, "to ride into a herd of tame cattle and commence shooting indiscriminately." The officers' analogies to domestic animals, which were protected in many states by anticruelty legislation, and their conclusion that the killing of bison was not simply needless but "wicked" (according to Hazen) and, more to the point, "cruel" (according to Brackett), revealed their debt to the arguments of the anticruelty advocates.[69] The officers' letters also

---

[67] Katherine C. Grier, "'Kindness to All Around': A Domestic Ethic of Kindness to Animals, 1820–1870," Paper presented to the Shelby Cullom Davis Center for Historical Studies seminar "Animals and Human Society," Princeton University, Princeton, N.J., April 25, 1997. Cited by permission of the author.

[68] Edward P. Buffett manuscript, "Bergh's War on Vested Cruelty," vol. 6, American Society for the Prevention of Cruelty to Animals Archives, New York. See also Zulma Steele, *Angel in Top Hat* (New York: Harper, 1942), 162.

[69] "Slaughter of Buffaloes," *Harper's Weekly,* 16 (24 February 1872), 165–166. A. G. Brackett, "Buffalo Slaughter," *New York Times* (7 February 1872). "Protection of Buffalo" *Congressional Record* (March 10, 1874), 2106.

THE LAST BUFFALO.
"Don't shoot, my good fellow! Here, take my 'robe,' save your ammunition, and let me go in peace."

Figure 5.3. Thomas Nast, "The Last Buffalo," Harper's Weekly, June 6, 1874

revealed that the extension of SPCA rhetoric of domestic kindness to a wild animal was expanding the organization's ideology in unanticipated ways.

Animal protection was a relatively new passion in the 1870s. So, too, was Indian humanitarianism. The 1870s were liminal years in United States Indian policy, marking a transformation from a policy of separation to one of assimilation. From the beginning of the nineteenth century until the Civil War, policymakers sought to confine Indian populations to reservations in order to segregate them from Euroamerican settlers. Indian policy in the 1870s was, in one sense, a continuation of this program. "Our civilization is ever aggressive, while the savage nature is tenacious of traditional customs and rights," wrote Columbus Delano, the Secretary of the Interior, in 1873. "This condition of things calls loudly for more efficient efforts to separate Indians from whites by placing them on suit-able reservations."[70] Yet in the years after the Civil War, the United States also embarked on a so-called "peace policy," a cooperative effort between the federal government and Protestant missionaries to Christianize and educate reserva-tion Indians. The peace policy foreshadowed the ambitious, albeit deeply flawed program of Indian assimilation that began in the 1880s and continued into the twentieth century.[71]

To a considerable extent, Indian humanitarianism emerged from the United States' experience in the Civil War. Tired of bloodshed, the editors of the *New York Times* condemned an army attack on a Piegan winter camp in 1870 as a "sickening slaughter" – the same terms the Freeport women used to describe the killing of bison. To subdue Indians by violence imperiled "our standing before the world as a Christian nation." The heightened interest in racial justice for recently emancipated slaves also influenced Indian humanitarianism. "We have long been doing justice to the negro," the *Times* wrote later in 1870, on the occa-sion of a visit to Washington by the Oglala leader Red Cloud. "Is it not almost time to see what we can do for the Indian?"[72]

The humanitarianism of the peace policy was not, however, a complete depar-ture from the history of hostilities between Indians and Euroamericans. "What we must do if we mean to save the remnant of the Indians," the *Times* editorial-ized in 1870, "is to gather them all into a small district which we can really police and protect, and there teach them the arts of civilized life." What the *Times* euphemistically termed "gathering" was, in plain words, the application of mil-itary force. Indeed, the editors endorsed military efforts to confine the plains nomads to reservations; they approved of the 1876 campaign to subdue the "hos-tile," off-reservation Sioux led by Crazy Horse and Sitting Bull. As far as the reformers were concerned, only reservation Indians deserved the benefits of material support and Christian education. Those nomads who continued to resist the pressure to go to reservations, the *Times* concluded, remained "utterly out of the reach of every humanizing influence." Following the Sioux defeat of Custer at the Little Bighorn in June, 1876, this already straitened channel of humanity was closed. In the wake of Custer's death, the *Times* counseled that the off-reservation Sioux deserved "condign" punishment.[73]

---

[70] *Annual Report of the Secretary of the Interior, 1873*, 43rd Cong., 1st Sess. (Serial 1601), ix.

[71] For nineteenth-century Indian assimilation, see Frederick E. Hoxie, *A Final Promise: The Cam-paign to Assimilate the Indians, 1880–1920* (Lincoln: University of Nebraska Press, 1984); Henry E. Fritz, *The Movement for Indian Assimilation, 1860–1890* (Philadelphia: University of Pennsyl-vania Press, 1963).

[72] "The Slaughter of the Piegans," *New York Times* (24 February 1870), 4; "The Piegan Slaughter and Its Apologists," Ibid. (10 March 1870), 4; "The Montana Massacre–Col. Baker's Report," Ibid. (12 March 1870), 4; "The Last Appeal of Red Cloud," Ibid. (17 June 1870), 4.

[73] "The Oldest of American Difficulties," Ibid. (22 May 1870), 4; "The Indian War," Ibid. (17 July 1876), 2.

Although all humanitarians wanted Indians of the western plains eventually to renounce nomadic bison hunting in favor of agriculture, some strongly advocated immediate cessation of the slaughter of the bison. They believed that such destruction was counterproductive, driving desperate Indians to acts of violence. The editors of *Harper's Weekly* contended in 1874 that "the indiscriminate slaughter of the buffalo ... has been the direct occasion of many Indian wars. Deprived of one of their chief means of subsistence through the agency of white men, the tribes naturally take revenge by making raids on white settlements and carrying off stocks."[74] *Harper's* asked its readers to take an unprecedented step: to extend the sentimentality and morality of animal protection and Indian humanitarianism from peaceful reservation Indians to off-reservation hunters, and from domestic to wild animals. More typical was the view of the *Nation*, however, which like *Harper's* attributed Indian violence to the demise of the bison. Far from criticizing the destruction of the nomads' resources, however, the *Nation* urged that nonreservation Indians first be "hunted down," and then subjected to a redoubled effort at cultural assimilation.[75] The wild Indians of the plains required taming.

These contradictions in the reformers' approach to Indians, which would eventually be the undoing of the effort to halt the hide hunters, were embodied in the bison's unlikely legislative champion, United States Representative Greenburg Lafayette Fort. A Republican from central Illinois, Fort's four terms in the House between 1873 and 1881 were the pinnacle of his political career. Two characteristics distinguished Fort's tenure in Congress. First, he was a practitioner of symbolic politics: the introduction of divisive, openly partisan legislation that stirred his supporters, irritated his opponents, and had little hope of passage. Fort, like many Republicans, most often engaged in such political symbolism when he "waved the bloody shirt," a postwar euphemism for the appeal to wartime loyalties. A Union veteran who had answered the call for volunteers in April, 1861, Fort introduced a resolution requiring members of the House to give preference to wounded Union soldiers when appointing aides and subordinates. He repeatedly proposed legislation granting pensions to all disabled, honorably discharged Union veterans. Although his bills ultimately failed, they galvanized Fort's supporters and won him national recognition from Union veterans.

Second, Fort saw himself as a reformer, while many of his colleagues saw him as no more than a crank. His oftentimes inane motions, amendments, and objections ("I object to everything that is out of order," he once said in debate) provoked the exasperation of the chamber. Arriving in Washington to take his seat in Congress in 1873, when Republican strength and enthusiasm for Reconstruction

---

[74] *Harper's Weekly* (12 December 1874), 1022–1023.
[75] "Our Indian Wards," *The Nation* (13 July 1876), 20–22.

in the South was waning, he initially turned his attention to the reform of the Western territories. The West in the 1870s was riddled with corruption. Territorial governments and the Indian Office were filled with inept political appointees; politicians at all levels of government enriched themselves by corrupt dealings in railroad construction. Indeed, Western railroad graft reached the highest levels of the Grant administration. Fort introduced bills – none of which became law – designed to prevent territories or municipalities in the territories from entering into debt to finance railroad construction; to create a new government for the Indian Territory; and to eliminate the corruption of territorial governments entirely by rapidly admitting territories to statehood. By 1877, however, Fort had shifted his reformist energies to the advocacy of paper currency and the coinage of silver. Although these positions put him at odds with the tight money policies of leading Republicans, they were politically astute stances for a representative from rural Illinois where farmers organized powerful political lobbies opposing the deflation of the currency.[76] Fort's ultimate shift from Western issues to inflation demonstrated that his reformism, although probably genuine, was nonetheless flexible enough to appeal to the shifting concerns of his constituents.

At almost every turn, Fort's grandstanding encountered the opposition of Columbus Delano, the Secretary of the Interior between 1870 and 1875. Fort regularly seized on popular causes to further his appeal, but Delano's career was an embattled one, characterized by his unflinching advocacy of unpopular positions. Before joining Grant's cabinet, Delano served three terms as an Ohio Congressional representative; from 1845–47 as a Whig from a largely Democratic district, and from 1865–69 as a Republican. Like Fort, he shaped his political views around sectional issues, antagonizing not only Southerners but Northern Democrats in the process. Unlike Fort, he was not adept at bolstering his popularity among his constituents. In his first term in Congress, he opposed the Mexican War as a Southern conspiracy. After the Civil War, he often sided with the radical faction of House Republicans on issues concerning the Reconstruction of the South. After leaving the House to join the Grant administration, as Commissioner of Internal Revenue from 1869 to 1870 and thereafter as Secretary of the Interior, Delano brought contention with him. Internal Revenue and Interior were two of the most venal branches of the federal government in a period distinguished for its extensive public corruption. Although Delano was probably an honest man – a rare commodity in Grant's cabinet – he was unmindful of his subordinates' corruption and uninterested in rooting it out. The liberal press and backbenchers such as Fort therefore subjected Delano to a barrage of criticism for his failure to weed out corruption. Criticism of Delano peaked in 1875. In April, the *New York Tribune* accused the Secretary's son,

---

[76] *Congressional Record*, 44th Cong., 1st Sess. (January 31, March 13, April 24, 1876), 773, 1678, 1813; Ibid., 45th Cong., 1st Sess. (November 23, 1877), 622–631.

John, of benefiting from corrupt Interior Department transactions in Wyoming. That summer, the House investigated Delano's supervision of contracts to supply Indian reservations with beef. Although concluding that Delano had awarded contracts to high bidders, the House exonerated him of any technical wrongdoing.[77] In September, however, the Yale paleontologist O. C. Marsh renewed the charges against Delano during an interview with Grant. The *Nation* reported on the exchange and called for Delano to resign. Under unrelenting pressure, Delano offered his resignation, but Grant refused to accept it. Delano therefore soldiered on in a job he no longer desired, inured to criticism, resigned to his unpopularity, and, quite unlike Fort, unmovable in his policies despite his many detractors in the government and the press.[78]

The slaughter of the bison brought Fort and Delano into direct opposition. Fort introduced bills in Congress in 1874 and 1876 making it "unlawful for any person who is not an Indian to kill, wound, or in any manner destroy any female buffalo, of any age, found at large within the boundaries of any of the Territories of the United States." Fort's idiosyncratic brand of reformism and symbolic politics, although alienating members of both parties, also garnered initial widespread, if shallow, support for his bison legislation. As symbolic politics, the bills offered Fort's reform-minded colleagues in the House the opportunity to castigate the Secretary of the Interior on another matter related to Indian subsistence. To Indian humanitarians, the bills restored the integrity of the treaties of Medicine Lodge and Fort Laramie. To anticruelty advocates, the bills outlawed an ignoble carnage. Reformers in both parties supported the bills. In 1874, when Republicans were in the majority in the House, and 1876, when Democrats were in the majority, the Committee on the Territories unanimously approved the bills and a majority of the House supported the legislation; a majority of the Senate voted in favor of the 1874 bill.[79]

The bills drew support because they marshaled the arguments for both animal protection and Indian humanitarianism. Fort made his sympathies plain in 1876, saying "For my part I favor the society which has in view the prevention of cruelty to animals." Most legislators who spoke in favor of the bills were Northeastern or Midwestern reformers with similar sentiments. George Hoskins, a Republican from New York, perhaps taking his cue from the letter of Lieutenant-Colonel Brackett, which was read into the record during the course of the 1874

---

[77] "Contracts for Indian Supplies and Transportation for the Fiscal Years Ending June 30, 1873, and June 30, 1874," House Report No. 778, 43rd Cong., 1st Sess. (Serial 1627).

[78] Daniel W. Delano, Jr., *Franklin Roosevelt and the Delano Influence* (Pittsburgh: James S. Nudi, 1946), 101–133. Allan Nevins, *Hamilton Fish: The Inside History of the Grant Administration*, vol. 2 (New York: Frederick Ungar, 1936).

[79] In 1874, House Republicans held a 100-seat majority, and Fort's bison bill passed by a voice vote. In 1876, House Democrats held a 60-seat majority, and the bison bill passed by a nearly two-to-one vote. For the debates on the bison bills, see *Congressional Record* (March 10, 1874), 2105–2109; "Slaughter of Buffaloes," Ibid. (February 23, 1876), 1237–1241.

debate, compared Fort's bill to extant state game- and animal-protection laws. Fort, who preferred a hyperbolic style of debate, described the killing of bison as "wanton wickedness," a term usually found in the SPCA's tracts. One of Fort's reform-minded colleagues in the House, the Republican Joseph Hawley of Connecticut, brought the issue closer to home, alluding both to motherhood and rural innocence in describing a hide hunter as a man likely to "shoot down his mother's cow in the barn-yard." Invoking the high moral ground of the SPCA, the supporters of Fort's bill portrayed the killing of bison as a thoroughly sordid business. Supporters of the bill further appealed to the arguments of Indian humanitarians. In his opening address on his 1874 bill, Fort articulated the strongest argument of the humanitarians: "I am not in favor of civilizing the Indian by starving him to death." Fort's colleague, the Republican David Lowe of Kansas, chimed in that the destruction of the nomads' means of subsistence "will not do in this age of civilization and Christianity."

On the floor of the House the question of animal protection was morally – or at least politically – unassailable, but Indian policy was a nettlesome problem. Fort's supporters were uncomfortable as partisans of the Indians. Lowe denied that his support of the bill was "simply a matter of sentiment in behalf of the Indian." In 1876, Fort declared that "I have no especial sentimentality in my bosom for the Indian; I have no especially friendly feeling for the savage." In the course of the 1874 debates, the Ohio Republican James Garfield – who six years later would be elected president – echoed Secretary Delano, posing the question that ultimately derailed Fort's legislation. However cruel the actions of the hide hunters may be, he pointed out, they were destroying the primary resource of the plains nomads and thereby forcing them to reservations. "If the barbarism of killing buffalo for mere wanton sport has any compensation in it," he suggested, "perhaps it may be this is a compensation worthy of our consideration."[80]

The effort to confine Indians of the plains to reservations posed a dilemma to Indian humanitarians. Forcing Indians to reservations and the aims of the peace policy were indeed complementary. Quite apart from the peace policy's hostility to Indian cultural traditions, it was not the entirely benign program that its appellation suggested. As Delano explained in 1873, the "so-called peace policy sought, first, to place the Indians upon reservations as rapidly as possible." Only on reservations were Indians treated to the government-sponsored advice and aid of missionaries. Toward nonreservation Indians, the federal government's policy was punitive. Delano wrote, "whenever it is found that any tribe or band of Indians persistently refuse to go upon a reservation and determine to continue their nomadic habits ... then the policy contemplates the treatment of such tribe or band with all needed severity ... thereby teaching them that it is better to follow the advice of the government." Delano saw the destruction of the bison as

---

[80] *Congressional Record* 43rd Cong., 1st Sess. (March 10, 1874), 2106–2107.

a means of pacification: "The rapid disappearance of game from the former hunting-grounds must operate largely in favor of our efforts to confine the Indians to smaller areas, and compel them to abandon their nomadic customs."[81]

Delano interpreted the treaties of Medicine Lodge and Fort Laramie as permitting the destruction of the bison by Euroamerican hide hunters. He applauded the results of their efforts, writing that he "would not seriously regret the total disappearance of the buffalo from our western prairies, in its effect on the Indians, regarding it rather as a means of hastening their sense of dependence upon the products of the soil and their own labors." He deplored the presence of hide hunters on Indian reservations but noted that the Treaties of Medicine Lodge did not exclude them from the area south of the Arkansas River designated as the hunting territory of the southern plains nomads. In regard to the northern plains, he regretted the stipulation of the Treaty of Fort Laramie of 1868 granting the Sioux the exclusive right to hunt north of the Platte River so long as the bison remained there in significant numbers. He therefore stated – quite unilaterally – that the number of bison ranging north of the Platte was insufficient to support the Sioux, and recommended in both his 1873 and 1874 reports that Congress abrogate that article of the treaty.[82] Congress did not act, so in 1875, Delano and Grant told a Sioux delegation to Washington led by Red Cloud and Spotted Tail that the region between the Platte and Niobrara rivers no longer contained enough bison to support the Sioux and must be ceded to the United States.[83]

Delano had many sympathizers in Congress. In 1874, the Missouri Republican Isaac Parker called his policy sound. In 1876, the Texas Democrat John Hancock explicitly rejected humanitarianism in favor of Delano's policies. "I hope, sir, there is no humanitarian sentimentality that would induce legislation for the protection of the buffalo," he said to Fort. "If the theory upon which the Government is now treating the Indians is a proper one, and I am inclined to believe it is the best, the sooner we get rid of the buffalo entirely the better it will be for the Indian and for the white man, too." Although Fort's support was strong enough to ensure passage in both houses in 1874 and in the House in 1876, well-placed opponents defeated the bills. President Grant, who had made his support for Delano's policy plain to Indian delegations to Washington, killed the 1874 bill with a pocket veto.[84] In February, 1876, Fort's bill passed in the House but never came to a vote in the Senate Committee on the Territories. After Custer's defeat at the Little Bighorn in late June, the bill had no chance of passage.

---

[81] Delano, *Annual Report of the Secretary of the Interior, 1873*, iii–ix; Ibid., *1872*, 42nd Cong., 1st Sess. (Serial 1560), 5.

[82] Ibid., *1873*, vi–viii; Ibid., *1874*, 43rd Cong., 2nd Sess. (Serial 1639), xi.

[83] "The President's Last Interview with the Sioux," *New York Times* (3 June 1875), 1.

[84] "Slaughter of Buffaloes," *Congressional Record*, 44th Cong., 1st Sess. (February 23, 1876),1239; "Red Cloud: The Indians in Washington Visit the White House," Ibid. (29 May 1872), 1; "The Sioux and the White House," Ibid. (27 May 1875), 5.

Delano's policy of relying on the exhaustion of the herds in order to relegate Indians to reservations was entirely consistent with a mid-century image of the bison that was radically different from the SPCA's depiction of a gentle ruminant. Popular accounts of the bison described a violent species consistently losing its battles against human hunters and the forces of nature. This view of the bison pervaded an 1869 description in a popular journal. Theodore Davis, the author of the article, argued that "the buffalo is fast disappearing." To the pressure of Euroamerican hunters Davis added Indian hunters and environmental factors: blizzard, drowning, and the predation of wolves. The bison competed among themselves as well. Describing the contests between bulls to establish a rank order during the rutting season, Davis wrote: "The bulls fight viciously, and are attended during these combats by an admiring concourse of wolves, who are ever ready to come in at the death of either of the combatants, or will even take a chance in and finish any killing that has been imperfectly done." One of the illustrations accompanying the article showed a "Battle for Life": a bison fighting off an attack by a pack of wolves.[85] In the 1860s and 1870s, such scenes were a staple of popular depictions of the bison.[86] (See Figure 5.4.)

The inevitability of the bison's extinction pervaded an 1876 study of the species by Joel Allen, a Harvard University zoologist. Allen's book was a hybrid of neo-Lamarckian and natural selection theories and a combination of scientific and popular accounts of the bison. Allen came to his subject while analyzing the fossil remains of extinct species of bison; the extirpation of *Bison latifrons* and *Bison antiquus* foreshadowed the fate of *Bison americanus*. His study was largely a recitation of the bison's disappearance from one region of North America after another, owing to both Euroamerican and Indian hunters and environmental pressures. He called the species "sluggish" – in other words, unfit – and concluded that "the period of extinction will soon be reached."[87] Allen's views exemplified both the popular and academic understanding of Charles Darwin's theories of natural selection. Most Americans conflated Darwin's ideas with those of Herbert Spencer and the neo-Lamarckian naturalists such as Edward Cope and Alpheus Hyatt, viewing natural selection as a process that weeded out the unfit in favor of ever-more-excellent forms of life. According to the neo-Lamarckians, the process leading from bison to cattle paralleled the replacement of Indians by Euroamericans.[88] Ten years after the hide hunters' slaughter ended,

---

[85] Theodore R. Davis, "The Buffalo Range," *Harper's New Monthly Magazine*, 38 (January 1869), 147–163. The predation of wolves was real, but late twentieth-century zoologists and wildlife biologists attest that contests between bulls to establish rank order are brief and almost never deadly.

[86] See Larry Barsness, *The Bison in Art: A Graphic Chronicle of the American Bison* (Fort Worth, Tex.: Amon Carter Museum of Western Art, 1977), 62–63, 80–81.

[87] Allen, *American Bisons*, 35, 56, 180–181.

[88] Peter J. Bowler, *Evolution: The History of an Idea*, rev. ed. (Berkeley: University of California Press, 1989), 24, 258. For the neo-Lamarckians, see also Edward J. Pfeifer, "United States," in Thomas F. Glick, ed., *The Comparative Reception of Darwinism* (Chicago: University of Chicago Press, 1988), 168–206.

Figure 5.4. William M. Cary, "Buffalo Bulls Protecting a Herd from Wolves," Harper's Weekly, August 5, 1871.

the University of Wisconsin historian Frederick Jackson Turner formalized this Spencerian interpretation of western settlement in his influential essay, "The Significance of the Frontier in American History."[89] Turner's interpretations of the history of the American West prevailed well into the twentieth century.

Lawmakers friendly to Delano's Indian policy embraced the idea that the destruction of the bison was an inevitable part of the advance of civilization. They were particularly attracted to the notion that domestic cattle made a higher use of the range than bison. Representative Omar Conger of Michigan said in 1874 that "there is no law which a Congress of men can enact, that will stay the disappearance of these wild animals before civilization. They eat the grass. They trample upon the plains upon which our settlers desire to herd their cattle and their sheep.... They are as uncivilized as the Indian."[90] Hancock of Texas seconded that sentiment in 1876; saying the bison "are, at most, but game. Men have not been able to domesticate them so as to make them useful in any respect as a domestic animal. They take up as much room and consume as much provender as cattle and horses or any other character of useful domestic animals."[91] Relying on popular and scientific accounts of the bison's tenacity to contrast the bison with familiar domesticated species, Conger and Hancock rejected the SPCA's depiction of the bison as nearly tame. They argued, in short, that the untamed bison was the resource of the savages; the bison's displacement by domestic cattle was a victory for civilization.

Ratification of Fort's bills may not have mattered, because most army officers in the plains were disinclined to enforce them. They were as enthusiastic as Delano about the disappearance of the bison. Colonel Richard Irving Dodge did not prevent hide hunters from entering the Indians' preserve south of the Arkansas River. In 1873, he reportedly told Josiah Wright Mooar, who had come to inquire about the propriety of hunting south of the Arkansas, "If I were a buffalo hunter, I would hunt where the buffaloes are."[92] When Sir William F. Butler, a British officer, confessed to Dodge that he had shot more than thirty bison on the North Platte, Dodge was gleeful. Butler wrote, "I could not but feel some qualms of conscience at the thought of the destruction of so much animal life, but Colonel Dodge held different views. 'Kill every buffalo you can,' he said; 'every buffalo dead is an Indian gone.'"[93]

The army adhered to Delano's policy of allowing the exploitation of the herds to proceed unfettered. Even some hide hunters ascribed to this view of the slaughter. "The buffalo didn't fit in so well with the white man's encroaching

[89] Frederick Jackson Turner, "The Significance of the Frontier in American History," *American Historical Association Annual Report* (1893), 199–227.

[90] *Congressional Record*, (March 10, 1874), 2107.

[91] *Congressional Record*, (February 23, 1876), 1239.

[92] J. Wright Mooar, "Buffalo Days," as told to James Winford Hunt, *Holland's*, 52 (February 1933), 10, 44.

[93] *Sir William Butler: An Autobiography* (New York: Scribner, 1913), 97.

civilization," argued Mayer. "So he had to go."[94] Although he recognized that
hide hunters deprived the plains nomads of their subsistence, John Cook reflected that the "ruthless slaughter" was "simply a case of the survival of the
fittest. Too late to stop and moralize now."[95] Eastern reformers reluctantly
agreed. In the Black Hills, the *New York Times* editorialized in 1875, "the red
man will be driven out, and the white man will take possession. This is not
justice, but it is destiny."[96] These rationalizations rested on the assumption of
the innate superiority of Euroamericans and their land use strategies. The belief
in Euroamerican progress assumed an inevitable advancement toward higher
forms: from Indians and bison to Euroamericans and domestic livestock. For
Delano, as for Sherman – who had been among the first to predict the demise
of the bison – extinction of the bison was not only an inevitability but a solution
to the problem of domesticating the western plains.

III

The political economy of the 1870s pitted not only Euroamerican bison hunters
against the plains nomads, but Euroamericans against each other. Bison hunters
rarely encroached upon each others' hunting territory, but they often found
themselves engaged in usually losing battles against hide dealers, freighters, and
retailers. Exorbitant prices for supplies and a glutted market in hides in the mid-
1870s broke many bison hunters. The destruction of and competition for the
bison not only deprived the plains nomads of their primary resource, but also
deprived many hide hunters of the rewards of their labors.

Josiah Wright Mooar was among the first hunters to turn to the procurement
of hides. Beginning in 1870, he provided bison meat at three cents a pound to
construction workers on the Santa Fe and Kansas Pacific railroads and soldiers
at Fort Dodge.[97] When the railroads laid off their construction workers for the
season in the fall of 1872, many entered the field as bison hunters and skinners.[98]
Theodore Raymond and the brothers Ed and Bat Masterson were typical; they
came to the southern plains in 1872 with a grading subcontract for the Santa
Fe Railroad before turning to bison hunting.[99] Richard Bussell, a "bull-whacker"
hauling freight between Fort Laramie, Salt Lake City, and Leavenworth, Kansas,

---

[94] Mayer and Roth, *Buffalo Harvest*, 27–28.
[95] Cook, *Border and the Buffalo*, 166–167.
[96] "Taming the Savage," *New York Times* (15 April 1875), 6.
[97] Odie B. Faulk, *Dodge City: The Most Western Town of All* (New York: Oxford University Press, 1977), 31.
[98] William E. Connelley, ed., "Life and Adventures of George W. Brown, Soldier, Pioneer, Scout, Plainsman, and Buffalo Hunter," *Collections of the Kansas State Historical Society*, 17 (1926–28), 116–117.
[99] Raymond, "Diary of a Buffalo Hunter, 345–346.

switched from freighting to bison hunting in 1868. His forays into hunting were sporadic, however; he continued hauling intermittently until 1872. Like the other bison hunters in the southern plains, he gradually drifted south in pursuit of the herds, moving from Dodge City to Fort Griffin in the Texas Panhandle. Often unable to sell his hides for a suitable price in Fort Griffin, Bussell hauled them to Dallas. Even so, Bussell lamented that he earned less for his labors than he had hoped.[100] Bussell's experiences exemplified bison hunting in many ways: transitory, episodic, and often unprofitable. Yet to poor men, bison hunting seemed to promise great and instant wealth. By the winter of 1872–73, according to the Newton *Kansan*, between one and two thousand hide hunters were pursuing bison in western Kansas. The economic depression that began in 1873 drove still more hunters into the southern plains. The rancher Charles Goodnight estimated that there were three thousand hunters in the Texas Panhandle in the mid-1870s.[101]

For a few years, the slaughter produced tremendous profits, but not necessarily for the hunters. From 1870 to early 1872, the price of a bull hide stood at $3.50, for that of a cow and calf slightly less. Frank Mayer calculated that inasmuch as cartridges cost 25 cents each, "every time I fired one I got my investment back twelve times over." If he could kill one hundred bison every day – which did not seem an unreasonable figure to him when he embarked on his career as a bison hunter – he figured to earn $200 a day. Mayer vastly overestimated the number of bison he could kill in a day, however. He also failed to consider that commercial hide hunting required a considerable investment: $400-$650 for a good wagon and $125 for a .50-caliber Sharp or Remington rifle. Altogether, it cost Mayer $2,000 to outfit himself for the hunt.[102] The large initial investment meant that many independent hunters went broke. Others judged themselves fortunate just to break even.[103]

Even after outfitting themselves, hunters, like miners in gold-rush boomtowns, paid inflated prices for ordinary goods and services. Prices in Dodge City were scandalously inflated. Wentin Wilson reported in 1876 that in Dodge, "everything is high: 25 cents for a shave; 75 cents for a haircut, whiskey 25 and 50 cents a drink."[104] The builders of a wooden bridge across the Arkansas at Dodge City charged bison hunters $1.50 to haul their hides across the river and into town.[105]

[100] Bussell, "Hunting Buffalo in the Panhandle," Panhandle-Plains Historical Society.
[101] Claude *News*, 13 March 1931. Bussell estimated that between fifteen thousand and twenty thousand men were engaged in the business of bison hunting – a not entirely unreasonable figure if one includes not only shooters but skinners, haulers, dealers, and the various merchants in the hide towns. Bussell, "Hunting Buffalo in the Panhandle," Panhandle-Plains Historical Society.
[102] Mayer and Roth, *Buffalo Harvest*, 49–52.
[103] Connelley, ed., "Life of George W. Brown," 111, 123.
[104] Wilson, "Details of a Buffalo Hunt of 1876 in Kansas," Kansas State Historical Society, Topeka.
[105] Connelley, ed., "Life of George W. Brown," 118.

The economic insecurities of hunting outfits inspired one anonymous bison skinner in the 1870s to modify the lyrics to "Canada-I-O," a Northern New England folksong which laments the hardships of seasonal work logging in Quebec. The revised song, "Buffalo Range," tells of an unemployed Texan who is enticed by the promise of "good wages" to join a hunting outfit headed for the Panhandle. After the outfit endures Indians' bullets, mosquitoes, and poor rations, however, the merchant who had organized the outfit declares bankruptcy. "Now we're back across Peace [sic] River and homeward we are bound," the song concludes, "In that forsaken country may I never more be found. / If you see anyone bound out there pray warn them not to go / To that forsaken country, the land of buffalo."[106]

The lament of the skinner in "Buffalo Range" would have been familiar to James Cator. Although Cator did not keep an account book, he saved many of his receipts from his bison hunting career between 1874 and 1878. In his first year as a hunter, he almost certainly failed to break even. His receipts – probably incomplete – show that he sold nearly $1,100 worth of hides to A.C. Myers and Charles Rath of Dodge City, but he also purchased nearly $2,900 worth of supplies. In 1875 and 1876, he looked to increase his profits by selling not only hides but meat, tongues, and the occasional wolf or coyote pelt. As prices dropped, Cator, like Bussell, hauled his hides to competing, far-flung dealers in search of the best price, selling his hides in New Mexico and Colorado.[107] By the late 1870s, Cator had abandoned hunting and, with his brother, established a trading post on one of the main wagon trails connecting Dodge City to the Texas Panhandle.[108]

Bussell and Cator were fortunate in that they hauled their own hides to Dodge City, Fort Griffin, or wherever they could find the best price. Freighters and merchants often went directly to the outfits camped on the plains to eliminate competition.[109] The hide dealer Charles Rath dispatched teams to the bison range to buy hides directly from hunting outfits for as little as 75 cents per hide.[110] At Rath/Reynolds City in the Texas Panhandle, prices were extortionate; tobacco sold at $2 per pound, corn at 5 cents a pound. The dealers, meanwhile, paid from 50 to 90 cents for bison hides that sold for perhaps twice as much in Fort Griffin. The dealers nonetheless accumulated large numbers of hides. A visitor reported "buffalo hides piled up here as high as a house."[111]

As hunters flooded the market with hides, the value of the product steadily declined. A tanner who experimented with bison hides in 1871 paid Josiah Wright

[106] N. Howard Thorp, *Songs of the Cowboys* (New York: Clarkson N. Potter, 1966), 195–218.
[107] Cator Family Papers, Panhandle-Plains Historical Society.
[108] C. Robert Haywood, *Trails South: The Wagon-Road Economy in the Dodge City-Panhandle Region* (Norman: University of Oklahoma Press, 1986), 107–108.
[109] J. W. Woody, interview with Haley, 19 October 1926; John Wood interview with L. F. Sheffy, Canadian, Texas, 28 December 1929, Panhandle-Plains Historical Society.
[110] Bussell, "Hunting Buffalo in the Panhandle," Panhandle-Plains Historical Society.
[111] Wilson, "Details of a Buffalo Hunt," Kansas State Historical Society.

Mooar $2.25 per hide. In 1872, before the rush of hunters into the southern plains had begun in earnest, Mooar sold his hides to a tannery in Pennsylvania for $3.50 per hide.[112] By 1874 and continuing until 1876, however, the price of a bull hide in the glutted market had fallen to $1.15, and that of a cow or calf hide to 65 cents.[113] In December, 1874, Dodge City dealers paid James Cator $2.15 for his bull hides. Two years later, the price had fallen to 80 cents per hide.[114]

The falling value of the hides drove some hunters to greater devastation by expanding their carnage to include the poisoning of wolves, foxes, and coyotes. The hunters stocked up on poison – usually strychnine – before setting out for a hunting excursion. At the end of a day's labor of shooting and skinning bison, they laced pieces of bison meat with the poison and left them for scavengers. Using this technique during a hunting trip in Kansas in 1879, Arthur Bill's outfit killed four hundred bison and fifty wolves in twelve days.[115] As the number of bison declined, "wolf-trapping" was so remunerative, the bison hunter George Simpson claimed, that some hunters concentrated on poisoning wolves during the winter.[116]

This ancillary destruction signaled the decline of southern plains bison hunting. Josiah Wright Mooar and his brother and partner John Wesley Mooar had the foresight to invest their profits from bison hunting in other business ventures. By 1877, they had purchased a cattle ranch and had begun to request cash payments from hide dealers, rather than leave their money on account against future purchases of supplies. By 1879, John Mooar reported to his mother, he and his brother had abandoned bison hunting: Josiah Wright was hauling supplies to the Colorado mines while John managed the ranch.[117] By 1880, Fort Griffin, Rath/Reynolds City, Buffalo Gap, and Hide Town were nearly deserted.[118] The bison hunters returned to work for the Santa Fe Railroad, went to the silver mines of Arizona, or moved north to pursue the bison in Montana and Wyoming.[119]

After the bison had been hunted out by 1883, the plains were strewn with their bones. A. M. Bede, a county judge from Fort Yates, North Dakota, recalled of his early days in the northern plains, "the country out here used to look like a charnel house with so many skulls staring at a man, and so many bones that

[112] Faulk, *Dodge City*, 32–33.
[113] H. B. Lovett, interview with L. F. Sheffy, 23 June 1934, Pampa, Texas, Panhandle-Plains Historical Society.
[114] Cator Family Papers, Panhandle-Plains Historical Society.
[115] Arthur C. Bill, "The Buffalo Hunt," Kansas State Historical Society.
[116] Simpson, interview with Haley, Canadian, Texas, 18 July 1926, Panhandle-Plains Historical Society. For the poisoning of wolves, see also Frank J. North Papers, State Historical Society of Nebraska; and Wentin Wilson, "Details of a Buffalo Hunt," Kansas State Historical Society.
[117] John W. Mooar, Fort Griffin, to his mother, Pownal, Vermont, 5 March 1879, John W. Mooar Papers, Southwest Collection, Texas Tech University, Lubbock, Texas.
[118] Dary, *Buffalo Book*, 114.
[119] Frank Collinson Papers, Panhandle-Plains Historical Society.

newcomers felt nervous, and, in some cases, could hardly plow the land."[120] L. C. Fouquet of Kansas also noted that the bones were "a nuisance to our breaking of the sod."[121] Poor homesteaders and Indians soon found a use for the bones, however, particularly during the drought years of the 1880s. They scavenged the plains for bison bones, which they sold to bone dealers for delivery to sugar refineries or fertilizer plants. It took one hundred skeletons to amass one ton of bones, which sold for $4 to $12. Although the scavengers did not become wealthy, the bone trade sustained many poor families. An early settler in North Dakota recalled that his family "hauled fourteen tons of buffalo bones. . . . I don't know how we would have lived if it had not been for the money we got that way."[122] Robert Wright of Dodge City believed that "if it had not been for the bone industry, many poor families would have suffered for the very necessaries of life. It looked like a wise dispensation of Providence."[123]

The bone trade was immense. In 1886, a resident of Dodge City saw a rick of bison bones a quarter of a mile long and as high as the bones could be thrown.[124] Bone dealers, such as the Northwestern Bone Syndicate of North Dakota, purchased thousands of tons of bones each year. Railroad companies annually shipped nearly five thousand boxcars of bones. The cargo was destined for the Michigan Carbon Works in Detroit and the Northwestern Fertilizer Company and Empire Carbon Works of East St. Louis, Illinois. (See Figure 5.5.) By the mid-1880s, the Michigan Carbon Works produced five thousand tons of bone black (a pigment) and four thousand tons of bone ash (a fertilizer) every year.[125] The bone trade was the final episode in the reduction of the most prominent resource of the plains to its salable parts and their incorporation into the American industrial economy.

The hide hunters' slaughter of the bison was a boon to Eastern tanneries, who had paid an average of $4.20 per hide in 1870, but were paying only $3.40 a decade later.[126] Moreover, the destruction of the bison accomplished the aims of the policymakers who sought to pacify the plains nomads. Once the hunters had eradicated the herds, the nomads had no recourse but to go to the reservations. Like poor Euroamerican farmers, the Indians gathered bison bones for sale to

---

[120] Bede, Fort Yates, North Dakota, to Edmund Seymour, New York City, 29 October 1919, American Bison Society Papers, Conservation Collection, Western History Department, Denver Public Library, Box 275, File 14.

[121] Fouquet, "Buffalo Days," *Collections of the Kansas Historical Society*, 16 (1923–25), 347.

[122] Quoted in LeRoy Barnett, "The Buffalo Bone Commerce on the Northern Plains," *North Dakota History*, 39 (Winter 1972), 23–41.

[123] Wright, *Dodge City*, 154.

[124] O. H. Simpson, Dodge City, Kansas, to the American Bison Society, 19 January 1934, American Bison Society Papers, Box 276, File 7. See also Joe Killough, interview with D. T. Leachman, 16 December 1945, Panhandle-Plains Historical Society.

[125] Barnett, "Buffalo Bone Commerce," 23–41. Bone black and bone ash are both produced by calcining bones, the former in closed vessels and the latter in open air.

[126] McMartin, *Hides, Hemlocks*, 88.

Figure 5.5. Bones at the Michigan Carbon Works, Detroit. Courtesy of the Detroit Public Library.

dealers. A reporter for *Harper's* magazine asked in 1893, "Do the Indians make a living gathering these bones?" Yes, replied a railroad inspector, "but it is a mercy that they can't eat bones. We were never able to control the savages until their supply of meat was cut off. We have had no trouble worth speaking of since 1883, however."[127] On the reservations, the Indians' existence was meager. They subsisted in part on government beef. At the Red Cloud Agency in western Nebraska, Oglala Sioux hunters prepared for the delivery of cattle from the government as they had once prepared for a summer bison hunt. As the cattle were released into the corral, the Indians set after them on horseback, slaughtering them in imitation – culturally rich but economically impoverished – of the communal bison hunts of the past.[128] Government authorities permitted the communal hunts to continue until 1897 when, in an effort to stifle this form of cultural expression, they built a slaughterhouse and began distributing butchered meat to the Indians. The Oglalas responded by setting fire to the slaughterhouse one night.[129]

The costs of the near-extermination of the bison were not shared equally. The plains nomads suffered the loss of their primary resource and consequently of most of their lands and economic autonomy. The benefits of the destruction of the bison were likewise inequitably distributed. Hunters transformed millions of bison into profitable commodities, yet merchants and industrialists appropriated most of the wealth generated by the destruction of the herds. While poor Euroamericans and Indians scavenged the plains for bison bones, industrialists added to their wealth by transforming the bones into fertilizer. In the plains, the slaughter left in its wake not wealth but poverty and misery.

Euroamericans did not slaughter millions of bison between 1870 and 1883 believing that nature provided an inexhaustible supply. Rather, they anticipated the extinction of the species. They regarded the disappearance of the herds as a triumph of civilization over savagery, because the extermination of the bison removed the nomads' primary resource and cleared the plains for Euroamericans. Hide hunters harbored little apprehension that the late nineteenth-century legal order might rein in the slaughter. Legal and extra-legal authorities in the nineteenth-century United States were the partisans of Euroamericans in their struggle to wrest control of resources from the Indians.[130]

The erosion of the nomads' hunting territory presaged the triumph – an

---

[127] Hamlin Russell, "The Story of the Buffalo," *Harper's New Monthly Magazine*, 86 (April 1893), 798. See also Mrs. Mae Tubb Dolcater, interview with Morris Dolby, 1 January 1948, Panhandle-Plains Historical Society.

[128] Collinson Papers, Panhandle-Plains Historical Society.

[129] James R. Walker, "The No Ears, Short Man, and Iron Crow Winter Counts," in *Lakota Society*, ed. Raymond J. DeMallie (Lincoln: University of Nebraska Press, 1982), 153.

[130] See McEvoy, *Fisherman's Problem*, 93–119.

inevitable triumph, in the minds of many contemporaries – of Euroamericans. The engine of the advancement of Euroamericans into the plains was the ability of an industrial society to destroy thoroughly the bison herds and thus deny their use to the nomads. A few lawmakers saw the destruction as deplorable – a violation of the treaties, a provocation to Indian war, and a profligate waste – but others saw it as a salient example of Euroamerican industriousness. The plains had remained a wilderness while in Indians hands, but hide hunters extracted extraordinary wealth from the grasslands – even if most of them failed to keep that wealth for themselves.

At the root of the failure to regulate bison hunting was the mid-century belief in economic competition. Everyone, Indian or Euroamerican included, was engaged in a race to exploit resources for individual gain. To reserve resources for anybody's exclusive use violated the competitive ideal; to reserve them for social outcasts such as Indians was unthinkable. Euroamericans waged a scorched-earth campaign against the Indians who impeded the expansion of industry. Yet the hide hunters' victory was hollow; when the campaign was over, most of the hunters found themselves no wealthier than before.

6

The Returns of the Bison

The itinerant artist George Catlin reflected, while touring the Missouri River valley in 1832, that the bison was "so rapidly wasting from the world, that its species must soon be extinguished." To save the herds, Catlin recommended that the federal government create "a *nation's Park*" in the grasslands. He imagined that both the bison and the Indians who hunted them "might in future be seen (by some great protecting policy of government) preserved in their pristine beauty and wildness, in a magnificent park."[1] For the next forty years, however, the United States government declined to pursue Catlin's vision. Rather, federal authorities welcomed the diminution of the herds because it forced famished Indians of the western plains to submit to the reservation system. Yellowstone, the United States' first national park, was located in the scenic Mountain West, far from the bison's range in the shortgrass plains. In the late nineteenth century, however, Yellowstone National Park, established in 1872, was the only public refuge for the bison apart from city zoos.[2] By the 1880s, a few hundred bison – the largest group of survivors in the United States – had found refuge there from commercial hunters, drought, and the destruction of grazing lands by farmers and livestock.

This remnant herd and other scattered survivors might eventually have perished as well had it not been for the efforts of a handful of Americans and Canadians. These advocates of the preservation of the bison were primarily Western ranchers who speculated that ownership of the few remaining bison could be profitable and elite Easterners possessed of a nostalgic urge to recreate a facsimile of the frontier. Beginning in the first decade of the twentieth century, the

[1] George Catlin, *North American Indians: Being Letters and Notes on their Manners, Customs, and Conditions, Written During Eight Years' Travel Amongst the Wildest Tribes of Indians in North America, 1832–1839*, vol. 1 (Philadelphia: Leary, Stuart, 1913), 294–295.

[2] The National Zoological Park in Washington, D.C., was established in 1889 to preserve North American animals. The park, founded largely in reaction to the diminution of the bison, was originally intended as a preserve largely closed to the public. Congressional pressure, however, forced the park organizers to open most of the grounds to visitors. See Helen Lefkowitz Horowitz, "The National Zoological Park: 'City of Refuge' or Zoo?" and Heather Ewing, "The Architecture of the National Zoological Park," in R. J. Hoage and William A. Deiss, eds., *New Worlds, New Animals: From Menagerie to Zoological Park in the Nineteenth Century* (Baltimore: Johns Hopkins University Press, 1996), 126–129, 151–157.

combination of Eastern sentiment and Western cupidity was instrumental in persuading the United States and Canadian governments to create national reserves for the bison. The Canadian government established Buffalo National Park near Wainwright, Alberta, in 1907, and Wood Buffalo National Park on the Alberta-Northwest Territories border in 1922. The United States government stocked Yellowstone Park with bison in 1902, and, between 1905 and 1914, founded bison preserves in Oklahoma (Wichita Mountains National Wildlife Refuge), Montana (National Bison Range), South Dakota (atop Wind Cave National Park), and Nebraska (Fort Niobrara National Wildlife Refuge).

The preservation of the bison in parks and reserves was on a significantly reduced scale from what Catlin imagined and what might have been possible in 1832 when he first suggested the idea. Preservationists confined the bison to small reservations often outside or on the fringes of the shortgrass plains. Tourism, recreation, and sport hunting were the preservationists' primary considerations. Moreover, by conforming their effort to save the species from extinction to the ecological transformation of the grasslands from a bison range to ranches and farms – a transformation Catlin had sought to pre-empt – preservationists were able to salvage but a fraction of the species' genetic pool and natural habitat. As a result, by the first decades of the twentieth century the bison had become an imprisoned species maintained only by the constant intervention of human keepers. Although Western ranchers and Eastern philanthropists combined to save the bison, they preserved the species not as Catlin imagined, but as bartered, domesticated captives. The turn-of-the-century preservationists were thus unlike both Catlin and recent wilderness advocates who have called for the establishment of a "Buffalo Commons" in large areas of the Great Plains.[3]

Despite these differences a number of environmental historians have seen the preservation of the bison as a precursor of the environmental movement. The historian Roderick Nash interpreted the Congressional endorsement in 1886 of the harboring of bison in Yellowstone – the lawmakers refused to allow a railroad line to cross the park because of its threat to the bison – as a formative moment in the development of "wilderness values." According to Nash, this secular creed became more popular but remained more or less unchanged from the late nineteenth century to the passage of the Wilderness Act in 1964.[4] Other

---

[3] For the original "Buffalo Commons" proposal, see Deborah Epstein Popper and Frank J. Popper, "The Great Plains: From Dust to Dust," *Planning*, 53 (December 1987), 12–18. For a critique, see Karen De Bres and Mark Guizlo, "A Daring Proposal for Dealing with an Inevitable Disaster? A Review of the Buffalo Commons Proposal," *Great Plains Research*, 2 (August 1992), 165–178. For the response of plains residents to the Poppers' plan, see Anne Matthews, *Where the Buffalo Roam* (New York: Grove Weidenfeld, 1992). For a similar proposal, see Ernest Callenbach, *Bring Back the Buffalo! A Sustainable Future for America's Great Plains* (Washington, D.C.: Island Press, 1996).

[4] Roderick Nash, *Wilderness and the American Mind*, 3d ed. (New Haven: Yale University Press, 1982), 115. For the Congressional dispute, see *Congressional Record*, 49th Cong., 2nd Sess. (14 December 1886), 94–95, 149–154.

environmental historians have similarly seen turn-of-the-century preservationism – particularly the protection of wildlife – as the antithesis of resource
exploitation, and as the foundation of twentieth-century environmentalism.[5]
This tendency to see preservationism as part of an ideologically consistent con-
tinuum of wilderness protection has obscured both the evolution of wilderness
ideology and the complicated motivations for preservationism that were specific
to the culture and economy of the late nineteenth and early twentieth centuries.[6]

Superficially at least, preservationists echoed Catlin and portrayed the effort
to save the bison from extinction as a rejection of the unrestrained exploitation of
nature that had depleted the herds in the nineteenth century. In 1908, William
Temple Hornaday, the director of the New York Zoological Park and president
of the American Bison Society, an organization founded in 1905 to preserve the
bison, wrote dozens of letters to wealthy Americans soliciting contributions to
establish a preserve in Montana. His indictments of materialism were scathing.
"It was the business interests of the country, represented by men who wished to
procure buffalo hides to sell at $2.50 each, that practically exterminated the
American Bison millions," he wrote in a typical letter to H. S. Herring of the
New Orleans Board of Trade. "Now that an effort is being made to preserve the
species for the benefit of posterity, the businessmen of the United States have
no option but to take hold and help!"[7] Many preservationists conceded, however, that the commercial slaughter of the herds in the nineteenth century had
been a necessary condition of American economic development. In one of his
most powerful essays, "The American Forests," John Muir wrote, "I suppose
we need not go mourning the buffaloes. In the nature of things they had to give
place to better cattle, though the change might have been made without bar-
barous wickedness."[8] George Bird Grinnell, the natural history editor of *Forest
and Stream* and a founder of both the Audubon Society and the Boone and
Crockett Club of sport hunters, maintained that the extermination of the bison

[5] See Douglas H. Strong, *Dreamers and Defenders: American Conservationists* (Lincoln: University
of Nebraska Press, 1988), 7. For wildlife protection, see John F. Reiger, *American Sportsmen and
the Origins of Conservation*, rev. ed. (Norman: University of Oklahoma Press, 1986), 25–49; James
Trefethan, *An American Crusade for Wildlife* (New York: Winchester Press and the Boone and
Crockett Club, 1975); Lisa Mighetto, *Wild Animals and American Environmental Ethics* (Tucson:
University of Arizona Press, 1991).

[6] Some historians have placed preservationism in its historical context. See Thomas Dunlap, *Saving America's Wildlife* (Princeton: Princeton University Press, 1988); Peter Schmitt, *Back to
Nature: The Arcadian Myth in Urban America* (Baltimore: Johns Hopkins University Press, 1990);
Hal Rothman, *Preserving Different Pasts: The American National Monuments* (Urbana: University
of Illinois Press, 1989). Also see William Cronon, "The Trouble with Wilderness, or, Getting
Back to the Wrong Nature," *Environmental History*, 1 (January 1996), 7–28. The essay is also
found in Cronon, ed., *Uncommon Ground: Toward Reinventing Nature* (New York: Norton, 1995),
69–90.

[7] Hornaday to Herring, 3 October 1908, Letterbooks, American Bison Society Papers, Box 273.
Denver Public Library, Western History Department, Conservation Collection.

[8] Muir, *Our National Parks* (Boston: Houghton Mifflin, 1901), 335, 364.

was "necessary" to economic growth.[9] The naturalist Ernest Thompson Seton similarly believed that the bison was "incompatible" with "higher productivity of the soil."[10] Finally, President Theodore Roosevelt – who was instrumental in reintroducing bison to Yellowstone and Oklahoma during his administration – concluded as early as 1885 that the bison had to make way for Euroamerican settlers.[11] The advocates of the preservation of the bison supported both the Euroamerican conquest of the western grasslands and the preservation of the dominant species of the preconquest plains. These contradictory ideals exemplified the dual vision of the North American frontier at the turn of the century: as a progression toward the modern age and as a refuge from modernism.

These goals were fundamentally irreconcilable. The preservationists probably saved the bison from extinction, but their conflicted views on the Euroamerican conquest of the West imposed limitations on the return of the species. Despite Hornaday's browbeating of business leaders, the primary animus of the preservationists was not a repugnance for the hide hunters who destroyed millions of bison in the 1870s and 1880s. Although the preservationists regretted the decline of the bison, they never criticized the ranchers who had replaced the bison with domesticated cattle. Not only did the preservationists admire the image of the cowboy, but as early as 1889, *Forest and Stream* – the "Weekly Journal of the Rod and Gun" whose editors were at the forefront of the movement to preserve the bison – argued that one of the benefits of the perpetuation of the bison should be the development of a profitable cattle-bison hybrid.[12] The preservationists were uneasy with urban, industrial society. They sought to establish public herds that could serve as places of historical and moral education for Euroamericans nostalgic for an imagined, pristine, Western frontier. Tourists validated the preservationists' program, just as the preservationists, in turn, legitimized the traffic in bison that stocked the preserves.[13] Indeed, preservationist sentimentality readily accommodated itself to the economic interests of ranchers and promoters of tourism. Thus, the movement to preserve the bison installed the species in small, accessible reservations, some of which were outside the shortgrass plains, and that altogether constituted a tiny fraction of the species' former range. Once these few, small, scattered preserves had been established, the enthusiasm of the preservationists for the perpetuation of the bison dissipated.

[9] Grinnell, "American Game Protection: A Sketch," in Grinnell and Charles Sheldon, eds., *Hunting and Conservation: The Book of the Boone and Crockett Club* (New Haven: Yale University Press, 1925), 219–220.

[10] Seton, "The American Bison or Buffalo," *Scribner's Magazine*, 40 (October 1906), 404.

[11] Roosevelt, *Hunting Trips of a Ranchman* (New York: G. P. Putnam's Sons, 1885), in Mario R. DiNunzio, ed., *Theodore Roosevelt: An American Mind* (New York: Penguin, 1994), 245.

[12] "The Domesticated Buffalo," *Forest and Stream*, 32 (9 May 1889), 313.

[13] For an analysis of tourism and preservation, see Kerwin L. Klein, "Frontier Products: Tourism, Consumerism, and the Southwestern Public Lands, 1890–1990," *Pacific Historical Review*, 62 (February 1993), 39–71.

I

Patricia N. Limerick, a historian of the American West, wrote in 1987: "Every human group has a creation myth – a tale explaining where its members came from and why they are special, chosen by providence for a special destiny."[14] More accurately, perhaps, one might say that every human group maintains many creation myths suited to different needs, or that individuals identify themselves as belonging to various groups with different creation myths. Such myths are, in any event, significant aspects of culture. They are reference points to which people periodically return to reaffirm or revise their identities. Both Indians of the western plains and Euroamericans incorporated the bison into some of their most important creation myths. For many Indian societies of the plains, the bison was a mythical source of prosperity and social organization.[15] For Euroamericans, the bison was a symbol of untamed nature, the frontier, and masculinity – since they considered the conquest of the frontier a male endeavor. The preservation of the bison was not an end in itself but a means to an end: the preservation of an imagined, masculine, frontier culture.

The University of Wisconsin historian Frederick Jackson Turner cogently articulated the frontier creation myth in 1893, declaring that the development of American democracy and individualism had depended on the rugged conditions of the recently closed Western frontier.[16] The American Bison Society echoed Turner's view. Like Turner, the members of the Society believed that the West was the locus of American identity. Based in New York City, the Society was both geographically and economically exclusive. In 1908, 79 percent of its members – and 85 percent of its Life Members – lived in New York, New Jersey, Pennsylvania, and New England. Only 6 of the 723 members in 1908 were residents of one of the Great Plains states.[17] The concentration of American Bison Society

---

[14] Patricia Nelson Limerick, *The Legacy of Conquest: The Unbroken Past of the American West* (New York: Norton, 1987), 322.

[15] See A. L. Kroeber, *Gros Ventre Myths and Tales*. Anthropological Papers of the American Museum of Natural History, vol. 1, pt. 3 (New York: American Museum of Natural History, 1907), 66–67; Clark Wissler and D. C. Duvall, *Mythology of the Blackfeet*. Anthropological Papers of the American Museum of Natural History, vol. 2, pt. 1 (New York: American Museum of Natural History, 1908), 121–125; George A. Dorsey, *The Cheyenne*. Field Columbia Museum Anthropological Series, vol. 9, nos. 1–2 (Chicago, 1905), 47–48; Elaine A. Jahner, "Lakota Genesis: The Oral Tradition," in Raymond J. DeMallie and Douglas R. Parks, eds., *Sioux Indian Religion* (Norman: University of Oklahoma Press, 1987), 48.

[16] Frederick Jackson Turner, "The Significance of the Frontier in American History," American Historical Association *Annual Report* (1893), 217, 227. Turner concentrated on the frontier's influence on American political traditions in "Contributions of the West to American Democracy," *Atlantic Monthly*, 92 (January 1903).

[17] "American Bison Society Organized," *New York Times* (9 December 1905), 18; "Hope to Buy All the Bison: American Society Wants to Save Them from Commercial Greed," Ibid. (11 January 1907), 3. See also "To Establish a Permanent National Bison Range," 60th Cong., 1st Sess., Senate Report 467 (Serial 5219), 1, and the appended membership list.

members in the Northeast left it more regionally restricted than even the Audubon Society, 72 percent of whose members lived in New York, New Jersey, New England, or Pennsylvania.[18] The American Bison Society membership included several wealthy, socially prominent, and notable Americans: Theodore Roosevelt as honorary president; Gifford Pinchot, a wealthy Pennsylvanian and the first chief of the United States Forest Service; the artist Frederic Remington; and the industrialist Andrew Carnegie. Carnegie's onetime business associate J. Pierpont Morgan, although not a member, was nonetheless sympathetic with the Society's goals. In 1910, Morgan enclosed a twenty thousand-acre tract in Colorado and stocked it with bison.[19]

It was precisely their station in life – refined, cosmopolitan, and comfortable but also, they feared, overfed, effete, and pampered – that caused these privileged Easterners to romanticize the supposedly hardier days when bison roamed the plains. Theodore Roosevelt epitomized this perspective. One of the formative influences on his character was a two-year stint as a North Dakota rancher, sheriff, and hunter in the early 1880s. Roosevelt might have drawn on this experience in 1907, when he wrote that "it would be a real misfortune to permit the [bison] to become extinct" because the herds "most deeply imprest the imagination of all the old hunters and early settlers."[20] Seton – a nature writer, one of the founders of the Boy Scouts of America, and a member of the American Bison Society – echoed Roosevelt's nostalgia for the West. In an article in *Scribner's Magazine* in 1906, Seton compared "all the hungry regret that Sir Walter Scott felt over the departed glories of the feudal life" to "the Buffalo days and the stirring times of the by-gone wildest West."[21] To the Easterners of the American Bison Society, the bison was a living icon of an imagined heroic West.

Some advocates of preservation believed that the reintroduction of the bison to its former range would restore a semblance of frontier wildness to the United States. In 1907, the cowboy Frank Rush enthusiastically welcomed the establishment of a federal bison reserve in western Oklahoma. He said: "The cowboy is rapidly becoming ... as extinct as ... the buffalo.... Back there on the range these buffalo ... will be attended to by some of the old cowboys who hunted buffalo on the plains in pioneer days."[22] Thus the preservation of one icon of the old West – the bison – would help to preserve another – the cowboy – at the very time when some Americans believed that the disappearance of frontier conditions threatened American culture.

[18] Stephen Fox, *John Muir and His Legacy: The American Conservation Movement* (Boston: Little, Brown, 1981), 158.

[19] "Buffalo for Morgan Estate: Large Herd to be Sent to His Game Preserve in Colorado," *New York Times* (5 July 1910), 8.

[20] Roosevelt, letter to Ernest Harold Baynes (24 October 1907), in *Annual Report of the American Bison Society, 1905–1907* (New York: American Bison Society, 1908), 9.

[21] Seton, "The American Bison or Buffalo," 403.

[22] "15 Buffalo to Go Back to the Ranges: Cowboy Rush Here to Take Part of the Zoo Back to Oklahoma; Old Hunters as Guards," *New York Times* (6 October 1907), 17.

The rapid urbanization of the United States at the turn of the century caused elite Easterners to fear that in congested cities Turner's warnings about the consequences of the closing of the frontier had been realized. What Hornaday wrote of the bison in captivity in 1887 he might just as well have written of urban Americans: "In captivity he fails to develop as finely as in his wild state, and with the loss of liberty he becomes a tame-looking animal. He gets fat and short-bodied, and the lack of vigorous and constant exercise prevents the development of bone and muscle which made the prairie animal what he was."[23] Theodore Roosevelt told the naturalist John Burroughs in 1892 that by the middle of the nineteenth century, "the physical type in the Eastern States had undoubtedly degenerated."[24] If their virility were to be salvaged, the men of the cosmopolitan East needed to imitate the experiences of their frontiersmen forebears. Hornaday followed this advice when he took a hunting trip in the Missouri River Badlands with the photographer L. A. Huffman in 1901, camping with the market hunter Max Sieber. One of Huffman's photographs from the trip shows the three men outside Sieber's cabin. Hornaday, dressed in fringed buckskins, cradles his rifle, surrounded by the skulls and antlers of assorted wildlife.[25] (See Figure 6.1.)

Hornaday, Roosevelt, Seton, and others agonized over what they perceived to be the waning of American masculinity. Such fixations were common in the late nineteenth and early twentieth centuries, when an aggressively masculine popular culture arose in reaction to the mechanization of life in an industrializing society.[26] Masculine adventure stories, such as those by H. Rider Haggard, Rudyard Kipling, and Edgar Rice Burroughs proliferated. Interest and participation in sports and outdoor recreation exploded.[27] In tune with this cultural shift, the preservation of the bison was a decidedly male concern. In 1908, over 85 percent of the members of the American Bison Society were men; many of the female members were wives or relatives of the men who belonged to the organization.[28] Men occupied all the important leadership positions. This preponderance of men was by no means typical of preservationist or conservationist organizations.

---

[23] Hornaday, "Extermination of the American Bison, with a Sketch of its Discovery and Life History," *Annual Report of the Smithsonian Institution, 1887*, vol. II (Washington D.C.: Government Printing Office, 1889), 394. A review of "Extermination of the American Bison" in *Forest and Stream* challenged the idea that captivity had a deleterious effect on the animal. See "Buffalo Types," Ibid., 36 (30 January 1890), 24.

[24] John Burroughs, *Camping and Tramping with Roosevelt* (Boston: Houghton Mifflin, 1906), xiv.

[25] Mark H. Brown and W. R. Felton, *The Frontier Years: L. A. Huffman, Photographer of the Plains* (New York: Bramhall House, 1955), 87.

[26] See T. J. Jackson Lears, *No Place of Grace: Antimodernism and the Transformation of American Culture, 1880–1920* (Chicago: University of Chicago Press, 1994).

[27] John Higham, "The Reorientation of American Culture in the 1890's," *Writing American History: Essays on Modern Scholarship* (Bloomington: Indiana University Press, 1970), 73–102; Michael Kimmel, *Manhood in America: A Cultural History* (New York: Free Press, 1996), 117–155.

[28] "To Establish a Permanent Bison Range," 28–34.

Figure 6.1. L. A. Huffman, Max Sieber, and William T. Hornaday, outside of Sieber's cabin in Montana, 1901. Courtesy of the Montana Historical Society, Helena.

Many women were enthusiastic participants in other such groups, such as the Society for the Prevention of Cruelty to Animals.[29] Preservationists, however, depicted the salvation of the bison as a task that demanded manliness. They persisted in this belief although many women managed or co-managed the ranches that raised bison.[30] Hornaday and Seton, for example, celebrated the capture of bison for preserves as an example of masculine frontier courage. In 1909, they both lauded Charles Jesse "Buffalo" Jones, a Kansas rancher and former hide hunter, for his capture of feral bison. Hornaday called the bison "as dangerous as the lion," and applauded Jones's "heroism." Seton praised Jones for liberating the bison from the clutches of "hostile" Indians, on whose reservations they had been grazing, and bringing them to the safety of domestication.[31] A 1909 watercolor by the artist Charles Russell emphasized the daring of cowboys who participated in a roundup of bison for a Canadian preserve.[32]

Preservationists worried that, unlike Buffalo Jones, urban Euroamericans had little recourse to the invigorating influence of the outdoors. Hornaday explored that problem in his 1896 novel, *The Man Who Became a Savage*. The novel opens with the protagonist, Jeremiah Rock, suffering from mid-life torpor. "[S]urfeited, cloyed, bored to death with rank luxuries, and soft living," Rock flees an upstate New York city and its "desperate strikes, failures, bread riots, the odors of bad politics, and other aggravations of many kinds," to become the major-domo to the chief of a group of headhunters in Borneo.[33] Hornaday, not coincidentally, had trained as a taxidermist and had once visited Borneo to collect specimens. Like the protagonists of Burroughs's Africa or Turner's American West, Hornaday's Rock is an Anglo-Saxon cast into a primitive environment. Urban comforts had softened him, but Rock's encounter with the wilderness restores to him the qualities that enable Anglo-Saxons to dominate. According to Hornaday, in order to maintain their advantage in the universal struggle for domination, Euroamerican men needed to renew their connection with the wilderness.

Most preservationists imagined that the restorative effects of nature could be obtained closer to home than Hornaday's Borneo. Franklin Hooper, who succeeded Hornaday as the president of the American Bison Society, wrote in 1914,

---

[29] Carolyn Merchant, "The Women of the Progressive Conservation Crusade, 1900–1915," in Kendall E. Bailes, ed., *Environmental History: Critical Issues in Comparative Perspective* (Lanham, Md.: University Press of America, 1985), 153–170; Vera Norwood, "Women's Roles in Nature Study and Environmental Protection," *OAH Magazine of History*, 10 (Spring 1996), 12–17.

[30] See Ken Zontek, "Hunt, Capture, Raise, Increase: The People Who Saved the Bison," *Great Plains Quarterly*, 15 (Spring 1995), 133–149.

[31] "Camp Fire Dinner for Buffalo Jones: Naturalists and Hunters Praise His Work in Preserving the American Bison," *New York Times* (5 December 1909), pt. 3, 1.

[32] Larry Barsness, *The Bison in Art: A Graphic Chronicle of the American Bison* (Flagstaff, Ariz.: Northland, 1977), 128–129.

[33] Hornaday, *The Man Who Became a Savage: A Story of Our Times* (Buffalo, N.Y.: Peter Paul Book Co., 1896), 5, 7.

"[T]here has been a danger during the past fifty years lest we lose our respect and love for the animal life of the field and forest, and that, blind to the great lessons of nature, we may lose ourselves in the artificial maze and swirl of city life." Echoing the wilderness advocate John Muir, Hooper wrote that the foremost duty of the American Bison Society was to "[bring] men back to nature."[34] Like Muir, the Society proposed to bring Americans back to nature as tourists. When an agent of the Society surveyed a location in Montana for a bison preserve in 1908, he wrote, "to be of the greatest use, the range should be reasonably near to the railroad. . . . [T]he public will want to visit the animals and see them on the range, and will desire to reach them easily from the railway."[35] Five years later, when the Society was engaged in an effort to create a bison refuge in Nebraska, it argued that the Montana preserve was too remote for tourists. The new refuge, however, "will be more readily accessible."[36] Later, the Society proposed building a hotel on the Montana bison range to lure tourists traveling between Yellowstone and Glacier national parks.[37] The Society was pleased to note, in 1911, that the site for a proposed bison refuge in South Dakota was near Hot Springs, a health resort that attracted numerous tourists from nearby states.[38]

While the preservationists labored to bring urban Americans to the bison, others brought the bison to urban Americans. Bison played an important part in Buffalo Bill's Wild West – the most successful popularizer of the frontier creation myth in the late nineteenth- and early twentieth-century United States. The renown of William "Buffalo Bill" Cody – a former Pony Express rider, bison hunter, and Army scout – rested largely on dime novels and stage melodramas that inflated or fabricated his achievements as a hunter and Indian fighter. Cody, in his autobiographies and stage appearances, enthusiastically participated in the exaggeration of his exploits in the West and his elevation to the status of an American folk hero. Cody exploited that exaggeration when, in 1882, he shifted from playing himself on stage to producing elaborate rodeo-style shows. From that time until 1913, Buffalo Bill's Wild West – a combination of trick-riding, -roping, and -shooting exhibitions, pseudo-historical reenactments, and Cody's stage melodramas – toured the United States and Europe.[39]

[34] Franklin Hooper, "President's Annual Report," *Seventh Annual Report of the American Bison Society* (New York: American Bison Society, 1914), 9.
[35] Morton J. Elrod, "The Flathead Buffalo Range: A Report to the American Bison Society of an Inspection of the Flathead Indian Reservation, Montana, for the Purpose of Selecting a Suitable Location for a National Buffalo Range," *Annual Report of the American Bison Society, 1905–1907*, 15.
[36] Fred M. Dille, "The Niobrara Reservation," *Sixth Annual Report of the American Bison Society* (New York: American Bison Society, 1913), 37.
[37] Edmund Seymour, New York City, to T. S. Palmer, Bureau of Biological Survey, Washington, D.C., 29 December 1924, American Bison Society Papers, Box 275, File 38.
[38] J. Alden Loring, *Report on Certain Lands in South Dakota Suitable for a Buffalo and Game Preserve* (New York: American Bison Society, 1911), 27.
[39] Sarah J. Blackstone, *Buckskins, Bullets, and Business: A History of Buffalo Bill's Wild West* (New York: Greenwood, 1986), 74.

Cody envisioned his show as more than mere entertainment; he touted it as historical education. Buffalo Bill's Wild West intended to instruct its viewers in what Cody understood to be the central drama of American history: the conquest of the wilderness and its indigenous inhabitants. That conquest, according to Cody, produced the ideal Euroamerican man: the indefatigable, practical, and courageous frontier scout.[40] Unfortunately, the scout belonged "to a class that is rapidly disappearing from our country."[41] Cody's mission, as he saw it, was to instruct city-dwellers in the virtues that the winning of the West, including the hunting of the bison, had produced.[42] In one of the Wild West acts, handlers drove a small herd of bison into an arena that contained a water tank made to simulate a spring. Once the animals had congregated around the spring for a drink, Cody, sometimes accompanied by cowboys or Indians, charged the herd firing blanks. With Buffalo Bill in pursuit, the bison fled the arena and headed back to their corrals.[43] More than eighty Western rodeo and theatrical companies much like Buffalo Bill's Wild West toured the United States and Europe in the late nineteenth and early twentieth centuries.[44] Many of the shows included an exhibition of bison. The experience of a Wild West show made tangible the myths of frontier masculinity.[45]

The feminizing ideology of the SPCA had failed to halt the destruction of the bison in the 1870s. Only by embracing the masculine ideology of frontier conquest did Euroamericans invest enough cultural significance in the bison to warrant its preservation. Preservationists and showmen such as Cody saw the species as a living reminder of the illustrious days of the nineteenth-century West. In the absence of a frontier to conquer, the survival of the bison in readily accessible parks would, like Buffalo Bill's Wild West, instill in urban Euroamericans the muscular spirit of the past. Attendance at Cody's show or a tour of a bison preserve was a ritual that, like the Oglala Sun Dance, for instance, reaffirmed the role of nature in human life. Those rituals were embedded in

[40] Richard Slotkin, *Gunfighter Nation: The Myth of the Frontier in Twentieth-Century America* (New York: HarperCollins, 1992), 63–87. See also Richard White, "Frederick Jackson Turner and Buffalo Bill," in *The Frontier in American Culture*, ed. James R. Grossman (Berkeley: University of California Press, 1994), 7–65. Both Slotkin and White drew many important distinctions between Turner and Cody: for instance, Turner's frontier was largely bloodless and faceless; Cody's was generally violent and individualized. Yet both Turner and Cody responded to similar fears about the closing of the frontier, and there are numerous similarities between their depictions of the frontier.

[41] John M. Burke, "Salutory," *Buffalo Bill's Wild West: America's National Entertainment* (Hartford, Conn.: Calhoun, 1884).

[42] See, for instance, Cody's 1898 program: *Buffalo Bill's Wild West and Congress of Rough Riders of the World* (Buffalo, N.Y.: Courier, 1898).

[43] Henry Blackman Sell and Victor Wellbright, *Buffalo Bill and the Wild West* (New York: Oxford University Press, 1955), 133.

[44] Blackstone, *Buckskins, Bullets, and Business*, 8–9.

[45] For a similar phenomenon, see Clifford Geertz's analysis of a village cockfight in Bali: "Deep Play: Notes on a Balinese Cockfight," *The Interpretation of Cultures* (New York: Basic Books, 1973), 443–444.

myths – the Oglala's tales of the buffalo people and the pseudo-history of Buffalo Bill – that assigned to the bison a central role in the creation of society. For the Euroamerican men of the American Bison Society, the preservation of the bison would sustain into the twentieth century the imagined, masculine frontier culture of Cody, Roosevelt, and Turner. It was the extinction of that culture, more than the disappearance of the bison, that the preservationists feared.

II

The first preserve exclusively for bison emerged in reaction to a Western show that blurred the distinction between myth and reality. In June, 1905, sixty-five thousand spectators flocked to the Miller Brothers 101 Ranch Show in Oklahoma for a rodeo and Western theatrical performance complete with trick riding, roping, and three hundred Ponca Indians who staged an attack on a wagon train. The highlight of the day was a so-called "last buffalo hunt." The show had recruited none other than Geronimo, the Chiricahua Apache, to dispatch some bison purchased from Charles Goodnight's ranch in Texas.[46] Many preservationists, however, recoiled from the killing of bison for popular amusement. *Forest and Stream* condemned the Miller Brothers show on the basis of its promotion. *Forest and Stream* editor George Bird Grinnell compared the event to the working-class amusements of "a Coney Island show," and concluded "the whole disgusting advertisement emphasizes again what we have so often pointed out – the importance of action by Congress to preserve the few remaining buffalo."[47] Theodore Roosevelt called the show a "disgraceful exhibition."[48] In his annual message to Congress on December 5, 1905, he went further, saying, "Either on some reservation or on some forest reserve ... or on some refuge, provision should be made for the preservation of the bison."[49] Thus the renewal of Catlin's call for government protection of the bison was born of a patrician revulsion against the killing of bison for vulgar entertainment.

Reaction to the Miller Brothers' show revealed that Euroamericans interested in the bison were divided into two groups: Easterners who sought to preserve it as a symbol of masculine frontier culture, and Western ranchers who sought to profit from the species. James McKay and William Alloway were typical of the ranchers who rounded up a few bison and raised them alongside their cattle.

[46] Norman B. Wood, *Lives of Famous Indian Chiefs* (Aurora, Ill.: Indian Historical Publishing Company, 1906), cited in Angie Debo, *Geronimo: The Man, His Time, His Place* (Norman: University of Oklahoma Press, 1976), 423–424. For Indians in Wild West shows, see L. G. Moses, *Wild West Shows and the Images of American Indians, 1883–1933* (Albuquerque: University of New Mexico Press, 1996).

[47] "A Buffalo Hunt in 1905," *Forest and Stream*, 64 (10 June 1905), 449.

[48] Debo, *Geronimo*, 424.

[49] *Congressional Record*, 59th Cong., 1st Sess. (5 December 1905), 103.

While hunting bison in the Red River valley in 1873 and 1874, McKay and Alloway captured a few bison calves and brought them to Alloway's ranch on the Assiniboine River. The routine of the ranch eventually reduced the bison to tame animals; Alloway told the Winnipeg *Tribune* in 1925 that "we fed them hay and tended them in shelters much the same as domestic cattle." In 1880, when the partners sold their small herd, Colonel Samuel Bedson, the warden of the penitentiary at Stony Mountain, Manitoba, purchased eight of the bison. Bedson pastured the animals on the prison grounds, the constricted range foreshadowing the fenced-in government preserves of the early twentieth century.[50]

In the United States as in Canada, western plains ranchers – whose cattle now occupied the bison's range – calculated that the novelty value of the bison might be high. Accordingly, Charles Goodnight captured a few bison calves in 1878 near his ranch in the Palo Duro Canyon in the Texas Panhandle. Frederick Dupree captured six calves in Montana in 1882 and brought them to his ranch in South Dakota. In 1901, Dupree sold his herd, which had grown to fifty-seven animals, to "Scotty" Philip, another South Dakota rancher.[51] Many of the bison that eventually populated government preserves descended from the herd of two Montana ranchers of Indian-Euroamerican ancestry, Charles Allard and Michel Pablo. In 1884, Allard and Pablo bought thirteen bison from a Pend d'Oreille Indian for two thousand dollars. In 1893 they added to their herd twenty-six more bison purchased from Buffalo Jones.[52] Jones was the most colorful rancher – albeit not the most successful – to raise bison. In 1885–86, a severe winter devastated domestic cattle in the plains. Impressed by the bison's ability to endure the winter storms, Jones captured fourteen calves in 1887. He added a few dozen more each year until by 1889 his herd numbered fifty-six. He eventually purchased Warden Bedson's herd and extradited the animals from their Canadian prison.[53]

Profit was the primary motivation for these keepers of the bison, just as it had animated hide hunters in the 1870s and early 1880s. Goodnight maintained that "the buffalo is the most profitable farm animal in America today."[54] Ranchers transformed their bison into commodities in numerous ways. Philip advertised the pleasures of both viewing and eating bison: "We supply Buffalo for Zoos, Parks, Circuses, and Barbecues."[55] Indeed, the commerce in exotic animals was

[50] Winnipeg *Tribune* (24 June 1925), quoted in George D. Coder, "The National Movement to Preserve the American Buffalo in the United States and Canada between 1880 and 1920" (Ph.D. dissertation, Ohio State University, 1975), 4–5.
[51] Ibid., 13, 23.
[52] Ernest Thompson Seton, *Lives of Game Animals*, vol. 3 (Garden City: Doubleday, Doran, 1927), 658.
[53] Henry Inman, *Buffalo Jones' Forty Years of Adventure* (Topeka: Crane, 1899), 134.
[54] Ernest Harold Baynes, "Report of the Secretary," *Second Annual Report of the American Bison Society, 1908–1909* (New York: American Bison Society, 1909), 57.
[55] Letterhead, Philip Buffalo Ranch, South Dakota, c. 1910, American Bison Society Papers, Box 272.

a lucrative trade in late nineteenth- and early twentieth-century America.[56] Some ranchers relied on the sale of bison meat; in the late nineteenth and early twentieth centuries, bison was for many people customary fare for Christmas dinner. Owners of bison attempted to card the animal's thick hair to make wool. Some even tried to domesticate the bison as a beast of burden. Most often, however, ranchers attempted to crossbreed bison with their domestic cattle to create a hybrid – cattalo – that would combine the meat-producing capacity of domestic cattle with the efficient grazing ability of the bison. These attempts were largely a failure. The male offspring of a bison bull and a domestic cow frequently died shortly after birth, or its mother died late in her pregnancy; surviving calves were uniformly sterile. Crossings of domestic bulls with bison cows were more successful, but unless they had been raised alongside the bison from birth, domestic bulls shied away from the female bison.[57]

Although some ranchers continued to experiment with crossbreeding bison and cattle well into the twentieth century, most found that the way to profit from the bison was to sell them – or more accurately, the right to hunt them – to wealthy sport hunters. In 1902, a rancher in Montana allowed two sport hunters to kill six of his bison bulls – for a price.[58] Later, one of those hunters, Howard Eaton, acquired a number of bison himself. In 1904, he sold two bison to a visiting German aristocrat and his son, who stalked and killed the animals on Eaton's ranch. The going rate for a bison in 1904 was reported to be a thousand dollars.[59] Some sport hunters refused to kill bison, however, until they were assured that the species was safe from extinction. Theodore Roosevelt's son, Kermit Roosevelt, declined to shoot bison on a hunting trip to South Dakota in 1908. The *New York Times* published a front page report of his refusal "to kill any buffalo . . . in these days when buffalo are all but extinct."[60]

Eaton and Roosevelt represented opposing interests: those who hoped to extract a profit from the bison – most of them Westerners – and those who hoped

[56] Richard W. Flint, "American Showmen and European Dealers: Commerce in Wild Animals in Nineteenth-Century America," in Hoage and Deiss, eds., *New Worlds, New Animals*, 97–108.

[57] For bison meat at Christmas dinner, see Larry Barsness, *Heads, Hides, & Horns: The Compleat Buffalo Book* (Fort Worth: Texas Christian University Press, 1985), 169; see also E. Douglas Branch, *The Hunting of the Buffalo* (Lincoln: University of Nebraska Press, 1960), 230. For a booster's view of the profitability of raising bison or bison-cattle crossbreeds, see William T. Hornaday, "The Extermination of the American Bison," 449–458. See also "Buffalo Breeding," *Forest and Stream*, 31 (29 November 1888), 361; "The Domesticated Buffalo," Ibid., 32 (9 May 1889), 313; Arthur Erwin Brown, "Notes on Buffalo Breeding," Ibid., 49 (24 July, 1897), 63–64; "Buffalo Bred in Captivity," Ibid., 57 (31 August 1901), 166; Cabia Blanco, "Buffalo Domestication," Ibid, 60 (17 January 1903), 45. The Secretary of the American Bison Society, Ernest Harold Baynes, was particularly interested in producing bison wool and taming bison to the yoke. See Baynes, "In the Name of the American Bison: A Plea for the Preservation of the Buffalo, and Some Experiments in its Domestication," *Harper's Weekly*, 50 (24 March 1906), 404–406.

[58] "Montana Buffalo," *Forest and Stream*, 58 (12 April 1902).

[59] "Howard Eaton's Buffalo," Ibid, 64 (29 April 1905), 334.

[60] "Kermit Balks at Buffaloes: President's Son Refuses to Shoot Game That is Almost Extinct," *New York Times* (29 September 1908), 1.

to preserve the species – most of them Easterners. Eventually, however, the ranchers and the preservationists reached an accommodation. For the ranchers, cooperation with the preservationists transformed them from traffickers in an endangered species to guardians of America's frontier heritage. Their reconciliation was rapid. Only five months after the Miller Brothers' show, J. Alden Loring of the New York Zoological Society surveyed a site in Oklahoma for a bison preserve. In his report, he made a point of thanking both Charles Goodnight and Joseph Miller for their help.[61] Later, the Society awarded honorary membership to several bison ranchers.

Apart from the legitimacy that cooperation with the preservationists conferred on them, the ranchers who owned the few remaining bison had every incentive to be helpful: the sentiment for preservation was a lucrative business opportunity. Ranchers regularly attempted to sell their bison to the American Bison Society. In 1916, H. A. Stone of Middletown, Missouri, offered to "get [the Society] all the Buffalo you want if [the] price suits." John "Buffalo Ray" Spurrier of Bigheart, Oklahoma, wrote to the Society in 1917, "I have three two year old Buffalo Bulls for sale. They are dandies and would make fine herd Bulls for small herds."[62] C. C. Garland wrote to the Society in 1923, "We offer 1 pair pure bred Buffalo, born 1922, for $250.00." Although both ranchers in the West and wildlife advocates in the East sought to preserve the bison, they labored at opposite ends of an economic exchange. The ranchers produced a commodity for the consumption of the preservationists.

The Society rarely purchased bison directly, but it referred potential customers to the ranchers. In 1922, A. H. Leonard, sales manager for Scotty Philip's bison ranch in South Dakota, received an inquiry from an Elgin, Illinois, park superintendent. Leonard later wrote to Martin Garretson, Secretary of the Society, to thank him "for referring so many park boards to us."[63] Occasionally, the Society solicited customers for the ranchers. In 1910, Hornaday petitioned the State Game Warden of Michigan to establish a state bison preserve by purchasing the private herd of Joshua Hill of Pontiac, Michigan. To Hill, Hornaday wrote, "I have notified several people regarding your elk and bison that you wish to sell, and I am really doing my best to help you find a buyer for your stock."[64]

[61] Loring, "The Wichita Buffalo Range," *Tenth Annual Report of the New York Zoological Society, 1905* (New York, 1906), 200.

[62] Spurrier to American Bison Society, 14 May 1917; Garland, South Tacoma, Washington, to Edmund Seymour, New York City, 12 July 1923;, American Bison Society Papers, Box 272. H. A. Stone to Edmund Seymour, 27 November 1916, American Bison Society Papers, Box 274.

[63] Leonard to Garretson, 9 March 1922, American Bison Society Papers, Box 272. The acquisition of bison by zoos in the late nineteenth and early twentieth centuries was part of a transformation of the mission of zoos from menageries to scientific facilities. See Vernon N. Kisling, "The Origin and Development of American Zoological Parks to 1899," in Hoage and Deiss, eds., *New Worlds, New Animals*, 109–125.

[64] Hornaday to Charles S. Pierce, 14 February 1910; Hornaday to Hill, Paywood, New Mexico, 14 February 1910. Letterbooks, American Bison Society Papers, Box 273.

Hornaday probably wrote these letters in the interest of Hill's bison – in all likelihood, the only alternative to sale was slaughter. Unwittingly or not, however, Hornaday acted as the rancher's agent, employing the sentimental mission of preservation as a sales gimmick.

Hornaday's concern was grounded in the fear that the bison was doomed. He shared with many nineteenth-century naturalists the notion that the replacement of the bison by domestic livestock was an inevitable result of the survival of the fittest. *Forest and Stream* similarly argued in 1890 that the "natural type" of bison was a "short-bodied, round-hipped, ... fat, logy animal."[65] Naturalists believed that these specimens had died off, leaving only the fittest bison. Hornaday described the bison he had hunted in Montana in 1886 as "perfect representations of the species. ... Out of the millions which once composed the great northern herd, those represented the survival of the fittest."[66] He argued again in 1912 that the remaining feral bison "surely represented the survival of the fittest ... in the soundness of that Darwinian principle."[67] However swift and strong the surviving bison had been forced to become, the organizing principle of the Society was that the extinction of the bison was inevitable unless civilized people intervened. Grinnell, editorializing in 1905 in favor of the establishment of bison preserves, argued that the bison's "fitness for longer survival in the wild state was long ago thoroughly disproved."[68] The aim of the American Bison Society was thus to stave off the extinction of a species whose time had passed. Rather than a repudiation of the nineteenth-century view that the bison was ultimately unfit, the efforts of the bison preservationists were an endorsement of that notion.

As if to confirm the naturalists' belief that the bison was unfit for survival, the largest herd of feral bison in the United States in the late nineteenth century steadily fell to poachers. Between 1889 and 1894, the population of wild bison in Yellowstone National Park declined from about two hundred to twenty-five. The Yellowstone bison were prime targets for market hunters. The potential profit was enormous and the risks were minimal. In the 1890s, a bison head could be sold for as much as fifteen hundred dollars. The punishments for poaching in Yellowstone were limited to confiscation of equipment and expulsion from the park. Sport hunters and wildlife preservationists lobbied Congress to stiffen the penalties for poaching in Yellowstone and in May, 1894, the federal government enacted a law providing for a thousand dollar fine, or two years in prison, or both, for killing a Yellowstone Park bison.[69]

[65] "Buffalo Types," *Forest and Stream*, 36 (30 January 1890), 24.
[66] Hornaday, "The Extermination of the American Bison," 395.
[67] William T. Hornaday, "The 'Outlaw' Remnant of the Pablo Bison Herd," *Fifth Annual Report of the American Bison Society* (New York: American Bison Society, 1912).
[68] "Pleading for the Buffalo," *Forest and Stream*, 65 (8 July 1905) 27.
[69] Hornaday, "Extermination of the American Bison," 464; T. S. Palmer, "Our National Herds of Buffalo," *Tenth Annual Report of the American Bison Society, 1915–1916* (New York: American

The 1894 law targeted market hunters, usually poor men who killed game on public lands for commercial profit.[70] Sport hunters – unless they were as scrupulous as Kermit Roosevelt – could continue to pay the fees charged by ranchers to hunt privately owned bison. Indeed, such distinctions of wealth – and of ethnicity, as most sport hunters were Anglos and many market hunters were not – tainted much of the Progressive-era regulation of commercial hunting. In a series of lectures delivered at the Yale University Forest School in 1914, Hornaday argued that the destruction of American birds "has been caused by the slaughter of them for food, in the North by the Italians and in the South by negroes."[71] He wrote in 1913 that "all members of the lower classes of southern Europe are a dangerous menace to our wildlife." He praised a Pennsylvania law that made it illegal for unnaturalized immigrants to hunt game.[72] *Forest and Stream* noted in 1898 that Montana game wardens arrested "a lot of Crees and half-breeds" for poaching bison, but rarely punished Euroamericans.[73] Outlawing market hunting opened the field for wealthy sport hunters. John Burroughs, while contemptuous of market hunters, claimed to "have never been disturbed" by big-game hunters such as Theodore Roosevelt. While visiting Yellowstone with Roosevelt in 1903, he wrote that, "It is to such men as he that the big game legitimately belongs."[74]

In 1902, in an effort to restore the bison, President Roosevelt appointed Buffalo Jones to the newly created position of Game Warden of Yellowstone. Jones had previously dabbled in crossbreeding cattle and bison, but had lost his sizable fortune on an irrigation scheme and had sold his bison and cattalo herd. In Yellowstone, Jones fenced in part of Mammoth Valley and stocked it with bison. With fifteen thousand dollars appropriated by the federal government, he purchased eighteen cows from Howard Eaton and three bulls from Charles Goodnight. Jones's herd resembled an earlier one established in the park in 1896 by E. C. Waters, who operated a steamboat that ferried tourists across Lake Yellowstone. To lure passengers aboard the steamboat, Waters purchased four bison from Goodnight, installed them on Dot Island in Lake Yellowstone, and,

Bison Society, 1916), 43. See also Barsness, *Heads, Hides & Horns*, 154–155; see also Martin Garretson, *The American Bison: The Story of its Extermination as a Wild Species and its Restoration under Federal Protection* (New York: New York Zoological Society, 1938), 196–200.

[70] For poaching of bison in Montana and Colorado before and after the 1894 law, see "The Lost Park Buffalo," *Forest and Stream*, 39 (13 October 1892), 314; "The Lost Park Buffalo," Ibid., 39 (20 October 1892), 331; "The Lost Park Buffalo," Ibid., 39 (27 October 1892), 353; "The Lost Park Buffalo Again," Ibid., 39 (1 December 1892), 466; "The Buffalo Remnant," Ibid., 41 (23 November 1893), 449; William N. Byers, "Buffalo in Colorado," Ibid., 42 (24 February 1894), 158; "Buffalo in the National Park," Ibid., 46 (18 January 1896), 45; "Yellowstone Park Buffalo," Ibid., 47 (8 August 1896), 101; "The Lost Park Buffalo Herd," Ibid., 48 (22 May 1897), 404.

[71] Hornaday, *Wildlife Conservation in Theory and Practice: Lectures Delivered Before the Forest School of Yale University, 1914* (New Haven: Yale University Press, 1914), 61.

[72] Hornaday, *Our Vanishing Wildlife: Its Extermination and Preservation* (New York: New York Zoological Society, 1913), 100, 103.

[73] *Forest and Stream*, 50 (1898), 61.

[74] Burroughs, *Camping and Tramping*, 7.

until 1907, operated a "game show" there.[75] Like Waters, Jones designed his little corral of bison in Yellowstone to attract tourists, locating the corral near Mammoth Hot Springs – not a site preferred by the few wild bison remaining in the park, but near the park's busiest entrance and therefore most accessible to visitors. Near the corral Jones established a private museum and souvenir shop. For these endeavors, the Park Superintendent accused Jones of "selling mementoes to tourists and generally prostituting himself for commercial gain."[76]

Unlike Waters, who abused and neglected his animals, Jones cared for the herd, furthering their domestication in the process, however. Shelters protected the herd from the elements in the winter. Keepers fed the animals hay when forage was thin, corralled rambunctious bulls separately, and bottle-fed milk to sickly calves.[77] Eventually, park authorities overcame their resistance to Jones and adopted his tame herd as a tourist attraction. Jones resigned his position in 1905; two years later park authorities moved the bison to a more suitable location in the Lamar Valley, but continued to drive a number of bulls to the old enclosure near Mammoth Hot Springs each year. The bison in the enclosure, the American Bison Society happily reported in 1915, "form one of the principal points of attraction during the tourist season."[78] In 1919, Horace M. Albright, then Superintendent of Yellowstone, wrote that "the visitors to the park are becoming more and more interested in the bison herd and henceforth it will play a much more important part in the operation of the park as a playground than it ever has before."[79] In the semidomesticated bison of Yellowstone, the Society realized its ambition to bring Americans "back to nature."

The strongest supporters of Yellowstone Park were by no means averse to using the park – and the bison – for commercial gain. Western railroads in particular promoted the ideals of recreation and the appreciation of scenic beauty. The Northern Pacific Railroad had been instrumental in the foundation of Yellowstone. In 1871, an agent of the Northern Pacific had enjoined the geologist Ferdinand Hayden to lobby Congress to create the park. Congress founded the park in 1872, and thereafter the Northern Pacific – whose line ran within a few miles of Yellowstone – promoted it heavily. After the establishment of Jones's herd, the Northern Pacific capitalized on the interest in the preservation of the bison. A 1904 advertisement read: "BISON once roamed the country now traversed by the Northern Pacific. The remnant of these Noble Beasts is now found in Yellowstone Park reached directly only by this line."[80]

[75] Aubrey L. Haines, *The Yellowstone Story: A History of Our First National Park*, vol. 2 (Yellowstone Library and Museum Association in cooperation with Colorado Associated University Press, 1977), 70–77.

[76] John Pitcher, quoted in Barsness, *Heads, Hides & Horns*, 156.

[77] Tom McHugh, *The Time of the Buffalo* (Lincoln: University of Nebraska Press, 1972), 302.

[78] Palmer, "Our National Herds of Buffalo," 44.

[79] Albright to Edmund Seymour, 3 December 1919, American Bison Society Papers, Box 274.

[80] Alfred Runte, *Trains of Discovery: Western Railroads and the National Parks* (Niwot, Col.: Roberts Rinehart, 1990), 19–21.

In the eleven years after the establishment of the Yellowstone herd the federal government provided for four more bison preserves. The government carved the first preserve out of the Kiowa-Comanche Indian reservation in south-western Oklahoma. Allotment – the policy, initiated with the passage of the Dawes Severalty Act of 1887, of distributing 160-acre homesteads to Indians and returning unallotted lands to the federal government – had destroyed the reservation in 1901. Congress later created a sixty thousand-acre National Forest Reserve out of the Indians' former holdings. President Roosevelt proclaimed the Forest Reserve a national game preserve in June, 1905 – shortly after the killing of bison in the Miller Brothers' show. Hornaday, in his capacity as director of the New York Zoological Park, offered fifteen of the zoo's bison to stock the preserve.[81] Most of the fifteen bison donated to Wichita by Hornaday had been given to the New York Zoological Park in 1903 by William Whitney, a Massachusetts wildlife advocate and a member of the American Bison Society. Whitney had purchased the animals from a Wyoming rancher in 1897.[82]

Following the pattern established in Oklahoma, the preservationists and the federal government established a second bison preserve on unallotted Indian lands in Montana. Bison belonging to the ranchers Michel Pablo and Charles Allard had grazed on the Flathead reservation since 1884. After Allard died in 1895, his heirs disposed of his half of the herd, but Pablo continued the speculative venture in bison ranching and profited handsomely. By 1902, he had sold fifty-seven bison to various zoos and menageries.[83] In 1906, however, the federal government allotted parts of the reservation to the Indians and opened the rest to Euroamerican settlement. Having lost his range, Pablo approached the Canadian government in an attempt to lease land in Canada for his bison herd. When the Canadians offered to buy his bison for $245 a head, Pablo agreed. Between 1907 and 1912, he delivered 672 bison to Elk Island and Buffalo national parks in Alberta.[84] The Canadian government paid Pablo over one hundred and sixty thousand dollars for the herd.

The sale of Pablo's herd to Canada animated the American Bison Society to do what Pablo had been unable to accomplish: continue to graze bison on what had been the Flathead reservation. The transaction had offended the preservationists' prickly nationalism: "The Pablo herd should not have been permitted to leave the country," complained Morton J. Elrod, the Society's agent in Montana. Hornaday – whose efforts to preserve the bison following Pablo's sale were described by the *New York Times* as a "patriotic labor" – lobbied Congress to establish a National Bison Range (an obvious rejoinder to the Canadians' Buffalo

[81] Hornaday, "The Founding of the Wichita National Bison Range," *Annual Report of the American Bison Society, 1905–1907*, 55–64; Hornaday, *Thirty Years War for Wildlife*, 167–169; Palmer, "Our National Herds of Buffalo," 44–46.

[82] Garretson, *American Bison*, 220–222.

[83] Seton, *Lives of Game Animals*, vol. 3 (Garden City: Doubleday, Doran, 1927), 658.

[84] For Canadian wildlife preservation, see Janet Foster, *Working for Wildlife: The Beginning of Preservation in Canada* (Toronto: University of Toronto Press, 1978).

National Park) on the former Flathead reservation.[85] "It is no exaggeration," he wrote to one senator, "to say that many Americans have been greatly disappointed by the sale of the Pablo herd of bison to the Canadian government."[86]

In 1908, Hornaday persuaded Congress to establish a preserve on the former Flathead reservation. The new National Bison Range reflected the Society's emphasis on tourism. The Society commissioned Elrod, a professor of biology at the University of Montana, to survey the site. Just as Buffalo Jones had selected Mammoth Valley for the Yellowstone herd because it was accessible to tourists, Elrod chose a site close to the railroad. He wrote of the twenty-nine-square-mile site he selected: "Tourists or visitors may step off the train at Ravalli and in five minutes be on the range. *They may look into the range for nine miles as they ride from Ravalli to Jocko!*"[87] The Society raised ten thousand dollars to provide the bison for the site. Most of the contributors were wealthy Easterners: Andrew Carnegie chipped in $250, approximately the cost of one bison. The Society purchased thirty-four bison from Alicia Conrad in Montana. She had purchased them some years earlier from Charles Allard's heirs.[88] Hornaday disdained to deal with Pablo, who still had some bison to sell. He refused, he explained, "to ask favors of a half-breed Mexican-Flathead."[89] Hornaday would not confer the Society's legitimacy on a non-Anglo who had dealt bison abroad, although Buffalo Jones, the Society's hero, had sold many bison to European zoos.

The establishment of the National Bison Range furthered the domestication of the bison, but did nothing to prevent the killing of bison outside the preserve. While the fence went up around the new preserve, about seventy-five of Pablo's bison still roamed the old Flathead reservation. Unable to round up this "outlaw remnant," for sale to Canada, Pablo proposed a "grand buffalo hunt" to eliminate them, at a cost to sport hunters of two hundred fifty dollars a head.[90] The State Game Warden of Montana declared the hunt illegal. Because Pablo had been unable to round up the remnant, the State deemed the animals to be wild. Montana asserted its protection of the unfenced bison – a protection it was completely unable to enforce. While thirty-seven bison remained confined inside the new National Bison Range, poachers steadily eradicated their seventy-five wild cousins outside the preserve, eliminating one of the largest remaining herds of undomesticated bison in North America.[91]

By the early 1920s, the bison population in the Montana preserve exceeded five hundred, and the Bureau of Biological Survey, which managed the range, began

[85] "The Bison Comes to Its Own," *New York Times* (28 May 1908), 6.

[86] Hornaday to Sen. Moses E. Clapp, 30 March 1908, "To Establish a National Bison Range," 3.

[87] Elrod, "The Flathead Buffalo Range," 25.

[88] Palmer, "Our National Herds of Buffalo," 46–48.

[89] Hornaday to Elrod, Missoula, Montana, 1 July 1908, American Bison Society Letterbooks, 2.

[90] Lincoln Ellsworth, *The Last Wild Buffalo Hunt* (New York, 1916).

[91] "President Hornaday's Report," *Fourth Annual Report of the American Bison Society, 1911* (New York: American Bison Society, 1911), 10–11; Hornaday, "The 'Outlaw' Remnant of the Pablo Bison Herd," 18–22; Barsness, *Heads, Hides & Horns*, 168. See also Hornaday to Henry Avare,

to slaughter surplus animals. Some of those excess bison became steaks and roasts on Northern Pacific dining cars, "as savory and tender as the Indians and pioneer hunters ever tasted," according to the railroad company. On a dining car menu card, the Northern Pacific assured its customers that serving bison meat was a sign of the species' return from the brink of extinction. It praised Theodore Roosevelt, the American Bison Society, and the Bureau of Biological Survey for saving the bison; it encouraged its customers to consume the meat both to savor the taste of the frontier and as a patriotic endorsement of preservationist ideals.[92] Like the ranchers who capitalized on the sentimentality of preservation as a sales tactic, the Northern Pacific used preservationism to sell bison meat.

In the end, the preservation of the bison brought in its train the same economic consequences that had attended its near-extermination in the nineteenth century; it benefited ranchers and railroads at the expense of Indians. In 1832, when Catlin had proposed a national park in the plains, he had imagined that it would include both Indians and bison. Instead, the Oklahoma and Montana preserves were established on lands alienated from the Kiowa-Comanche and Flathead reservations. Some members of the Society envisioned further enclosures; in 1911, Hornaday proposed establishing preserves in South Dakota when allotment came to the Sioux reservations.[93] In 1916, Charles Stonebridge, a founding member of the Society, made a similar suggestion when the Crow reservation in Montana was "thrown open to settlement."[94] The preservationists' attitude toward the Indians reflected both the frontier hostility to the native inhabitants of the West, and the late nineteenth- and early twentieth-century wilderness mentality, which found no place for Indians in its conception of a pristine, uninhabited North American environment.[95]

The bison preservationists acceded to the economic exploitation of the grasslands by the ranchers and farmers who had displaced the bison and the Indians in the nineteenth century. They sought only relatively small parcels of land for parks and game preserves, and were rather more concerned that the ranges be

Helena, Montana, 7 February 1912; Hornaday to Duncan McDonald, Ravalli, Montana, 7 February 1912; Hornaday to the Northern Pacific Railway, Ravalli, Montana, 7 February 1912; Hornaday to Lincoln Ellsworth, New York City, 29 February 1912; Henry Avare to Hornaday, 14 February 1912, Letterbooks, American Bison Society Papers, Box 273; Hornaday to Franklin Hooper, 18 December 1911, American Bison Society Papers, Box 272, File 19.

[92] For the serving of bison meat on Northern Pacific dining cars, see Northern Pacific flyer, c. 1925, American Bison Society Papers, Box 272, File 1; for the size of the bison population on the Montana range, see W. C. Henderson, Acting Chief of the Bureau of Biological Survey, Washington, D.C., to Hornaday, 20 November 1923, American Bison Society Papers, Box 272; E. W. Nelson, Chief, Bureau of Biological Survey, Washington, D.C., to Martin Garretson, Clifton, New Jersey, 25 January 1924, American Bison Society Papers, Box 272, File 27.

[93] "President Hornaday's Report," 27.

[94] Stonebridge, New York City, to Seymour, 11 December 1916, American Bison Society Papers, Box 274.

[95] For the wilderness ideology's disregard for Indians, see Cronon, "Trouble with Wilderness." Also see William M. Denevan, "The Pristine Myth: The Landscape of the Americas in 1492," *Annals of the Association of American Geographers*, 82 (1992), 369.

accessible to tourists. The leaders of the American Bison Society did not seek to profit from their efforts to preserve the bison, but their emphasis on tourism legitimated the economic interests of ranchers and railroad companies. The preservationists assented to the notion that the bison was an unfit species destined for extinction. Just as lawmakers in the 1870s and 1880s facilitated Euroamerican hide hunters' destruction of the bison in Indians' hunting territories, late nineteenth- and early twentieth-century legislators enacted game laws barring social outcasts from commercial hunting and making it all but impossible for anyone but a rancher or sport hunter to kill a bison. In sum, many of the social and economic forces that had contributed to the near-extermination of the bison also shaped the policies to preserve the species.

III

By 1911, Hornaday believed that "we need have no further fear that the American Bison will ever become extinct so long as civilized man inhabits the continent of North America." This declaration of the successful conclusion of their mission revealed the preservationists' conflicted loyalties to both progress and wilderness. Although "civilized man" had welcomed the destruction of the herds in the nineteenth century – indeed, had participated in it – in order to wrest control of the plains from the Indians, the preservation of the bison had, Hornaday argued, redeemed Euroamericans. Moreover, by salvaging a remnant of the herds, the preservationists legitimated the economic changes that "civilized man" had brought to the Great Plains. Hornaday resigned the presidency of the Society and, during the next two years, dissuaded his successors from establishing bison preserves in Colorado and North Dakota, believing that the work of bison preservation had been accomplished.[96] Despite Hornaday's discouragement, his successors in the Society helped to establish two more government herds in 1913: at Wind Cave National Park in South Dakota and at Fort Niobrara, a defunct Army post in Nebraska. The New York Zoological Park donated fourteen bison for Wind Cave. The six Fort Niobrara bison came from a private menagerist in Nebraska who had originally purchased them from Buffalo Jones.[97] By 1914, the federal government owned 10 percent of the captive bison in the United States: 15 at the National Zoological Park in Washington, D.C., 162 at Yellowstone, 48 at the Wichita Game Preserve, 96 at the Montana Bison Range, ten at Niobrara, and 14 at Wind Cave.[98]

In 1916, the American Bison Society looked back on its achievements and

[96] Hornaday to Walter N. Burns, 6 September 1911; Hornaday to T. S. Palmer, 29 April 1910; Hornaday to Franklin Hooper, 16 June 1913, Letterbook, American Bison Society Papers, Box 273.
[97] See Palmer, "Our National Herds of Buffalo," 48–50.
[98] D. F. Houston, "Letter from the Secretary of Agriculture," *Seventh Annual Report of the American Bison Society* (New York: American Bison Society, 1914), 51.

declared with satisfaction that "the Society has accomplished the main object for which it was established ten years ago; not only is the American bison no longer in danger of extinction but it is firmly established in all parts of the country."[99] Convinced that the bison's future as a tourist attraction was assured, the Society was unmoved in 1920 when in Utah the owner of a herd of over two hundred bison disposed of his animals by selling the right to hunt them for two hundred fifty dollars a head. Hornaday wrote to Edmund Seymour that "inasmuch as the owners ... find them an unbearable nuisance and an interference with their cattle-growing operations, what else is to be done than to get rid of them?"[100] In 1922, the Society acquiesced to the slaughter of surplus bison in Yellowstone and at Buffalo National Park. Seymour wrote that "it is a matter of gratification that the buffalo are becoming so numerous in some of the government herds that it presently will become necessary to treat the surplus bulls as so many domestic cattle."[101] The preservationists' objections to the killing of bison arose only when, as in the poaching in Yellowstone or the "last buffalo hunt" at the Miller Brothers' show in Oklahoma, it threatened the perpetuation of the species as a tourist attraction or sport hunters' quarry. By the 1920s, however, the salvation of the bison for those purposes was secure, and the zeal for the bison's preservation was exhausted. In 1936, the Society ceased to collect dues from its members, claiming that the preservation of the bison had been "placed upon a sound basis."[102] The legacy of the Society, however, was not to preserve the species as it had existed in the historic Great Plains, but to ratify the changes that Euroamerican conquest had wrought in the grasslands in the nineteenth century.

Those changes had left the bison and the grasslands irrevocably altered. Preservationism confirmed the nineteenth-century transformation of the bison from a species with continuous habitation of the plains to a fragmented population occupying disjunct "island" habitats.[103] The creation of refuges both limited the ability of the bison to seek new grasses and cemented the fragmentation of the bison population. The ecological consequences of the confinement of the bison to small refuges are significant. Despite the introduction of cattle to much of the bison's former range, the eradication of the bison, whose grazing had

---

[99] Henry Fairfield Osborn, "Report of the President for 1915," *Tenth Annual Report of the American Bison Society, 1915–1916*, 22.

[100] Hornaday to Seymour, 11 October 1920, American Bison Society Papers, Box 275, File 30. For the slaughter of the Utah bison herd, see William O. Stillman, President of the American Humane Association, Albany, New York, to Seymour, 6 November 1920; John E. Dooley, Salt Lake City, Utah, to Seymour, 10 November 1920; Stillman to Seymour, 17 November 1920; Stillman to Seymour, 28 March 1921, American Bison Society Papers, Box 275, File 30.

[101] Seymour, "Report of the President," *Report of the American Bison Society, 1922–23* (New York: American Bison Society, 1923), 12.

[102] Seymour, "To the Members of the American Bison Society," 25 January 1937, American Bison Society Papers, Box 272.

[103] Joel Berger and Carol Cunningham, *Bison: Mating and Conservation in Small Populations* (New York: Columbia University Press, 1994), 10.

favored the dominance of shortgrasses, allowed invading plant species to establish themselves in the western plains. Tall grasses expanded westward.[104] Aspen invaded a broad belt of the Canadian grasslands.[105] The loss of the bison permitted the spread of mesquite in the southern plains.[106] The disappearance of shortgrasses was apparent to the editors of *Forest and Stream* as early as 1891.[107] The bison was an integral part of the grassland environment. Although the preservationists saved a few bison from extinction, the elimination of the species from most of its habitat transformed the western plains.[108]

The fragmentation of the bison population into small, discrete herds has had a deleterious effect on the genetic diversity of the species. All bison in North America in the twentieth century descended from the roughly five hundred survivors of the commercial slaughter of the nineteenth century – a so-called "bottleneck" in the transfer of genes. The exile of bison to small, dispersed preserves has exacerbated this homogeneity. Bison, like 95 percent of all mammals, are polygynous – a small minority of dominant males are responsible for a majority of matings. In small, isolated herds, a single dominant male may sire every calf.[109]

A full understanding of the importance of genetic diversity emerged a decade or two after the establishment of bison preserves. Many members of the American Bison Society had a sophisticated understanding of the life sciences for their time. In the 1910s, the discovery of an apparent subspecies – the wood bison – in northern Canada energized the Society, prompting a spirited debate over the wood bison's apparent separate evolution.[110] The debate demonstrated that the preservationists understood the concepts of speciation and reproduction isolation, although they used different terms to represent these ideas. Prevailing notions of heredity convinced most preservationists, however, that the isolation

---

[104] Floyd Larson, "The Role of the Bison in Maintaining the Short Grass Plains," *Ecology*, 21 (April 1940), 113–121.

[105] See Charles Blyth, Celina Campbell, Ian Campbell, and John McAndrew, "Bison extirpation may have caused aspen expansion in western Canada," *Ecography*, 17 (1994), 360–362.

[106] For mesquite, see Dan Flores, *Caprock Canyonlands: Journeys into the Heart of the Southern Plains* (Austin: University of Texas Press, 1990), 31; Elinor Melville, *A Plague of Sheep: Environmental Consequences of the Conquest of Mexico* (New York: Cambridge University Press, 1994).

[107] See the editorial that cited the work of Professor A. R. Wallace, *Forest and Stream*, 37 (31 December 1891). A reader, William N. Byers, rebutted the editorial: "About Buffalo Grasses," Ibid., 38 (14 January 1892), 28.

[108] For a discussion of the ecological changes attendant on the replacement of bison by cattle, see Russel L. Barsh, "The Substitution of Cattle for Bison on the Great Plains," in Paul A. Olson, ed., *The Struggle for the Land: Indigenous Insight and Industrial Empire in the Semiarid World* (Lincoln: University of Nebraska Press, 1990), 103–126.

[109] Berger and Cunningham, *Bison*, 5–6.

[110] "Finds Wild Buffalo," *New York Times* (6 September 1912), 1; "New Herd of Bison Interests Scientists," Ibid. (9 September 1912), 7; "The Wood Bison," Ibid. (15 September 1913), 8. For the ongoing debate over the wood bison's status, see Valerius Geist, "Phantom Subspecies: The Wood Bison *Bison bison "athabascae" Rhoads 1897* is Not a Valid Taxon, but an Ecotype," *Arctic*, 44 (December 1991), 283–300.

of small herds in fenced preserves was no cause for alarm. Not until the 1920s did biologists develop the concept of a "gene pool." In the first two decades of the twentieth century, scientists concentrated not on collections of genes but on individual organisms.[111] The bison preservationists believed the organisms on their refuges to be superbly healthy; most of the preservationists, including Hornaday, adhered to the Darwinian notion that the surviving bison were the fittest of the species.

The preservationists' concerns were not for the as-yet-unknown concept of genetic diversity but for "inbreeding." Ranchers who raised bison certainly understood the dangers of inbreeding but many did little about it. A report on game preserves in 1897 noted this problem: "Aside from a few notable exceptions, there seems to have been little or no exchange of bulls among owners of buffalo, and though care has been taken to prevent intercourse between animals closely related, the blood of the herds now in existence is becoming more closely commingled each year."[112] Loss of genetic variation can lead to reduced fertility, increased mortality, and genetic anomalies. At the Sage Creek Wilderness Area near Badlands National Park in South Dakota, 9 of the 280 bison calves born between 1985 and 1990 suffered from morphological deformities. The anomalies included deformed or missing hooves and bowed, deformed, or missing legs.[113] The bison at Sage Creek were descended from the herd at Fort Niobrara, Nebraska, which began in 1913 with six animals, and from a private bison reserve in Colorado which began with one bull and two cows. The danger of inbreeding among the Niobrara herd was apparent as early as 1912, when Fred Dille of the Bureau of Biological Survey assessed the animals. He wrote that the bison "are now at just the point [where] we should arrange to ship in new blood either this fall or the next."[114] Two bison from Yellowstone joined the Niobrara herd in 1914, but they – like the movement to preserve the bison – arrived too late to halt the genetic drift of the herd.

The American Bison Society faded into irrelevance in the mid-1920s and finally folded in the mid-1930s, its limited mission accomplished. Without the help of the Society, the North American bison population continued to rise in the twentieth century; almost all the increase on private ranches. In the first decade of the twentieth century, ranchers sold their bison to government preserves, but by the 1910s and 1920s, as public herds reached their limited capacity, that flow

[111] Garland Allen, *Life Science in the Twentieth Century* (New York: Wiley, 1975), 126–134.
[112] D. F. Carlin, "American Game Parks: The 'Forest and Stream's' Fourth Annual Report on Game in Preserves," *Forest and Stream*, 49 (24 July 1897), 62.
[113] Berger and Cunningham, *Bison*, 47, 51–52, 246–249.
[114] Dille, "Report on the Gilbert Herd of Buffalo, Elk, and Deer, at Friend, Nebraska, May 23, 1912," American Bison Society Papers, Box 276, File 24.

reversed and state and federal authorities auctioned their surplus bison to ranchers. The flow of bison from public to private hands increased in the late 1940s. Whereas sport hunters and tourists had created the early twentieth-century market for bison preserves, a demand for bison meat in the dynamic postwar consumer economy created a new market for the species. Ranchers discovered that the cost of raising bison was roughly equal to that of raising cattle, but the novelty value of bison meat made it twice as profitable as beef. Because bison meat is lower in fat and cholesterol than beef, health-conscious consumers have boosted its sales in the last decades of the twentieth century. The number of bison on private ranches has risen from roughly thirty thousand in 1972 to an estimated ninety-eight thousand in 1989, to well over two hundred thousand in 1996. By the late 1990s, ranchers slaughtered approximately fifteen thousand bison every year, generating 7.5 million pounds of meat. That figure pales in comparison to the one hundred twenty-four thousand cattle slaughtered every day in the United States, yet the number of bison slaughtered every year for their meat exceeded the total number of bison in public herds in the United States in late 1997.[115]

Thus, over 90 percent of bison in North America in the late 1990s were privately rather than publicly owned, preserved not for their iconic significance or in the interest of biological diversity but simply raised to be slaughtered for their meat. In place of the American Bison Society there arose a ranchers' cooperative organization, the National Bison Association, founded in Denver in 1966. The Association generated mountains of instructional and promotional literature, schooling its members in cost-effective bison ranching techniques and advertising the healthfulness and tastiness of bison meat. The Association, in other words, treated the bison as domesticated livestock. To ease the qualms of potential bison ranchers, one promotional pamphlet asked rhetorically, "Are Bison Still Wild Animals?" and answered that, although less tame than cattle, "once they are used to being on a farm and seeing people regularly, they don't act very wild."[116] By the end of the twentieth century bison keepers had largely domesticated the species.

The eleven thousand bison in public herds were also constrained by the domesticated landscapes that surround them. Beginning in the mid-1920s and continuing until 1967, the National Park Service culled the Yellowstone bison herd, mostly by slaughter, in order to prevent the herd from spilling into neighboring areas. During those forty years rangers removed over nine thousand bison from Yellowstone. Some Indians of the plains eventually reaped some benefits from the culling programs. In 1934 and 1935, the Sioux (Pine Ridge)

---

[115] Vern Anderson and Dennis Sexhus, "The Bison Industry," *Bison World*, 22 (July/August/September 1997), 17. "Agricultural Alternatives: Bison Production," National Bison Association Information Packet.

[116] Judd Bunnage, "Introduction to Bison Management in Alberta" (September 1995), National Bison Association Information Packet.

and the Crow established bison herds on their reservations in South Dakota and Montana with surplus bison from Wind Cave and Yellowstone parks.[117] After the culling program ended in 1967, the Yellowstone bison population mushroomed from just over four hundred to well over three thousand by the late 1980s. During the twenty years following the end of the culling program, the killing of the Yellowstone bison occurred primarily in the winter, when some bison left the park in search of forage. Fearing that Yellowstone bison might spread brucellosis, a bovine disease, to domestic cattle, Montana game wardens quickly dispatched those that wandered north across park boundaries. Between 1967 and 1985, about six hundred bison – an average of thirty each year – were shot when they left Yellowstone Park in the winter. Ironically, the Yellowstone bison probably first contracted brucellosis from cattle corralled in Yellowstone in the 1910s for park employees.[118] The Yellowstone and Montana programs were less draconian than Canada's systematic slaughter of the entire bison population at Buffalo National Park in 1938–39. Canadian park authorities feared that the animals – the descendants of Michel Pablo's herd – might transmit bovine tuberculosis to domestic cattle.[119]

Following the example of Custer State Park in South Dakota, which first allowed public bison hunts in 1965, Montana amended its law in 1985 to allow private hunters to pay $200 each for the privilege of shooting the bison that left Yellowstone Park. The approach of the hunters generally did not alarm the bison, who were accustomed to the presence of tourists armed with cameras. In 1989, a manager for the Montana Department of Fish, Wildlife, and Parks said of the strange hunts, the bison "just kind of look at you, even after one of their mates is shot, wondering what the hell's going on."[120] In the winter of 1988–89, unusually large numbers of bison left the protection of the park to search for forage because drought and fires the previous summer had spoiled much of their range. By the end of the winter, Montana hunters had killed over five hundred, almost equaling in one season the number of Yellowstone bison killed outside the park over the previous twenty years.

The 1988–89 slaughter outside Yellowstone was exceeded by that of 1996–97. Although media reports of bison leaving Yellowstone indicated that the herd was too large to subsist on forage in the park, the migration had another cause. The bison's forage was adequate, but freezing rain had covered the grasses with a

[117] See Robert Yellowtail, Crow Agency, to Garretson, 15 December 1934; James H. McGregor, Superintendent of Pine Ridge Agency, South Dakota, to Garretson, 18 March 1935; and J. W. Emmert, Acting Superintendent of Yellowstone National Park, to Garretson, 6 February 1935, American Bison Society Papers, Box 276, Files 12, 24, 33.

[118] Mary Meagher and Margaret E. Meyer, "On the Origin of Brucellosis in Bison of Yellowstone National Park: A Review," *Conservation Biology*, 8 (September 1994), 645–653.

[119] William F. Lothian, *A Brief History of Canada's National Parks* (Ottawa: Environment Canada, Parks, 1987), 49.

[120] Timothy Egan, "Stray Buffalo Killed in Red Harvest on the Snow," *New York Times* (22 February 1989), 12.

sheet of ice. By the spring of 1997, hunters had killed over one thousand bison wandering out of Yellowstone.[121] In a failed effort to avoid the negative media coverage that had attended the 1988–89 shootings, park rangers undertook the 1996–97 killing. The justification remained the same: to protect Montana cattle from the remotest threat of bovine disease.[122] Prospective bison hunters no longer able to purchase permits to shoot bison outside of Yellowstone had other alternatives – if they could afford them. Both Custer State Park in South Dakota and the Perfect 10 Buffalo Ranch in Rose, Nebraska, charged $10,000 to hunt a trophy. The Perfect 10, which advertised on the Internet, promised: "The last great epoch in American History was the Wild West and now it can come back for you. For three days and two nights you can be a modern Buffalo Bill."[123]

As in 1989, the 1996–97 killings created an uproar among environmentalists and the progressive media.[124] In a sense, however, the hue and cry over the shooting of the Yellowstone bison was misplaced. One thousand bison died outside Yellowstone in 1997, but fifteen thousand perished in abattoirs around the country during the same year. The sensitivity of Americans to the Yellowstone bison, and corresponding blindness to the fate of bison on ranches, is a legacy of the early twentieth-century preservation of the species. Although the eleven thousand bison in public parks such as Yellowstone are no different biologically from the two hundred thousand on private ranches, Americans continue to regard them in very different ways. The Yellowstone bison are icons of the wilderness, to be protected from exploitation. Ranch bison are domesticated animals whose slaughter Americans perceive to be a necessary function of the United States economy.

The spectacle of hunters paying for the opportunity to shoot a bison, and of Americans simultaneously professing their love of wildlife while subordinating the interests of wild animals to the interests of ranchers, is reminiscent of the early twentieth century, when ranchers charged wealthy sport hunters for the right to shoot semi-domesticated bison. Mary Meagher, a biologist specializing in the bison, said of the 1988–89 slaughter outside Yellowstone: "There's a real mystique for these people who want to shoot a bison. We're not all that far removed from the frontier."[125] The persistence of the "mystique" of killing bison demonstrates that although preservationists probably saved the bison from

[121] Author's interview with Jim Angell, Sierra Club Legal Defense Fund, Atlanta, Georgia, June 21, 1997.

[122] "Slaughter of Errant Bison to Begin Near Yellowstone," *New York Times* (29 December 1996), 12; "Yellowstone Bison Cut in Half Over Winter," Ibid., (13 April 1997), 18.

[123] <http://si2000.inetncbr.com/buffalo/>. See also "Custer State Park Fall Classic" (advertisement) *Bison World*, 22 (July/August/September 1997), 34.

[124] Jim Robbins, "Slaughter of Errant Bison to Begin Near Yellowstone," *New York Times* (29 December 1996), 12; "Wild Bison Dispute Deepens as Montana Governor Faults U.S.," Ibid. (2 February 1997), 23; James Brooke, "Yellowstone Bison Herd Cut in Half Over Winter," Ibid. (13 April 1997), 13; "The Bison Killers," *Nation* (10 March 1997), 10.

[125] Egan, "Limited Winter Range Starves Yellowstone Elk," *New York Times* (20 February 1989), 8; Egan, "Stray Buffalo Killed," 12.

extinction, they saved the species not as a functioning part of the plains environment, but as a functioning part of the American economy: a curiosity, tourist
attraction, target for hunters, and domesticated beast. This piecemeal and com-
mercialized salvation owed itself to the limitations of an Eastern preservationist
ideology based on nostalgia and recreation, and to the perception of Western
ranchers that a profit could be made from the few remaining bison. This confused tangle of sentiment and cupidity has left a complex cultural and ecological
legacy; those complexities are revisited every year at any of the hundreds of
bison ranches in the United States and Canada and on the border of Yellowstone
Park in Montana. Those places, rather than an imagined "Buffalo Commons,"
are the true legacies of the turn-of-the-century preservationists.

Conclusion

The Indian hunters who came to the western plains in the eighteenth century encountered not only the villagers who already inhabited the region but other interlopers like themselves. The complex and multifaceted encounters that ensued among nomads and villagers became still more complex when Euroamericans arrived in the grasslands. The encounters among Indians and Euroamericans were both intercultural and environmental. Immigrants to the western plains introduced new animals, systems of resource use, and microbes to the region. The newcomers confronted not only other peoples but the semi-arid environment. As a result of these cultural and environmental encounters, villagers became nomads, farmers became bison hunters, and bison hunters became destroyers of a species.

The environmental history of the destruction of the bison thus unites two meta-narratives of eighteenth- and nineteenth-century history. First, imperial expansion brought Europeans, their economic system, and their biota into worldwide contact with non-Europeans. The conquest of indigenous peoples in North America was duplicated in South America, southern Africa, Australia, New Zealand, and elsewhere.[1] Second, the migration of European people, plants, animals, and economies overseas occasioned a global decline in biological diversity. Ultimately, European domesticated animals supplanted indigenous wildlife in many parts of the world. Domesticated livestock's displacement of bison in the Great Plains was but one example of this pattern of ecological simplification.[2]

[1] Howard Lamar and Leonard Thompson, "Comparative Frontier History," and "The North American and Southern African Frontiers," in Lamar and Thompson, eds., *The Frontier in History: North America and Southern Africa Compared* (New Haven: Yale University Press, 1981), 3–40; Walter Nugent, "Comparing Wests and Frontiers," in Clyde A. Milner II, Carol A. O'Connor, and Martha Sandweiss, eds., *The Oxford History of the American West* (New York: Oxford University Press, 1994), 803–833; James O. Gump, *The Dust Rose Like Smoke: The Subjugation of the Zulu and the Sioux* (Lincoln: University of Nebraska Press, 1994).

[2] See Alfred W. Crosby, *Ecological Imperialism: The Biological Expansion of Europe, 900–1900* (New York: Cambridge University Press, 1986); William Beinart and Peter Coates, *Environment and History: The Taming of Nature in the USA and South Africa* (London: Routledge, 1995); Elinor Melville, *A Plague of Sheep: Environmental Consequences of the Conquest of Mexico* (New York: Cambridge University Press, 1994).

The encounter between European and Indian societies was both a cultural and an ecological phenomenon, converging in the domestication of the plains environment: the transformation of the bison and the grasslands for human convenience. Indians in the plains initiated the process of domestication when they adopted the horse as a means of pursuing the bison. By the end of the eighteenth century, large Indian horse herds were competing with the bison for forage. As early as the 1820s, as domesticated cattle invaded the plains, bovine disease probably contributed to the diminution of the herds. From the 1840s to the 1880s, cattle and sheep increasingly crowded the bison's range. In combination with drought, domestic livestock's occupation of rangelands sped the decline of the herds. Preservationists who saved the bison from extinction at the beginning of the twentieth century ironically participated in the domestication of the species by confining them to managed preserves.

Over one hundred years ago, the frontier historian Frederick Jackson Turner understood the domestication of the Western environment as a transformation from wilderness to civilization.[3] Western and environmental historians now rely on terms other than Turner's, terms that carry more analytical subtlety, ecological sophistication, and cultural and moral complexity: encounter rather than frontier, environment rather than wilderness, and domestication rather than civilization.[4] The differences are not simply semantic. Nor are the new terms merely regressive counterpoints to Turner's celebratory, progressive understanding of the transformation of the West. Rather, encounter, environment, and domestication denote interrelations among human societies and the natural environment. Those interrelations were not unilinear, as in Turner's conception of the progressive transformation of the wilderness to civilization, but reciprocal.

Reciprocal relations were both intercultural and eco-social. The influence of the western plains environment pervaded human history in the region from the eighteenth to the early twentieth centuries. Climate, disease, and the migrations and aggregations of the bison influenced the cultures and economies of both Indian nomads and Euroamericans. The nomads adapted their societies to the movements of the bison. They felt the impact of Old World diseases. Drought assisted the Euroamericans who welcomed the destruction of the bison. The history of Indian and Euroamerican societies in the western plains is embedded in the complex ecology of the region.

Human embeddedness in the nonhuman natural world contradicts an old and deeply rooted concept in Western thought: the dualism of humanity and nature.

---

[3] Frederick Jackson Turner, "The Significance of the Frontier in American History," *American Historical Association Annual Report* (1893), 199–227.

[4] Patricia Nelson Limerick, "The Adventures of the Frontier in the Twentieth Century," in Limerick and Richard White, *The Frontier in American Culture* (Berkeley: University of California Press, 1994), 76.

Since George Perkins Marsh published *Man and Nature* in 1864, students of environmental history have challenged this dualism, which tempts historians to divorce human history from its environmental context. Advances in scientific study since the publication of *Man and Nature* have only underscored humanity's interconnectedness with the nonhuman natural world. Despite an ever-increasing awareness of humanity's dependence on nature for survival, and nature's sensitivity to human exploitation, a residue of dualism persists. Western tradition insists that whereas human culture is dynamic, nature is essentially stable. Even Marsh believed that "man is everywhere a disturbing agent. Wherever he plants his foot, the harmonies of nature are turned to discords."[5] The history of the bison, however, reveals a natural world characterized not by stability but by unpredictable change.

In recent years, some ecologists have advanced the idea that instability characterizes the global environment. These scientists' new emphasis on instability is the logical result of the erosion of the dualism between nature and human society. If everything is connected to everything else, then a trivial change in one part of the biosphere can result in change, even monumental change, elsewhere. One of the favorite metaphors of nonlinear dynamics, or chaos theory, is the "butterfly effect": a butterfly beating its wings in Asia, for example, may theoretically cause a tornado some time later in North America. To be embedded in such an interconnected, disharmonious natural world means that the environment is as changing and unpredictable as human history. It also means that a change somewhere in the global environment, however small, will eventually have an effect, however small, on everything else in the global environment.[6] The nature writer John Muir anticipated this insight in 1911 when he wrote, "When we try to pick out anything by itself, we find it hitched to everything else in the universe."[7]

Muir's observation is nowhere more relevant than to the history of the bison, a species seemingly connected to everything: grasses, drought, wolves, horses, smallpox, steamboats, railroads, the European conquest of North America, the expansion of the market, industrialization, and cultural constructions of gender. Accordingly, a host of environmental and human factors contributed to the destruction of the bison. Euroamerican hide hunters in the southern plains,

[5] George Perkins Marsh, *Man and Nature, Or, Physical Geography as Modified by Human Action*, ed. David Lowenthal (Cambridge: Harvard University Press, 1965), 36. For an analysis of disorder in nature and its implications for environmental history, see Donald Worster, "The Ecology of Order and Chaos," in *The Wealth of Nature: Environmental History and the Ecological Imagination* (New York: Oxford University Press, 1993), 156–170.

[6] For chaos theory, see James Gleick, *Chaos: Making a New Science* (New York: Penguin, 1987). For an environmental historian who has integrated an understanding of an inherently changing nature into his analysis, see Arthur F. McEvoy, *The Fisherman's Problem: Ecology and Law in the California Fisheries, 1850–1980* (New York: Cambridge University Press, 1986).

[7] John Muir, *My First Summer in the Sierra* (Boston: Houghton Mifflin, 1944), 157.

emigrants' livestock in the central plains, and Indian commercial hunters in the northern plains where the robe trade was most intense combined with regional drought, cold, habitat degradation, competition from domesticated livestock, and bovine disease to cause the near extinction of the species. To categorize human and environmental causes of bison mortality separately, however, reinforces the specious notion of human and natural dualism. The causes of the destruction of the bison were inextricably both anthropogenic and environmental. The rise of Indian commercial hunting, for instance, was rooted in a host of ecological forces, including the incursion of horses and disease into the western plains. In the 1870s, drought was most devastating to the bison where cattle ranches prevented the bison from migrating in search of forage.

Although a butterfly somewhere in the world might have inadvertently caused drought in the plains (if the chaos theoreticians are correct), no butterfly ever shouldered a .50-caliber rifle on the hide hunters' range. The destruction of the bison was a monumental environmental transformation: the near-extinction of an animal that was not only the largest land mammal in North America but the dominant animal species of the largest biome on the continent. The decline of the bison had an equally monumental primary cause. Without the rise of industry in the nineteenth-century United States, the bison would not have become nearly extinct, nor would its current habitation of the plains be so scant and confined. Yet, even commercial hunting, surely the primary cause of the destruction of the bison, was embedded in nature. A bison hide did not cease to be part of nature when it had been removed from the carcass and sold. The hide continued to flow through the environment like all energy and material. The passing of the bison from the natural environment to the human market was but incidental. Both Indian and Euroamerican hunters were, in this ecological sense, predators on the bison, and their exploitation of the animal was an ecological phenomenon. The market in bison robes and hides was not an exclusively anthropogenic cause of the bison's destruction, but the leading cause among several eco-social factors.

The hunting of the bison was bound to the encounter between Indians and Euroamericans. That encounter – the central event in the story of the destruction of the bison – can be understood variously. According to one version of environmentalist teleology, in the distant past, American Indians – a people presumed to possess a higher ecological consciousness than Europeans and their descendants – lived in harmony with nature. Some environmentalists assert that the coming of Europeans destroyed that balance and from the arrival of European colonists until the present American society's relationship with the environment has been unsustainable. Furthermore, they believe that it will continue to be so unto its own extinction, unless Americans reform their thought and behavior to achieve sustainability. This narrative – simultaneously retrospective and prospective – stems from patterns of thought that are as rooted in Western culture as the dualism between nature and humanity. Although its adherents may not recognize it as such, the narrative is essentially a secular form of Christian teleology: humankind sinned, fell from grace, and was banished from Eden; repentance, however, will bring a return to Paradise.[8]

Many environmental histories of the near-extinction and preservation of the bison parallel this environmentalist teleology. According to these interpretations, the Indians of the western plains maintained a sustainable reliance on the abundant bison until they were seduced into the bison robe trade in the 1830s; unsustainable exploitation of the bison by Euroamerican hide hunters peaked in the 1870s; ultimately, however, at the turn of the century enlightened proto-environmentalists rescued the species from extinction.[9] This narrative presumes that the bison population, when not subjected to unsustainable human hunting, was stable. It idealizes Indians, at one end of the story, and preservationists, at the other, while demonizing commercial hunters in the middle. It contextualizes neither Indian nor Euroamerican use of the bison; it does not recognize that bison hunters and conservationists, whether Indian or Euroamerican, were entangled in a host of social and economic concerns.

Nor does it recognize that, from the perspective of the bison, there were striking similarities between the nomads and the Euroamericans. Both were newcomers to the plains in the eighteenth century. Both employed new technologies and adopted new modes of production to hunt the bison. Both sacrificed bison to meet social demands of integration, prestige, or conquest. Both increasingly adapted to capitalism in the eighteenth and nineteenth centuries. In the end, that adaptation was fatal to millions of bison. Certainly, there were significant differences between Euroamericans and the various Indian societies of the plains – differences too obvious and lengthy to enumerate. But the differences must have seemed trivial to the bison during the height of the commerce in robes and hides.

The interaction between Indians and Euroamericans in the western plains created bison hunters on both sides of the encounter: notably equestrian Indian nomads and Euroamerican hide hunters. By the second half of the nineteenth century, however, Indians and Euroamericans were engaged in a destructive battle over control of resources in the plains. The peculiar tragedy of the slaughter of the bison is that both Indians and Euroamericans had the opportunity to regulate commercial hunters and, until the end of the nineteenth century, declined to do so. Like most questions about whether or how to conserve resources, the essential questions were about the distribution of wealth.[10] Although it is in

---

[8] For the tensions between environmentalism and environmental history, see William Cronon, "The Uses of Environmental History," *Environmental History Review*, 17 (Fall 1993), 1–22; for the influence of Christian thought on environmentalism, see Donald Worster, "John Muir and the Roots of American Environmentalism," in *Wealth of Nature*, 184–202.

[9] See, for instance, J. Donald Hughes, *American Indian Ecology* (El Paso: Texas Western Press, 1983).

[10] Hugh Stretton, *Capitalism, Socialism, and the Environment* (New York: Cambridge University Press, 1976), 5.

the interest of all to preserve common resources such as the bison, in a competitive economy it is in every individual's interest to exhaust available supplies in the pursuit of private wealth.[11] To a commercial hunter in the late nineteenth century, to leave a bison behind was to leave it for a competing hunter, or worse yet, if the hunter was a Euroamerican, for an Indian.

Underlying the Euroamerican destruction of the bison in the 1870s and 1880s was an ecological irony. In terms of resource management, by the mid-nineteenth century the plains nomads shared important similarities with their Euroamerican contemporaries. Like the industrial economy which relied on the unsustainable use of natural resources, the nomadic societies had come to rely overmuch on a narrow ecological foundation, the bison. Like Euroamerican industrial society, which felled trees and mined coal and iron ore at an alarmingly destructive pace, by the mid-nineteenth century the nomads' economy was based on the unsustainable exploitation of the herds. In the understanding of the Euroamericans, the nomads' reliance on the bison was the weakness of a savage society. But when Euroamericans slaughtered the bison to pacify the plains nomads they did not exploit the peculiar frailty of a primitive society; when they capitalized on the nomads' ecological Achilles' heel they exposed the fragility of all societies, including their own, that rely on the unsustainable exploitation of nature.

[11] McEvoy, *Fisherman's Problem*, 3–16.

Index